RENAISSANCE DRAMA

New Series 35   2006

Renaissance Drama

NEW SERIES 35

*Embodiment and Environment
in Early Modern Drama
and Performance*

Edited by Mary Floyd-Wilson
and Garrett A. Sullivan Jr.

Northwestern University Press

EVANSTON 2006

Title page image from Robert Fludd, *Utriusque cosmi maioris scilicet
et minores metaphysica, physica atque technica historia*
(1617). By permission of Duke University Library.

Contents

Editorial Note

Embodiment and Environment
in Early Modern Drama and Performance

The essays in this special issue of *Renaissance Drama* take up the challenge that Kristen Poole articulates in the essay that closes the volume: they explore and seek to delineate "an environmental, material consciousness and comprehension that differed radically from our own." In different ways, the volume's contributors each examine the environmentally situated nature of early modern psychology and physiology both as depicted in drama and as a condition of performance. What constitutes the "environmental" varies, ranging from cold air, hot drinks, English soil, sound, breath, and the devil himself. Uniting these essays, however, is the recognition that early modern conceptions of embodiment cannot be understood without attending to transactional relations between bodies and their environments.

Several of these essays examine the dramatic representation of ecologically embedded identities. The authors shed new light on the ways that travel and climatic conditions were understood to shape and reshape class status, gender, ethnicity, national identity, and subjectivity in the period. For Daryl Palmer, Hamlet's famed inwardness is the starting point for a broad survey of early modern northern engagements with the cold that aim to reconstitute a regionalized masculinity in outward terms. Ultimately the essay resituates Hamlet as an exoteric hero in an environment shared with northern voyagers. Jean Feerick moves the scene across the ocean to the exotic but unidentifiable islands of Shakespeare's *The Tempest* and Fletcher and Massinger's *The Sea Voyage,* where transplantation threatens to "reinscribe the physical and social identity" of the European settlers. In his reading of William Haughton's *English-men for My Money,* Alan Stewart also explores the challenges of transplantation, but shifts our attention to foreign, Jewish denizens attempting to root in stubbornly resistant English soil.

Many of the volume's essays focus in particular on theatrical ecologies, identifying the playhouse as a "special environment" or its own "ecosystem," where performances have material, formative effects on the bodies of actors and audience members. Paul Menzer's essay posits a theatrical environment of implicit mimetic contracts, where the actors seek to communicate strong passions through a coded rhetoric of increased restraint. Taking his cue from the physical placement of "understanders" in the theater, William West uncovers the surprisingly complex and somatic sense of early modern theatrical *understanding*—an ecological understanding indigenous to the shared community of the Elizabethan theater. Much in the same spirit, Carolyn Sale's essay views the theater as a communal space where transactions take place between the actors and the audience through the senses of smell and taste. The materializing language of *Hamlet,* she suggests, points to an ideal, liberatory theatrical experience of collective purification.

The final two essays of this collection consider transactions between theatrical, political, and cosmological environments. Jonathan Gil Harris assesses the dropsical bodies of *All's Well That Ends Well* in relation both to the theater's "ecosystem of sound" and to a body politic marked by monarchical "swellings" that could betoken illness rather than offspring. For Kristen Poole, *Dr. Faustus* offers a purchase on a metamorphic model of the cosmos, defined by what she terms "Ovidian physics." Faustus's contract appears in this analysis less as a prop shuttled between actors than as a trope for placing the theater itself in a transactional relation to the supernatural: the "bond" passes between this world and Hell, bearing evidence of the way in which theatrical ecologies are nested within a broader cosmic framework.

Poole sees an analogue between Ovidian physics and the tenets of

Galenic humoralism, which has been the subject of work by Gail Kern Paster and others. This work has shown how early modern beliefs about embodiment have shaped lived experience, and its influence is apparent in this volume. For instance, Palmer, Feerick, and Stewart explore how the environment reconstitutes the identity of a porous humoral body. Other contributors draw inspiration from Bruce Smith's acoustic world to imagine theatrical ecosystems of sense and sensation; cases in point are the essays by Harris and Sale. Most of these essays have a methodological interest in historical phenomenology; they understand that the historical retrieval of lived experience requires, as Poole puts it, "the work of fantasy." Anatomized, fragmented, and embarrassed, the body has long been fruitful ground for Renaissance drama scholars. What distinguishes the essays in this volume, however, is an early modern body explored primarily through its engagements with and operations in specific environments that it both shapes and is shaped by. Embodiment, our contributors remind us, is without borders.

Mary Floyd-Wilson and Garrett A. Sullivan Jr.
Guest Editors

An annual and interdisciplinary publication, *Renaissance Drama* invites submissions that investigate traditional canons of drama as well as the significance of performance, broadly construed, to early modern culture. We particularly welcome essays that examine the impact of new forms of interpretation on the study of Renaissance plays, theater, and performance; the cultural discourses that shaped and were shaped by drama and the institutional conditions in which it was produced; and the way that performance and performativity functioned both on and off the professional stage. Occasionally special issues of the journal are devoted to specific topics of current interest.

Renaissance Drama conforms to the stylistic guidelines of *The Chicago Manual of Style* (14th edition), including endnote reference citations. Scholars preparing manuscripts for submission should refer to this book. We prefer to receive manuscript submissions electronically: send a copy of the essay as an electronic file attachment (saved either as rich text [an .rtf file] or as a Microsoft Word file) to staff assistant Latonia Trimuel, l-trimuel@northwestern.edu, copied to j-masten@northwestern.edu. Submissions of essays in hard copy may be mailed to:

Renaissance Drama
Department of English
Northwestern University
1897 Sheridan Road
Evanston, IL 60208-2240
USA

The journal does not accept submissions of essays by fax. For initial review of essays, legible photocopies or electronic files of any illustrations are acceptable; authors of essays accepted for publication will be responsible for obtaining any necessary permissions.

Additional information on submissions, special issues, and forthcoming essays may be found at the Northwestern University English Department Web site, http://www.english.northwestern.edu/resources/journal.html.

RENAISSANCE DRAMA

New Series 35   2006

Hamlet's Northern Lineage: Masculinity, Climate, and the Mechanician in Early Modern Britain

DARYL W. PALMER

"That all mental form being indefinite and ideal, realities must needs become cold. . . ."

—Coleridge, *Coleridge's Shakespeare Criticism*

FOR CENTURIES, THE study of early modern men has been troubled by Hamlet's famous declaration of grief: "But I have that within which passes show, / These but the trappings and the suits of woe."[1] In the play, Hamlet needs to justify his dull behavior before an unsympathetic audience. In critical commentaries, scholars have accepted this fact and gone on to search for what was "within," even as others have protested that the search was hollow.[2] In the essay that follows, I propose that we would be better served by focusing on the way Hamlet's rhetoric of justification evolves over the course of the play. As early modern observers would have done, I am inclined to ground this inquiry in regional and lineal terms. I will suggest that, as *Hamlet* unfolds, the prince aligns himself with the active voyagers of the frozen north by engaging with his environment and redefining himself in exoteric, or outward terms. How, I want to ask, do Hamlet's northern predecessors—real and fictional—inform the play's innovative apologia for early modern man?

Of course the context for such questioning is both humoral and geographical. To an extent rarely remarked, we have tended to nationalize gender in this period even though early modern observers paid more attention to what Mary Floyd-Wilson has termed "geohumoralism,"[3] the classical notion that habitat shapes human being. Writers such as Jean Bodin and Levinus Lemnius drew on Aristotle, Hippocrates, and Galen in order to elaborate this zonal vision.[4] In the hands of these commentators,

3

classical notions of region (centered on the Mediterranean) merged with Macrobian cartography, which seemed to frame, even explain, fluidic and thermal variation in the human body. Other commentators, such as Giovanni Botero, paid scrupulous attention to the ways in which "situation" determined human being: "So we may see, that the Englishmen which inhabit a plaine and plentifull soile, have always prevailed against the Scots & Welshmen, who presuming upon the strength of their owne countrey, have divers times molested them."[5] According to these models, habitation exercised a profound and predictable influence on human behavior. In this context, Britain and its people were usually seen as "northern," an identity they shared with many other people who inhabited a region famous for its frostiness.[6] In *Famous Frosts and Frost Fairs in Great Britain,* William Andrews documents this thermal perception with a chronology of famous English winters, beginning in C.E. 134, when the Thames was frozen for two months.[7] With good reason, Macrobian cartographers located Britain in a larger territory they called "Europa Frigida." In his *Historia de gentibus septentrionalibus* (1555), Olaus Magnus describes the people of this region and celebrates their common identity:

I have written above about the various activities of the northern peoples, looking at their violent struggles in war, their buildings, their social intercourse, and also the cheerful processions that entertain this race, who live under the influence of the harsher planets, and how they celebrate their feast days in the regular yearly course, as other nations do.[8]

Having chronicled the violent animosities between Poles and Swedes and Russians, the writer looks back and declares with complete confidence that his great work deals with a single "race" of people. It is no coincidence, I suggest, that the most discussed character in English literature is a Dane.

And how did such theorizing matter to notions of northern masculinity? As Mark Breitenberg has pointed out, "Masculinity is inherently anxious. . . ."[9] Men fumbled about in the cold, searching for a way to justify their own versions of masculine identity. Climate only complicated this search. According to humoral theory, the steady dose of northern cold could either seal in a man's natural heat or undermine his masculinity. Floyd-Wilson describes another layer of permutation: "The logic of inversion fixed the white northerner and the black southerner in an interdependent relationship: if the southerner is hot and dry, then the northerner must be cold and moist; if the southerner is weak and wise, the northerner must be strong and witless."[10] To be sure, early modern Britons could find little comfort in this sort of identification. Floyd-Wilson writes, "to be white and British in the early modern period was not a badge of superiority but cast one instead on the margins as uncivil, slow-witted, and more bodily determined than those people living in more temperate zones."[11] The author of *Batman uppon Bartholome* declares, "in the bodies that colde hath the masterie over, the coulour is white, the haire soft and straight, the wit hard and forgetful, little appetite, much sleep, heavie in going and slow. . . ."[12] In this spirit, Lemnius points to northern "Dolts and Asseheads."[13] Bodin simply declares that people of the north tend to be beastly and cruel.[14]

Of course Britons resisted such verdicts, but the complexity of this opposition has only begun to be studied. Floyd-Wilson explains, "In both imaginative and non-imaginative literature, late sixteenth- and early seventeenth-century English writers struggle to stabilize and rehabilitate their northern identity."[15] We can mark the heterogeneity of this rhetoric in the writings of two men, Raphael Holinshed and Robert Burton. Holinshed recounts the year of Shakespeare's birth:

The one and twentith of December began a frost, which continued so extremlie, that on Newyeares even, people went over and alongst the Thames on the ise from London bridge to Westminster. Some plaied at the football as boldlie there, as if it had beene on the drie land: diverse of the court being then at Westminster, shot dailie at pricks set upon the Thames: and the people both men and women went on the Thames in greater numbers, than in anie street of the citie of London.[16]

In these and similar humoral histories, the chronicler records winter behavior alongside accessions and depositions. In fact, Holinshed savors the winter cold, relishing the way it continues "so extremlie," transforming their known world into a place of wonder. Thermal extremity inspires masculine activity as Holinshed celebrates people (men?) who play "boldlie" and shoot "at pricks." Unlike a number of his partisan colleagues, he makes no attempt to celebrate the masculine mind. Perhaps bold football will compensate for dull wits? Another version of this response can be found in Robert Burton's *Anatomy of Melancholy*. As leaf after leaf charts the fluidic instabilities of the masculine body, Burton arrives at a solution. Breitenberg explains, "How can such potent internal pressure be released? By writing about it, externalizing it, and especially by assigning it to someone other than oneself."[17] Of course Burton's efforts both underwrite and unsettle those of Holinshed. One man values thought, the other physical exertion. Both value writing, and the conversation proceeds in this manner. What stands out in the growing argument, as I hope to show, is a rather consistent attempt to emphasize the external.

Shakespeare, for his part, seems to have found this conversation irresistible. Cold permeates the plays. The word appears some 217 times, but more often—and with greater complexity—in the tragedies, histories, and romances. As a backdrop to these more complex invocations, Shakespeare invokes winter to sound an old seasonal note of lack, as when Cleopatra recollects Antony: "For his bounty, / There was no winter in't" (5.2.86–87). Or the playwright conjures up a chill when he wants to talk in traditional terms about justice and mortality. At the end of *Titus Andronicus*, Lucius addresses his dead father: "O, take this warm kiss on thy pale cold lips" (5.3.153). Likewise, Cleopatra gestures toward Antony's corpse: "This case of that huge spirit now is cold" (4.15.89). Quite suggestively, Shakespeare's characters use the same terms to talk about modesty. In this vein, Ferdinand tries to impress his purity upon his future father-in-law in *The Tempest*: "I warrant you, sir, / The white cold virgin snow upon my heart / Abates the ardor of my liver" (4.1.54–56). On the other hand, Shakespeare's women often seem cold. Isabella in *Measure for Measure* and Marina in *Pericles* come to mind (2.2.45; 4.6.139). In *Much Ado About Nothing*, Beatrice takes pride in her "cold blood" (1.1.130). But, as Paster points out, the codes of humoral temperature always seem to work against women, who are figured as inherently imperfect.[18]

In the comedies, men feel nipped and pinched by brumal experience that usually has much to do with failed romance and usually, via the discourse of humors, intimates a moist masculinity. When the King of Navarre and his cohorts don Muscovite costumes in order to woo the visiting ladies, the Princess sends them off in this spirit: "Twenty adieus, my frozen Muscovits" (5.2.265). Shakespeare carries the theme forward in *The Merchant of Venice*. Once the Moor discovers he has chosen the wrong casket and lost his chance for Portia's hand, he says, "Cold indeed, and labor lost: / Then farewell heat, and welcome frost!" (2.7.74–75).[19] Frost describes the suitor's penalty, for he has promised, if wrong, "Never to speak to lady afterward / In way of marriage" (2.1.41–42). In *All's Well That Ends Well*, the sage Lafew knows that the lords who prance before Helena will fail: "These boys are boys of ice, they'll none have [her]" (2.3.93–94). In *The Merry Wives of Windsor*, Falstaff cries, "Come, let me pour in some sack to the Thames water; for my belly's as cold as if I had swallow'd snowballs for pills to cool the reins" (3.5.21–24).

In his tragedies, Shakespeare leaves little doubt that inner cold cripples a man's capacity for violent action. In *Richard III*, the main character instructs Buckingham how to speak with Hastings: "If he be leaden, icy, cold, unwilling, / Be thou so too, and so break off the talk" (3.1.176–77). At the end of the play, Richard describes his own weakness to himself in the same evolving language: "Cold fearful drops stand on my trembling flesh. / What do I fear? Myself? There's none else by" (5.3.181–82). For Richard, the cold that seeps into a man makes him tremulous. When Mowbray confronts Bullingbrook at the beginning of *Richard II,* he shows in his public address that he understands the implications of this sensibility. He wants to speak less than his adversary, but he must excuse himself: "Let not my cold words here accuse my zeal" (1.1.47). A heroic version of this condition emerges when Richard declares his sudden judgment against Bullingbrook:

K. RICH: Six frozen winters spent
Return with welcome home from banishment.
BULL: How long a time lies in one little word!
Four lagging winters and four wanton springs
End in a word: such is the breath of kings. (1.3.211–15)

As the play commences, Bullingbrook's sense of deprivation and dislocation is perfectly rendered by the king's seasonal sentence. The predicament has a long history in English literature. Old English lyrics such as "The Wanderer" and "The Seafarer" describe imposed exiles in this fashion. When set against these examples, Bullingbrook's situation seems like destiny. He does not choose winter, but confronts exile as so much snow and ice. What sets Bullingbrook apart is the way he chafes at his fate, eventually returning to his people as their ruler. When we hear Macbeth and Iago use the same terms, a paradigm of tragic incapacity becomes clear. On the verge of killing Duncan, Macbeth chides himself: "Words to the heat of deeds too cold breath gives" (2.1.61). In precisely the same spirit, Iago urges himself: "Ay, that's the way; / Dull not device by coldness and delay" (2.3.387–88). Cold overwhelms the willing minds of these male characters when it creeps inside them, unsought. Indeed, according to geohumoral theory, it makes these men too effeminate to carry out bloody business. Such examples suggest that Shakespeare, on many occasions, was perfectly content to follow geohumoral fashions.

When the playwright begins to figure such predicaments in terms of voyaging, a remarkable pattern of innovation begins to unfold. The plight of Sir Andrew in *Twelfth Night* signals the change. Paster observes that Sir Andrew's name marks "his phallic deficiencies just as his small wit, dry hand, scanty hair, and inability to cut high-stepping capers do: they are the bodily and behavioral signifiers of his lack of manly heat."[20] In other words, traditional notions of geohumoral destiny can certainly explain the man; but Shakespeare sets a new course when Fabian describes Andrew's failure with Olivia: "you are now sail'd into the north of my lady's opinion, where you will hang like an icicle on a Dutchman's beard, unless you do redeem it by some laudable attempt either of valor or policy" (3.2.26–29). Andrew is northern man but also a failed mariner on a northerly course that will spell his doom. The reference to "a Dutchman's beard," as I discuss below, demands that the audience consider the character's masculinity in terms of contemporary voyage narratives, an interpretive leap that puts new emphasis on a man's outward and valorous engagement with the cold.

Of course northern voyaging begins with the 1553 expedition of Sir Hugh Willoughby which, under the London-based direction of Sebastian Cabot, aimed for Cathay. As old markets like Antwerp had begun to fail, English merchants pooled their funds in order to share the risk of seeking out eastern trading partners. Willoughby commanded the venture from the *Bona Esperanza*. Richard Chancellor, a skilled navigator, served as chief pilot and captain of the *Edward Bonaventure*. The *Bona Confidentia* completed the party, which departed on May 11. Here were Britons who, instead of simply accepting their fate, chose the frosty unknown.

Remarkable for its masculine boldness, the expedition also demands attention because of the way it counters the image of the dull-witted Englishman with the new "mechanician." The fact is, Willoughby and company were able to set sail because of a veritable explosion of English learning and technology in the 1540s.[21] John Dee seems to have orchestrated this ferment, which included the labor of skilled pilots, craftsmen, and mathematicians. Men such as Leonard Digges and Robert Recorde published important manuals that clearly demonstrated the Englishman's perspicacity. Chancellor, as well as anyone, seems to have embodied this new masculinity. Well known as a gifted pilot, a man capable of sailing boldly through frosty seas, Chancellor was much more. E.G.R. Taylor explains that the man "was a mathematician of such an order that Dee worked with him on equal terms, and he had a further talent, one which always commanded Dee's respect: he was a mechanician. . . ."[22] The *Oxford English Dictionary* (*OED*) quotes Dee and credits him with the invention of the word: "A Mechanicien, or a Mechanicall workman is he, whose skill is, without knowledge of Mathematicall demonstration, perfectly to worke and finishe any sensible worke. . . ."[23] In everything that happened during his northern voyages, Chancellor stood for this improved Englishman, the mechanician who converted theory into action. Of course it would be whimsical to argue that northern cold inspired this intellectual transformation, but the activities of Chancellor and his contemporaries certainly proved that male Britons could transcend the negative influences of their region.

Willoughby's great enterprise went forward without incident until the 30th of July, when the *Bona Esperanza* lost touch with the other ships in a heavy fog. After five days of searching for his companions, Willoughby pressed on to the east, wandering aimlessly for more than a month. Meanwhile, the winds grew contrary. The official log of the *Bona Esperanza* narrates the finale with a poet's eye for the exoteric:

The next day being the 18th of September, we entered into the haven, and there came to an anker at 6 fadoms. This haven runneth into the maine, about two leagues, and is in bredth halfe a league, wherein were very many seale fishes, & other great fishes, and upon the maine we saw beares, great deere, foxes, with divers strange beasts, as guloines, and such other which were to us unknowen, and also wonderfull. Thus remaining in this haven the space of a weeke, seeing the yeare farre spent, & also very evill wether, as frost, snow, and haile, as though it had beene the deepe of winter, we thought best to winter there.[24]

On that brutal September day, the men believe they have found a "haven," but come to the extraordinary conclusion that they have traveled into winter. Reduced to animal-like responses, they aim to hibernate for the season among the other animals that inspire their wonder. By way of conclusion, "winter" becomes both noun and verb. Because people thought of seasons as "natural," an order ordained by the God, it made sense to adduce the coming and going of winter as evidence of a divinely ruled cosmos. A man took his place in that order, and winter happened to him. By contrast, Willoughby and his company break out of the old seasonal order by discovering a "wonderfull" new winter that gives shape to their struggle for survival. In ways that later generations would imitate, they write their own failure as a winter's tale. If bold enough, a man could transcend his geohumoral origins and choose the season that would ultimately explain his behavior.

No less compelling was the experience of Chancellor, who pushed forward and found himself in the Muscovy of Ivan the Terrible. To be sure, the pilot saw much that could be called exotic, but nothing more so than the Muscovite winter. Elaborating on Chancellor's account of the voyage, Clement Adams (Master of the Queen's Henchmen) transforms the Petrarchan discourse of fire and ice:

> The north parts of the Countrey are reported to be so cold, that the very ice or water which distilleth out of the moist wood which they lay upon the fire is presently congealed and frozen: the diversitie growing suddenly to be so great, that in one and the selfe same fiebrand, a man shall see both fire and ice.[25]

The idea of winter in Russia gave the Englishman a profoundly concrete way of writing about the yoking of elemental opposites, of temperature, and finally of intensity. Indeed, one could say that Chancellor's experience gave Petrarchan psychology a local habitation and a name. But it fell to Giles Fletcher to formulate the evolving aesthetic in a way that points directly to Shakespeare's management of his masculine characters: "The whole countrie differeth very much from it selfe, by reason of the yeare: so that a man would mervaile to see the great alteration and difference betwixte the winter, and the sommer in *Russia.*"[26] Expanding on Adams's description of opposites, Fletcher concentrates on the problem of identity, on the problem of "selfe." Here was a Russian world whose climate modeled the unstable psychologies of human beings who live north of familiar civilizations and so very often "differ from themselves." By choosing to sail on into winter, Chancellor became a hero, but he also brought the English face to face with a disturbing reflection of themselves. To be northern is to differ from oneself. Famous for this behavior and his attempts to compensate for it, Hamlet might just as well have been a Russian.[27]

Surely, the advent of such frosty speculation would have been enough to mark an epoch, but the north called to a new generation of mariners whose exploits showed early modern men how to rewrite their masculinity. Some years after Willoughby's disaster, Richard Willes urged his contemporaries to seek a passage to the northwest, noting that "in the Northeast that noble Knight Syr Hugh Willoughbie perished for colde."[28] With visions of frozen failure fixed firmly in his mind, Martin Frobisher set out three times to triumph over the unseasonable cold. As Samuel Eliot Morison notes, Frobisher's exploits, along with those of Sir Humphrey Gilbert, constitute "a series of glorious failures."[29] Frost, snow, and ice sang like sirens to these men, whose journals echo each other with a poetics of entrapment and ruin that powerfully augment Surrey's new lyrics of failed love. What sonneteers merely thought, Frobisher and company enact with a highly evolved theatrical sense of ruin. Pointing to the way writers of voyage narratives shape their materials in terms of tragic conventions, Philip Edwards notes that such narratives "convert their own actions into theatre," with the failed hero at the center.[30] As Arthur Marotti, Martin Elsky, and Mary Fuller have pointed out, writing in the Renaissance is often about failure.[31] Whether the matter be lost labors of love or scuttled voyages of ambition, the writer's aim was often, in Fuller's words, to recuperate failure "by rhetoric, a rhetoric which in some ways even predicted failure."[32] It would seem that Shakespeare's Sir Andrew comes from a long line of losers and apologists.

Some years after the Willoughby tragedy, William Warner took up the matter of the leader's icy end in his *Albions England.* Warner's speaker envisions Willoughby and his crew as "Actors" whose deeds challenged the labors of Jason and Ulysses.[33] Willoughby was "a Knight both wise and stoute," and Chancellor was a kind of Arthur.[34] Willoughby and his party "weare in theat Climate Frozen dead, shut up with isie Driftes. / Thus died he and all with him, if so to die be death: / But no, faith Heaven, no faith their Fame, surviving there on Earth."[35] In these lines, Warner's speaker argues forcefully that men who hazard greatly and fail in the face of ice and snow must triumph for all eternity. Crucial to this rhetoric is the writer's insistence on the exoteric engagement as the measure of the man. "Isie Drifts" clearly ennoble defeat.

As well as any of his chilled brethren, Claudio, in *Measure for Measure,* illustrates Shakespeare's investment in this discourse of northern voyaging. Having violated Vienna's laws against premarital sex, Claudio will be executed. No one can fail to appreciate the extremity of the punishment, but Escalus creates a puzzle when he puts it into words:

> Well; heaven forgive him! and forgive us all!
> Some rise by sin, and some by virtue fall;
> Some run from brakes of ice and answer none,
> And some condemned for a fault alone. (2.1.37–40)

For generations of editors, this passage has proven opaque. Why ice? Editors have not been comfortable with the explanation. When they have been unable to account for the "ice," they have emended the text, as Kittredge did and the *Norton Shakespeare* does, to "vice."[36] Why would editors be insensitive to the cold? Or perhaps they are already too sensitive to the cold? Such whimsical questioning actually hints at the larger methodological issues addressed in this essay. Literary interpretation has always thrived on its special relationship with the esoteric, with inwardness, with entities we call "soul" and "spirit." When confronted with exoteric masculinity, the conscientious editor prefers "vice" to "ice."

We return to the "Dutchman's beard." Sarah M. Nutt has given us good reason to believe that Shakespeare was thinking of ice, more particularly Dutch explorer William Barents's experience of ice during three voyages to a string of islands off the northern coast of Russia, a region known as "Nova Zemlya." On the third voyage, in 1596, the expedition found itself trapped in the thickening ice. Against incredible odds, the party survived the winter there. De Veer published his narrative in Dutch in 1598; Latin, French, and German editions followed and circulated throughout Europe. An English translation, by William Phillip, appeared in 1609. For her part, Nutt has recounted this publishing history and described the detailed resemblances between De Veer's account and eight of Shakespeare's plays.[37] She urges us to read *Measure for Measure* alongside De Veer:

> The ice came so fast towards us, that all the ice whereon we lay with our scutes and our goods brake and ran one peece upon another, whereby we were in no small feare, for at that time most of our goods fell into the water. But we . . . drew our scutes further upon the ice towards the land . . . and as we went to fetch our goods we fell into the greatest trouble that ever we had before . . . [for] as we laid hold upon one peece thereof the rest sunke downe with the ice, and many times the ice brake under our owne feet. . . . And when we thought to draw up our boates upon the ice, the ice brake under us, and we were caried away with the scute and al by the driving ice.[38]

Escalus needs to explain how a man could end up in this preposterous position, and his language certainly draws from voyaging narratives of ensnarement, particularly De Veer's breathtaking prose of Arctic peril. What really confounds Escalus, however, is the irony that some (like De Veer and company?) are able to run safely from such pervasive disaster, while Claudio (like Willoughby and Frobisher?) find their fate sealed by something less, by "a fault alone." More than anything else, the invocation of northern voyaging foregrounds choice as an essential part of masculine definition. Barents and his company choose to sail north. Claudio simply discovers himself on thick ice. So much for puzzles.

More victim than champion, Claudio owes his predicament, in part, to a cold man. Lucio tells Isabella that Angelo is "a man whose blood / Is very snow-broth" (1.4.57–58). The wintery terms of Barents's Russian voyaging serve his theme as he concludes: "it is certain that when he [Angelo] makes water his urine is congeal'd ice, that I know to be true" (3.2.109–11). The utterly fallen angel, Angelo has succumbed to what Falstaff calls the cold of the belly. Like the Russian landscape, he differs from himself, demanding moral stricture while indulging his own licentiousness.

If Claudio turns out to be "better" than Angelo, this male aura depends on the way he comes to envision his fate: a boreality to be confronted. It is worth noting here that Claudio does not know what Escalus has said about ice; he does not borrow the figurative language of northern voyaging from the critical counselor. Instead, Shakespeare seems to be going out of his way to show Claudio choosing a frame for his plight as he talks to Isabella:

> Ay, but to die, and go we know not where;
> To lie in cold obstruction, and to rot;
> This sensible warm motion to become
> A kneaded clod; and the delighted spirit
> To bathe in fiery floods, or to reside
> In thrilling region of thick-ribbed ice;
> To be imprison'd in the viewless winds
> And blown with restless violence round about
> The pendent world: or to be worse than worst
> Of those that lawless and incertain thought
> Imagine howling—'tis too horrible! (3.1.117–27)

Perhaps setting the agenda for later scholars, Alexander Gerard pointed to this passage in 1774 and concluded: "tho' each of the ideas is subservient to the end in view, yet they are so incongruous that they cannot be all adopted with propriety."[39] By now it should be clear that what Gerard calls incongruity is really another example of Shakespeare's ongoing exploration of the way men explain their own endurance and worth. Ice is the proper region for northern man.

Just how horrible is this distinctively male predicament? Nutt points out that De Veer uses the descriptions of ice to heighten the drama of his chronicle: "'the ice came still more and more driving in, and made high hilles by sliding one upon the other.'"[40] In point of fact, De Veer adopts these icy terms in order to conjure up a stirring marvel: "'the ice was in such a wonderfull manner risen and piled up one upon the other that it was wonderfull, in such manner as if there had bin whole townes made of ice, with towres and bulwarkes round about them.'"[41] To be "incertain" and confront "cold obstruction" as Claudio does is to tap into the "wonderfull." By appropriating the popular Dutch discourse of northern voyaging, the prisoner can shift his consternation to a benumbed region of wonder that English travelers had described in vivid detail. In fact, Claudio recovers his will when he imagines himself a second De Veer: "Sweet sister, let me live" (3.1.132). Just as it does for Hamlet's temperament, the northern cold becomes a key to the moral mind of this character; and, like the Russian winter as Fletcher describes it, Claudio comes "to differ from himself." He seems to possess an interiority through that differing, and the wonder implicit in the experience of the exotic merges with his wonder at his "life."

Whatever the character gains through this matrix of reference, Shakespeare carefully husbands it over the remainder of the play. In the scene we have just been discussing, Isabella quickly chastises him for his self-interest. Claudio reconsiders and begs to speak with his sister, but the Duke ushers him away. The character speaks a few words in 4.2, and then remains silent until he takes his place in the Duke's orchestrations at the play's conclusion. Shakespeare has recuperated Claudio, after a fashion. What matters most for our discussion is the way this rehabilitation depends on an extraordinary synthesis of the old and the new. In Claudio, the ancient concern with internal cold merges with the contemporary interest in the exoteric assay.[42]

Sometime around 1599, in a burst of creative activity that produces *Julius Caesar* and *Hamlet,* Shakespeare sets his work apart from the ancient tradition when he divides the male population into men who are cold and men who choose the cold. (Claudio epitomizes the former category, while Willoughby and Chancellor embody the latter.) Near the beginning of *Julius Caesar,* Cassius invokes the rubric Hamlet will use when the prince attempts to justify his grief: "I know that virtue to be in you, Brutus, / As well as I do know your outward favor" (1.2.90-91). A man must be valued by some comparison of the inward and the outward. Caesar's confession to Antony frames Cassius's opinion:

> I do not know the man I should avoid
> So soon as that spare Cassius. He reads much,
> He is a great observer, and he looks
> Quite through the deeds of men.
> (1.2.200-3)

Regardless of how we judge him, Cassius surely lives up to Caesar's estimation as he explains masculinity to Brutus:

> I cannot tell what you or other men
> Think of this life; but, for my single self,
> I had as lief not be as live to be
> In awe of such a thing as I myself.
> I was born free as Caesar, so were you;
> We both have fed as well, and we can both
> Endure the winter's cold as well as he . . . (1.2.93–99)

No neutral observer, Cassius is all too aware that his fortunes have failed to keep pace with Caesar's, but this self-interest does not diminish his ability to scrutinize. Internal temperature does not matter in this analysis. Seeing through the deeds of men, for Cassius, means recognizing the male capacity for enduring winter's cold, a point the speaker supports with a story about swimming. He tells how Caesar, on a "raw and gusty day," said, " 'Dar'st thou, Cassius, now / Leap in with me into this angry flood' " (100, 102–3). The formula is simple: we can value men by studying how they dare to embrace the cold.[43] On that day, Caesar sank. That Cassius braved the icy waters to save this "god" is now proof (for him) that something is rotten in Rome. Indeed, invoking the language of encompassment (so prevalent in the voyaging narratives), Cassius asks, "When could they say, till now, that talk'd of Rome, / That her wide walks encompass'd but one man?" (1.2.154–55). According to Cassius, to be "incompass'd" is the fate—perhaps the birthright—of all men. He resists Caesar's claims to special status even as he inflates himself through his narrative of an icy swim.

What Cassius inaugurates, Hamlet may be said to complete. From the first moments of the play, Hamlet appears to encourage boundless speculation: "But I have that within which passes show" (1.2.85). For centuries, critics have tried to pursue this claim. In the wake of Charles Lamb and Samuel Coleridge, Edward Dowden thought the play epitomized the value of "obscurity": "Hamlet might so easily have been manufactured into an enigma or a puzzle; and then the puzzle, if sufficient pains were bestowed, could be completely taken to pieces and explained. But Shakspere created it a mystery, and therefore it is forever suggestive; forever suggestive, and never wholly explicable."[44] Sigmund Freud gave this "modern" appreciation of uncertainty a new twist when he began to detect Hamlet's unconscious desire for his mother, gradually coming to see himself in Hamlet. Freud concludes, "Here I have translated into conscious terms what was bound to remain unconscious in Hamlet's mind. . . ."[45] As a new century dawned, Hamlet possessed a willing mind whose obscurity could nonetheless be recovered by the aggressive analyst. Indeed it would be difficult to say whether Hamlet is the subject or the source of the analysis.[46] Bradley simply declares: "How many things still remain to say of Hamlet!"[47]

I begin with a simple fact: Hamlet, like everyone else in the tragedy, is cold. Who in Denmark would not want to go inside, whether we think of the interior space in terms of the mind or the edifice? When Kenneth Branagh directed his film version of the play, he whitened the landscape and the main character, perhaps setting a record for the use of artificial snow. The vision recalls the geohumoralism of *Batman uppon Bartholome,* with its emphasis on the whiteness of northern people. Branagh's screenplay begins in terms Willoughby could appreciate: "Darkness. Uneasy silence. The deep of a Winter's Night."[48] This seems right because the playwright takes pains to stress the frigidity of the environment from the opening lines. As Francisco says somewhat cryptically at the beginning of the drama, "For this relief much thanks. 'Tis bitter cold, / And I am sick at heart" (1.1.8–9). In Denmark, the cold indicates the condition of a solitary man, whose ailment will never be adequately communicated. Indeed, Francisco departs the stage and the play as a frosty cipher.

Garbed in an inky cloak, Hamlet takes Francisco's place, answering questions with riddles, quips, and puns. Sick at heart, he does not fit the old model of northern masculinity. Floyd-Wilson sharpens this sense: "In its representation of a melancholic *Dane,* Shakespeare's play tells the story of an extraordinary northerner—extraordinary because his inward melancholy has estranged him from his native, northern complexion."[49] Hamlet acts too little and thinks too much. Claudius makes the obvious point that the prince has given in to "unmanly grief" (1.2.94). By contrast, Hamlet's father embraced his native cold. Here was the traditional northern monarch, untroubled by cogitation, who "smote the sledded [Polacks] on the ice" (1.1.63). Here was the king who "Did slay this Fortinbras" (1.1.86) on the day of his son's birth. Hamlet, it seems, was born under the sign of his father's prowess. Measured against this example, Hamlet appears to be an extraordinary failure, a passive victim. And it is at this juncture in the play that Hamlet defends himself by claiming to "have that within which passes show." Left alone, the man reverts to the old indictment: "O that this too too sallied flesh would melt, / Thaw, and resolve itself into a dew!" (1.2.129–30). Hamlet longs to "melt" and "thaw," a desire that reveals much about the way he sees himself in the world. He is a man of ice who has nearly succumbed to the cold. As Sidney Warhaft pointed out some time ago, Hamlet's sense of his flesh as something that would melt (and here, I am inclined to favor "solid flesh") certainly suggests the character's humorous condition, namely the cold and congealed body of a melancholy man, the estranged Dane, a failed man whose only recourse is silence.[50]

In fact, Hamlet has already begun to tinker with the old rhetoric, thinking through the cold in unprecedented ways. Although an ardent spokesman for Hamlet's inwardness, Coleridge helps to explain this innovation when he remarks the way that Hamlet's "half embodyings of thoughts, that make them more than thoughts, give them an outness, a reality *sui generis,* and yet retain their correspondence and shadowy approach to the images and movements within."[51] Coleridge, I believe, has pinpointed Shakespeare's strategy of rapprochement. For example, Hamlet's decision to think about himself as snow and ice "half-embodies" his condition. In this spirit, Hamlet rattles Horatio by seeing his father. The friend looks about, but Hamlet explains, "In my mind's eye, Horatio" (1.2.185). Over the course of the play, Hamlet will justify himself by straddling thought and action, interiority and exteriority, erecting a field of "outness" around him that has stabilized his challenged masculinity for more than four centuries. The irony, of course, is that Hamlet's cognitive innovation does nothing to lessen the chill. With his usual intuitive genius, Coleridge, as quoted above in this essay's epigraph, diagnoses an "exhaustion of bodily feeling from perpetual exertion of mind," concluding "that all mental form being indefinite and ideal, realities must needs become cold." Hamlet attempts to survive his ordeal with half-embodying thought, but his behavior only heightens the cold.

When Hamlet decides to go out into the cold to confront the Ghost, he seems to accept the challenge set forth in the voyaging narratives. How appropriate then that as Hamlet waits for the Ghost, he declares: "The air bites shrowdly, it is very cold" (1.4.1). An Elizabethan might have wondered whether there was something effeminate in this cold, in its shrewishness, but Shakespeare emphasizes what is outside the man, namely the biting northern "air." Horatio foretells a change in the wind when he calls it a "nipping and eager air" (1.4.2). In the Danish chill, the men listen to the king's wassail, and Hamlet laments the northern propensity for "heavy-headed revel" (1.4.17). The proud prince aims for a better "attribute" (1.4.22). Indeed, we can mark his transformation when

Horatio and company try to prevent him from departing with the Ghost. Hamlet declares, "My fate cries out, / And makes each petty artere in this body / As hardy as the Nemean lion's nerve" (1.4.81–83). Cold actually fortifies his body. He seems ready to follow the example of his martial father as he learns of his uncle's crime: "And thy commandment all alone shall live" (1.5.102).

To be sure, Hamlet's half-embodying thoughts immediately complicate this agenda. Having promised action, Hamlet should gather his comrades. Marcellus yells, "Illo, ho, ho, my lord!" (1.5.115). Hamlet cries: "Hillo, ho, ho, boy! Come, [bird,] come" (1.5.116). The prince has not officially assumed his antic disposition, but his thinking seems already to have made it so. In his giddy mood, Hamlet half-embodies his newfound purpose. He plays the part of a falconer calling down his bird. The inspiration is aural, the application fair, the utility in question. As the group interview begins, Horatio begins to doubt: "These are but wild and whirling words" (1.5.133). Hamlet apologizes and comes to the purpose; but his survival strategy has already begun to emerge. Henceforth he will "bear" himself in a "strange or odd" fashion (1.5.170). He will, in other words, justify himself by casting his outness as madness. Claudius glosses the effect:

> Something have you heard
> Of Hamlet's transformation; so call it,
> Sith nor th' exterior nor the inward man
> Resembles that it was. (2.2.4–7)

No simple disguise, Hamlet's "transformation" unsettles Claudius because of the way he differs from himself, inside and out.

What we make of this strategy has everything to do with the way the playwright engages the discourse of northern voyaging. When Rosencrantz and Guildenstern come snooping, Hamlet clues them in with a famous line: "I am but mad north-north-west" (2.2.378). The declaration may suggest mere flippancy, but I hear Hamlet claiming his position as yet another northern male in Willoughby's line, encompassed by extremes, near mad with dejection, epitomizing the fate of heroic masculinity. We step back in awe at this transformation, but Hamlet remains unsatisfied and quite mad. It is worth noting in this context that, according to the *OED,* for centuries before the writing of *Hamlet,* "mad" referred not only to insanity but also to being "'Beside oneself' with anger; moved to uncontrollable rage; furious."[52] For Hamlet, the problem is how to translate mere (even effeminate) fury into the more masculine *wrath.*[53] His lack of success on this score finds voice as he prepares to depart Denmark for England, only to witness the army of Fortinbras and wonder "How all occasions do inform against me" (4.4.32). Like Willoughby and Frobisher, he claims our attention because he has failed. Environed by icy circumstance, he poses the obvious question: "What is a man . . . ?" (4.4.33).

Shakespeare's answer comes straight from the nexus of climate and voyaging that we have been charting. Indeed, Chancellor, the man who helped Dee invent the paradoxal compass, the man who combined action and thought in the role of the mechanician, serves as a key to Hamlet's evolving experiment. Long before he reaches the despair of 4.4, he writes to Ophelia and promises love "whilst this machine is to him" (2.2.124). Capable of half-materializing thought, of mingling the inward and the outward, Hamlet identifies his own body as a "machine." The *OED* credits Shakespeare with the invention of this notion and so calls attention to the playwright's real innovation. What is particularly remarkable about this tack is the way the word "machine" floats between the substantial and the insubstantial, referring (as the *OED* explains) to structures "of any kind, material or immaterial."[54] Confronting his native cold with a fluidic body that seems to have failed him, Hamlet reinvents the male body as a machine. Even more ambitiously, he becomes his own mechanician.

As Chancellor might have done, Shakespeare goes on to suggest that a man is a person who sets out on a voyage. Of course he does not choose the venture; but, once at sea, Hamlet performs deeds of valor. He reports to Horatio: "Finding ourselves too slow of sail, we put on a compell'd valor, and in the grapple I boarded them" (4.6.17–19). Inspired by his own swashbuckling, Hamlet now discerns his opportunity. When Shakespeare gets Hamlet out of Denmark and into the pirates' custody, he makes it possible for Hamlet to choose to return to the "bitter cold" of his homeland. Hamlet may possess a sense of his own inwardness, but his experience under sail exposes the exoteric protocols of masculinity that he needs. Back in Denmark, Hamlet writes to Claudius and signals his explicit transformation by promising to "recount the occasion of my sudden [and more strange] return" (4.7.46–47). Hamlet is now master of his own occasion, but Hamlet's penchant for outness makes him pause.

Hamlet returns to the old question with clarity: "What is a man?" No longer focused on rhetorics of self-justification and survival, Hamlet exploits his habitual outness with an eye toward more enduring questions:

"Why may not imagination trace the noble dust of Alexander, till 'a find it stopping a bunghole?" (5.1.203-4). Ever the pragmatist, Horatio counsels against such musing, but Hamlet proceeds to recast the old masculine engagement with winter:

Alexander died, Alexander was buried, Alexander returneth to dust, the dust is earth, of earth we make loam, and why of that loam whereto he was converted might they not stop a beer-barrel?
Imperious Caesar, dead and turn'd to clay,
Might stop a hole to keep the wind away.
O that that earth which kept the world in awe
Should patch a wall t' expel the [winter's] flaw! (5.1.208-16)

I quote the passage at length because Shakespeare's hand is so evidently marking the dynamic quality of this frosty speculation as a movement into lyrical resolution. Alexander is "converted" to loam, to matter for a "stop," in prose that suggests logical demonstration; but Hamlet reaches his conclusion in verse, in couplets that emphasize the utter mutability of life. Having chosen to face the cold of his native land with all the problems it holds for him, Hamlet has satisfied a certain standard of masculine behavior. Yet he has come to understand that a man may justify himself for a time and still end up a patch, a rich word, both noun and verb, that referred to both a mechanician's repair and a fool.[55] In this way, Hamlet's outness bears fruit in the shape of skeptical wisdom: Hamlet sees through the deeds of men. Botero helps us value the prince's achievement. Questioning whether a man requires courage or wisdom most, the writer opts for courage because "wisedome is given but to fewe, and that must be gotten too by travail."[56] At the end of the play, Hamlet has demonstrated both courage and wisdom. Like the accomplished mechanician, he can finish what he cannot demonstrate.

By the time Hamlet receives Osric, he has outmaneuvered the old thermal tests, and we measure his superiority against the lesser man. Osric thinks it very hot, but Hamlet applies correction: "No, believe me, 'tis very cold, the wind is northerly" (5.2.95). It is telling that both times Hamlet indicates direction (hearkening back to 2.2.378), he does it aggressively while in the company of lesser men who irritate him. In both scenes, the direction implies his superiority. He is not the muddled prince who cannot act, but a man encompassed by northern cold that elevates him even as it afflicts him. Such subtleties escape Osric's notice, and Hamlet toys with him. When the courtier agrees with Hamlet's temperature reading, the prince tells him, "But yet methinks it is very [sultry] and hot [for] my complexion" (5.2.98-99). Having mastered the old discourse of voyaging and cold, Hamlet amuses himself with a "yes man." After Osric departs, Hamlet comes to the point: "Thus has he, and many more of the same breed that I know the drossy age dotes on, only got the tune of the time, and out of an habit of encounter, a kind of [yesty] collection" (5.2.188-91). The Folio points more precisely to Hamlet's sentiments as he complains of this breed that has only got an "outward habit of encounter." Like Rosencrantz and Guildenstern, Osric thinks he can define his masculinity with little exoteric formulas of civility, but he seriously underestimates the venture.[57] These men stand as the real failures in the tragedy because they do not rescue their prince.

For his part, Hamlet has grown into the role of mechanician as Dee defined it. Shuttling between thought and action, the material and the immaterial, Hamlet discovers how to finish his "sensible work." With no boasts of what he holds within, he walks "here in the hall," in "the breathing time of day" (5.2.173-74). As the Folio emphasizes, Hamlet's attempt at a formal reconciliation with Laertes carries with it a nod to their quite public "audience" (5.2.240). Their contest occurs before judges who "bear a wary eye" (5.2.279). When the first hit comes, it is "palpable" (5.2.281). In the aftermath of the carnage, Fortinbras, who seems never to have questioned his outward obligations, gives the exoteric order: "Take up the bodies" (5.2.401). Branagh's film version of the play surely captures the exteriority of Hamlet's end as we look down on the pearly prince at rest in an open casket suspended above the snow.

In 1598, the Thames froze solid, as it had done many times before, and people probably tried to read the event as a sign of the times. Perhaps Shakespeare was thinking about *Hamlet*. Today, we may follow scientists who talk about our playwright's epoch as "The Little Ice Age," a chilly era that engulfed the whole of Europe. Most of us will continue to think about Hamlet, the supreme representative of this age, who takes his place in a long line of men who sought to redeem themselves through engagement with the frozen north. If he manages to rehabilitate northern masculinity, we must admit that it comes with the heavy burden of skepticism. Some 325 years later, Wallace Stevens was able to fathom the heart of this discourse for a warmer world, refashioning Hamlet's early modern speculations into a modern "mind of winter," "the listener, who listens in the snow, / And, nothing himself, beholds / Nothing that is not there and the nothing that is."[58]

Notes

1. William Shakespeare, *Hamlet*, in *The Riverside Shakespeare*, ed. G. Blakemore Evans (New York: Houghton Mifflin, 1974), 1.2.85–86. Subsequent references to the plays of Shakespeare will be from this edition and appear parenthetically in the text.

2. The scholarship devoted to this question is extensive, to say the least. One might well begin with Sigmund Freud, who has seemed to underwrite the study of inwardness in the Renaissance, particularly with his reading of *Hamlet*. In fact, Freud points in another direction when he discusses being as an ego-effect. In "The Ego and the Id," he explains, "The ego is first and foremost a bodily ego; it is not merely a surface entity, but is itself the projection of a surface" (*The Standard Edition of the Complete Psychological Works of Sigmund Freud*, 24 vols., trans. and ed. James Strachey, [London: Hogarth Press, 1961], 19:26). Katharine Eisaman Maus offers perhaps the most cogent account of the controversy by arguing persuasively that the early modern stage afforded its audiences "inwardness displayed: an inwardness, in other words, that has already ceased to exist" (*Inwardness and Theater in the English Renaissance* [Chicago: University of Chicago Press, 1996], 32). Other crucial discussions of this problem include Francis Barker, *The Tremulous Private Body* (London: Methuen, 1984); Cynthia Marshall, "Man of Steel Done Got the Blues: Melancholic Subversion of Presence in *Antony and Cleopatra*," *Shakespeare Quarterly* 44.4 (1993): 386; Mark Breitenberg, *Anxious Masculinity in Early Modern England* (Cambridge: Cambridge University Press, 1996), 15; and Michael C. Schoenfeldt, *Bodies and Selves in Early Modern England: Physiology and Inwardness in Spenser, Shakespeare, Herbert, and Milton* (Cambridge: Cambridge University Press, 1999), 2, 76.

3. Mary Floyd-Wilson, *English Ethnicity and Race in Early Modern Drama* (Cambridge: Cambridge University Press, 2003), 2. See also Mary Floyd-Wilson, "Transmigrations: Crossing Regional and Gender Boundaries in *Antony and Cleopatra*," *Enacting Gender on the English Renaissance Stage*, ed. Viviana Comensoli and Anne Russell (Urbana: University of Illinois Press, 1999), 77.

4. John Wands, "The Theory of Climate in the English Renaissance and *Mundus Alter et Idem*," *Acta Conventus Neo-Latini Sanctandreani, Medieval and Renaissance Texts and Studies*, ed. I. D. McFarlane, vol. 38 (Binghamton, N.Y.: Medieval and Renaissance Texts and Studies, 1986), 519–20. Floyd-Wilson provides a useful bibliography for this tradition (*English Ethnicity*, 3).

5. Giovanni Botero, *Historicall Description of the Most Famous Kingdomes and Common-weales in the World* (London, 1603), 7.

6. Botero, by contrast, seems content to include Britain in Europe, which he describes as "passing good, holsome, temperate, and the soile exceeding fertile" (*Historicall Description of the Most Famous Kingdomes*, 10).

7. William Andrews, *Famous Frosts and Frost Fairs in Great Britain* (London: George Redway, 1887).

8. Olaus Magnus, *Historia de Gentibus Septentrionalibus,* trans. Peter Fisher and Humphrey Higgens, ed. Peter Foote (London: Hakluyt Society, 1998), 3:771.

9. Breitenberg, *Anxious Masculinity,* 2. In recent years, scholars have paid increasing attention to the unstable nature of masculinity, particularly in the plays of Shakespeare. See, for example, Coppélia Kahn, *Roman Shakespeare: Warriors, Wounds, and Women* (London and New York: Routledge, 1997); Geraldo U. de Sousa, *Shakespeare's Cross-Cultural Encounters* (Houndmills and London: Macmillan, 1999); *The Image of Manhood in Early Modern Literature,* ed. Andrew P. Williams (Westport, Conn.: Greenwood Press, 1999); Bruce R. Smith, *Shakespeare and Masculinity* (Oxford: Oxford University Press, 2000); Robin Headlam Wells, *Shakespeare on Masculinity* (Cambridge: Cambridge University Press, 2000); Alexandra Shepard, *Meanings of Manhood in Early Modern England* (Oxford: Oxford University Press, 2003).

10. Floyd-Wilson, *English Ethnicity,* 3. Of course all recent studies of humoral theory in the Renaissance owe something to the work of Gail Kern Paster. See, for example, Gail Kern Paster, "The Unbearable Coldness of Female Being: Women's Imperfection and the Humoral Economy," *English Literary Renaissance* 28.3 (1998): 416.

11. Floyd-Wilson, *English Ethnicity,* 4-5. See also Floyd-Wilson, "Transmigrations," 75.

12. Stephen Batman, *Batman uppon Bartholome* (London, 1582), 26.

13. Levinus Lemnius, *The Touchstone of Complexions,* trans. Thomas Newton (London, 1633), 25.

14. Jean Bodin, *The Six Bookes of a Commonweale,* ed. Kenneth Douglas McRae (Cambridge: Harvard University Press, 1962), 99.

15. Floyd-Wilson, *English Ethnicity,* 4.

16. *Holinshed's Chronicles,* 6 vols. (London: Johnson, 1808), 4:228; qtd. in Andrews, *Frost Fairs,* 8.

17. Breitenberg, *Anxious Masculinity,* 68.

18. Paster, "The Unbearable Coldness of Female Being," 439-40.

19. For an important geohumoral revision of the usual reading of Morocco's failure, see Floyd-Wilson, *English Ethnicity,* 42-43.

20. Paster, "The Unbearable Coldness of Female Being," 435.

21. On this phenomenon in particular and English contact with Russia in general, see Daryl W. Palmer, *Writing Russia in the Age of Shakespeare* (Aldershot and Burlington, U.K.: Ashgate, 2004), 9-11, and passim.

22. E.G.R. Taylor, *Tudor Geography 1485-1583* (London: Methuen, 1930), 91.

23. *Oxford English Dictionary,* s.v. "mechanician," n.1.

24. Hakluyt, *Principal Navigations, Voyages, Traffiques, and Discoveries of the English Nation,* 8 vols. (London: J. M. Dent, 1927), 1:253.

25. Hakluyt, *Principal Navigations,* 1:279.

26. Giles Fletcher, *The English Works of Giles Fletcher, the Elder,* ed. Lloyd E. Berry (Madison: University of Wisconsin Press, 1964), 175.

27. Moved by ethological similarities, nineteenth-century writer and artist William Morris declared to Georgiana Burne-Jones that "Hamlet . . . should have been a Russian, not a Dane" (March 17, 1888, letter 1470, *The Collected Letters of William Morris,* ed. Norman Kelvin, vol. 2, pt. b, 1885–88 [Princeton: Princeton University Press, 1987], 755).

28. Hakluyt, *Principal Navigations,* 5:121.

29. Samuel Eliot Morison, *The Great Explorers* (New York: Oxford University Press, 1978), 277.

30. Philip Edwards, "Tragic Form and the Voyagers," *Travel and Drama in Shakespeare's Time,* ed. Jean-Pierre Maquerlot and Michele Willems (Cambridge: Cambridge University Press, 1996), 82.

31. Arthur Marotti, " 'Love is not Love': Elizabethan Sonnet Sequences and the Social Order," *ELH* 49.2 (1982): 398; Martin Elsky, *Authorizing Words: Speech, Writing, and Print in the English Renaissance* (Ithaca, N.Y.: Cornell University Press, 1989), 188–89; Mary Fuller, *Voyages in Print: English Travel to America, 1576-1624* (Cambridge: Cambridge University Press, 1995), 12.

32. Fuller, *Voyages in Print,* 12.

33. William Warner, *Albions England* (London, 1597), 273–74.

34. Warner, *Albions England,* 274.

35. Warner, *Albions England,* 274.

36. *The Complete Works of Shakespeare,* ed. George Lyman Kittredge (Boston: Ginn, 1936): 2.1.39; *The Norton Shakespeare,* gen. ed. Stephen Greenblatt (New York and London: Norton, 1997), 2.1.39, n. 2.

37. Sarah M. Nutt, "The Arctic Voyages of William Barents in Probable Relation to Certain of Shakespeare's Plays," *SP* 39 (1942): 260. Perhaps the most comprehensive discussion of this sphere of exploration is found in Sir Clement R. Markham's *The Lands of Silence: A History of Arctic and Antarctic Exploration* (Cambridge: Cambridge University Press, 1921).

38. Qtd. by Nutt, "The Arctic Voyages of William Barents," 254.

39. Alexander Gerard, "An Essay on Genius," *Shakespeare, The Critical Heritage: 1774-1801,* ed. Brian Vickers, 6 vols. (London: Routledge, 1981), 6:114.

40. Qtd. by Nutt, "The Arctic Voyages of William Barents," 254.

41. Ibid.

42. It should be noted that I have chosen to treat Claudio as a kind of prologue to my discussion of Hamlet, even though *Measure for Measure* was written after the famous tragedy. I do this for the sake of clarity in my argument, but I realize that this example proves, yet again, that genealogy is rarely linear. Although I choose to see Shakespeare as an innovator in *Hamlet,* I can assume very little about the playwright's investment in that innovation.

43. Surely this credo informs Caesar's description of soldier Antony in the Alps in Shakespeare's play (1.4.66-71).

44. Dowden, *Shakespere: A Critical Study of His Mind and Art,* 3rd ed. (New York, Harper & Brothers, n.d.), 112.

45. Sigmund Freud, *The Interpretation of Dreams: The Complete Psychological Works of Sigmund Freud,* trans. James Strachey, 24 vols. (1900; London: Hogarth Press, 1953), 4:265.

46. Marjorie Garber, *Shakespeare's Ghost Writers* (New York: Routledge, 1987), 170. See also Julia Reinhard Lupton and Kenneth Reinhard, *After Oedipus: Shakespeare in Psychoanalysis* (Ithaca, N.Y.: Cornell University Press, 1993), 2.

47. A. C. Bradley, *Shakespearean Tragedy* (1904; New York: St. Martin's Press, 1969), 118.

48. Kenneth Branagh, *Hamlet, Screenplay and Introduction* (New York: Norton, 1996), 1. As Russell Jackson notes in "The Film Diary" from the same volume, the exterior filming at

Blenheim Palace was beset by "real snow" that "sweeps in off the lake, blanking out visibility in a blizzard that covers all of us" (190). The next day, Jackson remarks, "Dry, bitter wind. Frozen snow now like brittle wedding-cake icing, and mixed with our own foam, paper, and salt" (191). In this way, cinema elaborates the dreams of exoteric man.

49. Floyd-Wilson, *English Ethnicity*, 78.

50. Sidney Warhaft, "Hamlet's Solid Flesh Resolved," *ELH* 28.1 (1961), 22.

51. Coleridge, *Coleridge's Shakespeare Criticism*, 1:38–39.

52. S.v. "mad," 6.

53. Citing Helkiah Crooke's *Description of the Body of Man*, Paster notes that "anger" was associated with women while "wrath" was reserved for men ("The Unbearable Coldness of Female Being," 429).

54. S.v. "machine."

55. In *A Midsummer Night's Dream*, Puck uses these terms to describe Bottom and company as "A crew of patches, rude mechanicals" (3.2.9).

56. Botero, *Historicall Description*, 3.

57. John Lyly provides a comic prologue to these scenes in his *Gallathea* as Rafe, Robin, and Dick attempt to become real men after their ship sinks. Their doomed labor of masculine self- definition turns on their ability to speak in northerly terms:

DICK: I'll say it. North, northeast, northeast, nor'—nor' and by nor'east—I shall never do it.
MARINER: This is but one quarter.
ROBIN: I shall never learn a quarter of it. I will try. North, north-east, is by the west side, north and by north—
DICK: Passing ill. (*Drama of the English Renaissance*, ed. Russell A. Fraser and Norman Rabkin, 2 vols. [New York and London: Macmillan, 1976], 1:2.1.63–72).

The words of Rafe at the end of the lesson aptly sum up the condition of Rosencrantz, Guildenstern, and Osric: "I will never learn this language" (2.1.78).

58. Wallace Stevens, "The Snow Man," *The Palm at the End of the Mind*, ed. Holly Stevens (New York: Knopf, 1971), 54.

"Divided in Soyle":
Plantation and Degeneracy in
The Tempest *and* The Sea Voyage

JEAN FEERICK

"Sea-Changes" of Blood

In the account of his voyage to Barbados in 1631, Sir Henry Colt provides a detailed survey of the status of English planters abroad. In summarizing the quality of life available to them in the recently planted island—the foods the island can provide, the sustaining power of the soil, the qualities of the climate—Colt also observes how the island has affected the collective complexions, that is the tempers, of Englishmen. The already hot tempers of the island's young English planters, he notes at the start of his account, have grown dangerously fiery. Searching for explanations of this near-universal pattern, Colt turns first to humoralism and to the effects of consumption on the humors to account for the change. The distempered excesses of these men, he believes, derives in part from their overconsumption of hot drinks[1]—the rosemary water, angelica water, aniseed water, and aqua vitae that he will recommend his son include among his own staples should he set out on a future voyage. Not moderating their "younge & hott bloods" by drinking "cold water," these young planters have instead allowed themselves to become inflamed to passion and quarrelsomeness, spending their days in riot and idleness and allowing the duties of running a plantation to fall by the wayside.[2] Making his observations just a few years after the plantation of Barbados by Englishmen, Colt was describing part of a phenomenon that would eventually congeal in the phrase "Barbados distemper."[3]

27

Although Colt writes with a distinctly paternalistic concern, urging English planters to correct this mishap, he also seems to suggest they are destined to fail. Indeed, after detailing his various criticisms of their behavior, he comes forward with his own confession. He, too, it seems, underwent the same alienating transformation. Though he had always lived by habits "wise & temperate," while on the island he fell under the grip of these distempering behaviors, observing how his customary two drams of "hott water" rose to a frightening thirty drams in a matter of days.[4] In numbering himself among those who have declined, Colt seems to suggest that few English planters—young or old, gentle or base— can escape untouched by these lands' profound transformations. As if abandoning all hope, he gestures toward a metaphysical explanation of this heatedness to supplement the natural explanation he had earlier provided, noting:

Who is he [that] cann liue long in quiett in these parts? For all men are heer made subiect to ye power of this Infernall Spiritt. And fight they must, although it be wth ther owne frends.[5]

In observing the island's centripetal tug toward discord, heat, and disquiet, Colt contributed to a growing cultural obsession among the English of the early seventeenth century about how transplantation could effect reversals on "civil" planters. In observing transformations that affected the blood—changes that made the already hot blood of young Englishmen even hotter—Colt was addressing a problem that elsewhere was described through the language of degeneration. Just a few years before Colt's journey to Barbados, for instance, Purchas worried these unpredictable shifts in those migrating to Virginia, urging that adventures to the Americas not make "Savages and wild degenerate men of Christians, but Christians of those Savage, wild, degenerate men."[6] In this early period of English plantation, geographies as variable as Virginia, Bermuda, Ireland, and the West Indies were framed through this language of degeneration, which, I will argue, expressed in small a complex engagement with the challenge of maintaining English identity outside England.[7]

By the time the English began active settlements in the West Indies in the late 1620s and early 1630s, the question of how transplantation would affect the physical and social identity of Englishmen was already being explored on the Jacobean stage, dating from the period of Shakespeare's romances. Emerging as a dominant genre of the stage during the early period of Virginia's colonization, romance placed a premium on plots dramatizing social and physical displacement. They staged families divided, heirs seized, patriarchs displaced, obsessively circling around challenges to elite blood posed by, among other things, geographical obstacles. Both *The Tempest* and Fletcher and Massinger's *The Sea Voyage,* written a decade later, speak to this growing interest in the effects of transplantation on English bodies and English culture.[8] If *The Tempest* obliquely engages the question of whether and how foreign lands might reinscribe the physical and social identity of transplanted Europeans, *The Sea Voyage* makes this problem its central concern. Both plays are set on islands distant from Europe, and likewise both plays avoid precisely identifying the geography of their setting. Scholars have locked in debate over the location of the isle in Shakespeare's play. Some have tended to read the play as broadly allusive to events surrounding the early colonization of Virginia, producing readings that emphasize an Atlantic context and the play's implication in an emergent imperial discourse.[9] Others take note that the origin of the Italian fleet's journey in Tunis insists on the island's Mediterranean context and, more specifically, a location somewhere in the Sicilian archipelago.[10] Still others suggest that the island is all of these locations and more, identifying Ireland as yet another site allusively engaged by the play.[11] In a similar way, Fletcher and Massinger avoid specifying the precise location of the islands featured in their later play. We know little save that the colonists have fled from a plantation in "the happy Islands" (5.2.97) before arriving to the "unknown world" (5.4.32) of the twin islands they now inhabit. Working from these rather general references, a critic like McMullan posits that the islands are located near the coast of Guiana.[12] But an exact location is never named. As with Shakespeare's play, what we have is an "island play," one that rejects specificity of place and even conjures multiple locations.[13]

This obfuscation of geography is, for my purposes, of the essence. I suggest that to varying degrees these plays represent and seek to resolve the problematic of surviving not in any one specific place but rather in a place far from "home." The geographies they describe are linked in being alien to the native lands of the plays' respective protagonists. As Jerry Brotton has recently argued, we know for certain only that the islands represented are "distant, terrifying and bewildering places."[14] Together the plays constitute a sustained meditation on how alien soils affect elite Europeans, exploring the effects transplantation might have on elite blood.

Through the French, Italian, and Portuguese figures depicted in these plays, the English playwrights project onto an earlier round of European colonizers challenges that the English were newly facing at the start of the seventeenth century in moving to plant abroad.

And yet despite their similarities, *The Tempest* and *The Sea Voyage* represent two rather divergent figurative resolutions of the problems posed by plantation. *The Tempest,* produced in the context of Virginia's earliest settlement, evokes, even as it sidesteps, the question of how living and reproducing beyond English borders might affect identity. The play gives us reason to believe that inhabiting a different climate, soil, and air could well be a veritable Pandora's box for identity. It is hardly inconsequential that Prospero's magic is founded on his control of the natural elements, granting him the power to produce or withhold the alterity of the island's geography. And it is the qualities of the isle's climate that first lock the newcomers in dispute (2.1.35-60).[15] If the optimism of Adrian and Gonzalo lead them to emphasize the landscape as temperate, lush, and capable of sustaining life, Antonio and Sebastian deflate this account with their own narrative of the isle as a barren and infecting landscape. For them the air is "rotten" and fenny and the land itself burned to a "tawny" (2.1.55) color. That this discussion implicitly mediates the problem of reproducing far from home, in a place alternately described as "inaccessible" and even "uninhabitable" (2.1.38), is expressed in the sudden turn of this conversation to the topic of marriage, heirs, and both Claribel and Dido. As figures who embody the disruption of patronym—whether that of Alonso or Aeneas—these famous queens serve to mark the crisis of lineage occasioned through prolonged contact with lands beyond "our Europe" (2.1.125). In the image that brings this classical digression to a close, the play's humorists conjure an alternate system of property transmission—one where distant isles can be transported, like any old apple, back "home in [one's] pocket" (2.1.90). In the image of island "kernels" generating "more islands" after being sown in the sea, we witness the play's wistful rewriting of migration and transplantation. In this reverie islands travel home, securing lineage and even empire, and thereby absorb the costs of reproduction from a nobility wary of displacement.

If I am right to infer that geographical alterity is this play's Pandora's box, it is a box closely guarded. Indeed, in this play, the elements are obedient; they submit to Prospero's power. Although Prospero raises a natural storm and, by implication, the "sea-change" (1.2.401) of a social calamity in the mariners' revolt against rank and royalty, he also makes it his task to quell both. He actively governs these storms, righting the wrongs he had allowed at home in his attempt to newly embody the role of duke. European social systems and their concomitant identities are produced on the island precisely as they should have been at home, and alterity—of clime and identity—is held at bay. The question of how to reproduce home abroad is not a problem this play seeks to resolve.

When *The Tempest* first appeared in print in the 1623 Folio—itself a collaborative production of Shakespeare's fellow King's Men, notably Condell and Heminge, but also, perhaps, Fletcher—two playwrights for the King's Men took it upon themselves to rewrite the play. In doing so, they fundamentally altered it, fixating on the geographical alterity that the earlier play had recoiled from in framing Europe as "home," as the locus of desire for the play's Italian characters as well as their ultimate destination. Fletcher and Massinger's play has a different trajectory. Using material clearly indebted to Shakespeare's play, they ask and attempt to imagine how Europeans might transport "home" to unfamiliar lands, both barren and idyllic, as embodied by the representation of the two different soils and climates of the play's sister islands. At a time when the Virginia Council began sending women and children in significant numbers to Virginia, Fletcher and Massinger were using romance to explore how women's presence in the colonies might implicate the colonial project. If *The Tempest* ultimately reads Italy as home—as the space where the play's romantic resolutions will bear their fruit—*The Sea Voyage* labors to make *the colony* a viable site of romance. Just as Shakespeare's imaginative engagement with colonial matters seems a response to the interest of his patrons Southampton and Pembroke in the Virginia Council, so Fletcher had a spur in his close ties to Henry Hastings, fifth earl of Huntingdon, who invested in the Virginia project in the early 1620s. A patron to a host of poets and dramatists—Donne, Drayton, Marston, and Massinger among them— Huntingdon had joined the Virginia Council in 1620 and was connected still further to Western enterprises in that his brother accompanied Sir Walter Raleigh in his second attempt on Guiana in 1617.[16] Taking up the conceptual problems posed by the colonialist project and the questions that forging a sustainable settlement newly raised, Fletcher and Massinger fix our attention on what it means not merely to sojourn for a time in a distant place, as Shakespeare had done in having Prospero reside on a distant island, but what it might mean to take root in an alien soil. As such, the "sea-changes" artificially circumscribed in Shakespeare's earlier play become the very condition of this later play. That is, *The Sea Voyage* insists that the extreme threat to identity posed by degeneracy assumes center stage.

If we take a few steps back and ask precisely what was described through this language of degeneracy, we would be well served by turning to the colonial context of Ireland. Here *degeneration* described a set of changes that were perceived to be closely connected to qualities of blood, although this association has often been overlooked. Through this word New English planters like Spenser, Sir John Davies, and Fynes Moryson puzzled over the Circean transformations that they observed among an earlier round of English colonists in Ireland, those they called the Old English. To New English eyes, reproducing abroad had forced these Old English colonists into a long and gradual process of decline. Fynes Moryson, secretary to Lord Deputy Mountjoy in the early 1600s, emphasized the extent to which the decline was related to processes of generation and, by implication, to blood when he observed:

As horses, cows, and sheep transported out of England into Ireland do each race and breeding decline worse and worse, till in few years they nothing differ from the races and breeds of the Irish horses and cattle, so the posterities of the English planted in Ireland do each descent grow more and more Irish, in nature, manners and customs . . .[17]

In noticing a decline to "races and breeds," Moryson was articulating a shift at the level of blood, that is, one that was capable of producing a break between parent and offspring. By choosing to live and, more important, *reproduce* beyond the pale of England's borders, it would seem, English planters implicitly invited genealogical disruption.

Degeneration—whether explicitly engaged as in Moryson's words or implicitly described as in Colt's—described more than just a transformation at the level of culture, more than just a shift to habits of dress, speech, and manner, as critics have thus far argued. If we persist in reading degeneration as a cultural phenomenon, we remain wed to nineteenth-century notions of the body and to a nineteenth-century discourse of "going native." Moryson's words tell us something different; they resist these characterizations, just as they derive from an early modern model of embodiment that openly expressed the articulation of nature to culture. That is, changes to culture were perceived to produce and express material shifts to nature. The

phenomenon that Moryson describes, and that countless proximate authors described as well, should not therefore be understood to limit itself
to "manners" and "customs." Rather for the early modern period, such
cultural indicators have a dynamic relationship to "nature," to conceptions
of the body, such that they express and in some cases help to produce
physical states. Moryson makes these connections overt in placing these
two terms beside the proximate term "nature." In this instance, moreover,
he seems to define nature as the causal agent, a change in nature here
producing a shift at the level of culture. In the homology he uses whereby
English people are to Irish manners and customs as English horses are to
Irish breeds, he defines the change these planters have undergone as one
originating in changes to nature, to the physical body. More specifically,
I suggest he was drawing on a widespread belief that the physical body
was shaped by a surrounding world and that it would absorb changes from
altered environments.[18]

Such ideas derived from early modern tendencies to understand the body
through the lens of humoralism. Never sealed off from its surroundings,
the humoral body was seen as continuous with the world, as positing a
radically porous set of boundaries dividing it from that world. Gail Kern
Paster has reminded us of these specific qualities in describing the humoral
body as "being open and fungible in its internal workings" as well as
"porous and thus able to be influenced by the immediate environment."
John Sutton builds on these observations in suggesting of this body that
"urgent steps could be taken to close off its vents and windows, barring
the orifices by which external dangers could intrude. But this seasonal
body was always vulnerable to climatic effects, and permeated by the
environment right through to its cognitive capacities."[19] In coining the
term "geohumoralism," moreover, Mary Floyd-Wilson has demonstrated
that in this early modern period different geographies were perceived to
produce widespread physical correspondences among populations, such
that people inhabiting cold climates were believed to demonstrate an
excess of phlegm or blood, while those in hot climates were thought to
have a preponderance of choler or black bile. She goes on to demonstrate
how these associations amount to an early, if estranging kind of ethnic
discourse, since the dominance of any given humor bespeaks a whole
range of intellectual and emotional traits in a population.[20]

To the extent that humoralism posited a porous boundary between body
and environment, as these critics contend, I suggest it elicits different

readings of degeneration than those that emerge at the end of the nineteenth century where the body is understood as a genetic entity. We may
laugh when Colt describes how his drinking habits abroad catch him off
guard, finding his worries quaint and pedestrian. But I will argue that to
do so is to miss the ontological charge of such concerns. For in worrying
changes to his humoral disposition through this language of temperance
and distemperance, Colt attempted to describe and to modulate physical
shifts structuring social identity. That he is particularly attuned to changes
of blood—a fluid that was both a humor and the basis for an entire social
system—warrants particular attention. In describing blood heated to an
extreme—whether by climate, diet, passion, or appetite—writers like Colt
sorted through the profound adjustments to identity that colonization
occasioned. By grappling with perceived changes to blood's temperature,
they worried the remaking of a substance that was intimately connected
both to their place within a social hierarchy (that is, as elite, middling, or
base men) and their sense of themselves as English.

Temperate Races

That divisions of rank were intimately connected to the qualities of one's
blood functioned as something of a commonplace for the early modern
period. Sir Thomas Smith, for instance, in articulating the distinctions
between different social ranks, defines them as originating in "blood and
race."[21] To be elite, to be of a race, was a function of blood. And to be of
the blood was to enjoy both a physical and metaphysical separation from
one's social inferiors. Sir Thomas Elyot would outline these associations
in *The Book Named the Governor,* his educational tract for gentlemen.
Here he would urge: "where vertue is in a gentyll man, it is commenly
mixte with more sufferance, more affabilitie, and myldenes, than for the
more parte it is in a persone rural, or of a very base linage."[22] These
virtues, moreover, stood in direct relation to the physical qualities of blood;
noble blood was thought to embody more closely a tempered ideal, as
compared with the intemperate condition of base blood which expressed
itself through "villainous" behavior.[23] Sir Thomas Elyot would articulate
what it might mean to have noble blood through the lens of humoralism.
In *The Book Named the Governor,* a text produced in and through the
medical knowledge that more explicitly informs Elyot's more popular
Castel of Health, the basis for nobility emerges as a kind of physiology: "a

gentyll wytte is . . . sone fatigate . . . lyke as a lyttel fyre is sone quenched with a great heape of small stickes."[24] If on a cultural plane noble blood was equated with great courage, Elyot translated what were once thought to be solely spiritual virtues into humoral physiology, reading nobility as the embodiment of subtle heat. His educational regime, moreover, was offered up to readers as a guide to achieving and sustaining this temperate condition, thus suggesting by implication that the "subtlety" of elite blood had to be actively supported.

As Englishmen ventured to plant abroad in the early part of the seventeenth century, this language of temperance took on new force, becoming a defining trope of colonialist literature.[25] Writing his own guide for gentlemen while serving as a planter in Ireland, for instance, Spenser placed temperance second only to holiness as an indispensable virtue.[26] While temperance is of course a virtue, scholars have tended to assume that because it follows so closely upon the heels of holiness, that Spenser wanted us to think of temperance in solely spiritual terms. Like Elyot, however, Spenser understands this virtue not only as a spiritual quality but also as a humoral condition.[27] Given the centrality of this virtue not just to Spenser but to an entire class of New English planters, one might wonder what cultural work this discourse of temperance was performing. I will argue that colonization opened this entire system of blood to profound scrutiny and that temperance is the language mediating these shifts. On the one hand, it did so by holding out the promise of landholdings to those not likely to inherit them at home—that is, to younger sons of the gentry and men of nongentle blood. By disarticulating these ancient connections, colonization undermined the sign system upon which accounts of blood were built. Such associations were reified by biblical exegesis, and were a structuring principle of early modern England. The story of Cain, for instance, functioned as an originary account of servitude, suggesting that those dispossessed of lands and estates had earned their status through deeds "unnoble" and "[dishonourable]."[28] By contrast, virtuous sons like Sem and Japhet were awarded a "free estate" and a "famous stocke" to carry them through time, their virtue imagined as descending uninterrupted through generations of offspring produced by the quasi-immaterial repository of their blood. The metaphysical qualities of blood came therefore to be reified in the physical world. Those of the blood were often also of the land, lords who possessed great estates. By distributing land less restrictively, colonization impeded these associations, placing a wedge between land and noble blood. That is, land could no longer be trusted as a stable sign of elite blood.

Colonization problematized blood in other ways as well. In fact, if the blood of elite Englishmen was reified in land, it was not reified in just *any* piece of land. Rather it gathered its particular attributes from the unique topography and climate of *Eng-land,* a geography granted considerable force by the period in constituting identity. As Floyd-Wilson has recently argued, England's climate—its cold and relatively damp qualities—were thought to produce a shared disposition among all her people, with smaller variations of dispositions suggestive of differences of rank, gender, and individual quirks. England's climate was the source of physiologies thought to express themselves through acts forthright and martial, if not politic and circumspect like their counterparts in more southerly climes.[29] Hence, to contemplate transplantation to a hot climate such as characterized Barbados was to contemplate a wholesale reorientation of identity. In the language of temperance and distemperance so prominent in texts of a colonialist nature, writers of the period express their imbrication in the moment's reorganization of blood's meanings. I read the repetition of these terms as indicative of this crisis, as attempts to secure the elite English blood of planters from its degeneration into alien blood—blood, that is, that could no longer demonstrate its distinction from base blood or, perhaps, from the choleric tinge of Spanish blood. Once Englishmen imagined planting themselves beyond the shores of England, I suggest, blood's meanings altered. Not entitled to colonial lands by virtue of old systems of blood, planters struggled for other languages, other systems of blood to justify the status imparted by landed possession. They also struggled for a language that would demonstrate their proximity to those who remained in England. Through the language of temperance, not only did they justify newly won landed possession, but they sought to identify themselves as properly English, as anything but alien. This language, however, required nothing less than constant vigilance, because blood could be profoundly altered, as Colt's account suggests, in no less than a "few dayes."[30]

Reproducing Abroad

If the self-identity of blood could be profoundly altered in so short a time as days, it is no wonder that colonists worried with particular force about the extent of alteration that might occur generationally to transplanted groups. Indeed, Moryson's words sound the alarm that plantations posed to blood across the generations, effectively urging English planters, following Spenser, to scrutinize carefully the conditions of their children's upbringing. Colt, too, seems to contemplate the risks of reproducing abroad, if only obliquely—for it is the *young* English planters about whom he expresses particular concern, just as it his youthful son who constitutes his immediate audience. How to guide this young generation in securing blood that he sees as both English and elite seems to motivate his writing. He advises: "you are all younge men, & of good desert, if you would but bridle ye excesse of drinkinge, together wth ye quarelsome conditions of your fyery spiritts."[31] By prefixing to his account a letter to his son outlining a detailed physical regimen should he consider moving abroad, Colt guards against the debasements to blood that he observed in and through the distempering excesses of the island's young English planters. In order to ensure that his son's "stomack" is "kept warme"—a hot physiology believed to be both a native condition of all Englishmen[32] and one necessary for proper digestion—he advises his son not only to wear a "wollen stomacher" and to consume foods spiced with hot pepper but suggests as well that he visit "Mr Wicks in black fryers beyond ye playhouse" who will furnish him with "his best hott waters at 7s ye gallon." Such waters, he makes clear, were "our principall prouision & dyett," and he urges his son to use them to aid digestion, "befoor meals & sometimes after."[33] But the same waters appear in his narrative as, potentially, "oyle" in the flame of the planters' "hott bloods." Paradoxically, the substance capable of supporting an English temperament was precisely that which might also bring it to "flame." Constant vigilance was one's only weapon. Only through careful attention to diet and purgation could these mishaps be avoided. It is suggestive that Colt recognizes only one person on the island as embodying this delicate temperate state—the island's young governor at the time, Henry Hawley. For Colt, the young governor's ability to temper his own passions was right and fit, the proper expression of his power to adjudicate the quarrels among the island's planters.[34]

If Colt is intent that his son guard against the potential debasement of the family's blood abroad, he is also hopeful that such blood may, God willing, even be ennobled abroad. Imagining himself lord over this fertile land, he urges "would it weer my owne & thus seated in any part of Europe. I will not say whatt I could be in short time, if ye princes of Europe by force or couetousnesse would not take it from me."[35] Though not "seated in any part of Europe" and, therefore, an implicit threat to English blood, Barbados also held the promise of rapid upward mobility. Not only does Colt imagine himself as on a par with Europe's monarchs, but he also imagines his son dining, like he had, on a "pye" so rare that "ther fathers & predecessors yt liued & dyed in England weer neuer fed dayly wth . . . Yett weer they farr better men"[36] than them both. If, then, he worries that his son not degenerate abroad, he also imagines the many ways that blood can be improved abroad.

In wondering about the potential alterations to his bloodline, Colt participated in a discourse about alien soils that would erupt in and through inquiries into natural science as well. In fact, alongside Colt's worries about his son's prospects abroad, we also can observe a detailed attention to how "English" plant and animal species are affected by these foreign conditions. If on the one hand Colt optimistically observes that "English cowes" produce milk that "tasts better then in England," he also notes that "our henns eggs heer are very smale."[37] Richard Ligon, who planted in Barbados nearly a decade later, would further develop these observations, noting that meat becomes "flat and insipid" in Barbados and that bread lacks the "full taste it has in England." Moreover, although Ligon observes that both plants and animals reproduce with great abundance in the tropical climate—ewes always bearing two lambs at once—he describes their offspring as "faint," presumably lesser specimens than their English counterparts.[38] I suggest that attention to the generative potential of English species abroad is symptomatic of attempts by these authors to work through the implications of alien soils and altered bloodlines. Like Moryson, they reason homologically, moving from plant and animal species to the human species.[39]

The crisis of reproduction that I have identified in association with this active period of colonization on the part of the English is legible as well in the documents surrounding the structural changes to settlement that the Virginia Council initiated in the early 1620s. In its *Declaration of the State of the Colony and Affaires in Virginia,* for instance, the council outlined broad shifts in policy to govern the plantation, high among them the decision to send a larger contingent of women to accompany the numbers of men flocking to the colony. Although some women had arrived earlier at the Virginia colony, in general women were the exception to a dominantly male planter class in the early years of settlement.[40] But this pattern was to shift in the years before and up through the 1620s. In enumerating the names and investments of those involved in the plantation effort, for instance, the *Declaration* identifies 90 women among a 1619 shipment of 650 people to the colony, suggesting a new emphasis on expanding the female population in Virginia. The council announced further that it planned to send an additional hundred "yong Maides" to "make wiues" for another shipment of eight hundred planters to be sent on behalf of the council.[41] That women were coming to play a more central role in the colony is suggested as well by the presence of their names among those whom the council identifies as having contributed to the plantation venture. The list that comprises the bulk of this *Declaration* records, for instance, Mary Robinson's donation of two hundred pounds toward the founding of a church in Virginia, as well as a fifty-pound contribution made by Mary, countesse of Shrewsbury, and a twenty-five-pound investment of Mistris Kath, West, now Lady Conway. Urging that "the Colony beginneth now to have the face and fashion of an orderly State, and such as is likely to grow and prosper" and affirming that efforts are now underway "to perpetuate the Plantation," the council suggests that women will be the key to accomplishing such goals.[42]

If women's reproductive role was deemed indispensable to the colony's longevity, however, that was not to say that the necessity of reproducing abroad did not occasion some uneasiness. In fact, worries are implicitly sounded in the very pages of the *Declaration,* immediately after women's contribution to the effort are outlined by the council. By insisting that the people of this plantation are "diuided in soyle oneley" from "this their natiue Countrey" and will "continue always as one and the same people with vs," the council was already insisting on the hope of reproducing a community of Englishmen abroad. Reading between the lines, we detect a council anticipating potential differences and disruptions between an imagined "us" and them. For, as Spenser and others had argued just twenty years earlier, being divided by "soyle oneley" had often resulted in the engendering of an alien people, the very antithesis of "us." The Virginia Council in this document and elsewhere makes clear its determination to guard against a reading that reproduction abroad might disrupt English consanguinity.[43] But these matters would assume center stage at the Blackfriars' Theater, in a play produced collaboratively by Fletcher and Massinger that speaks to plantations comprised of men, women, and children. In this context the problems and potential solutions of such settlements would be openly staged.

That this play responds to the conditions of this moment, when the survival of plantations was necessitating that planters embrace the prospect of reproducing abroad, cannot be overemphasized. *The Tempest*, by contrast, raises questions of reproduction abroad but deflects any sustained attention to the problem of degeneration they unleash. In fact, in localizing such threats to reproduction in the figure of Caliban—who, we are told, earned his enslavement through his attempted rape of Miranda (1.2.347-48)—Shakespeare's play engages contamination of elite blood in its most literal form—by rape—a threat conceivable in a range of contexts, both near and far. And significantly, this threat is one that Prospero contains. The play prefers instead to narrate reproduction as an event tied to home. Miranda, for instance, is nearly three years old when she travels to this island with her father, and the start of yet another generation is deferred at the play's close to a point following Miranda and Ferdinand's return home. In fact, though Prospero has celebrated their union in the play's masque, consummation has been guarded against in overdetermined ways; Prospero warns Ferdinand no less than three times to restrain his desire, asserting "Look thou be true; do not give dalliance / Too much the rein. The strongest oaths are straw / To th' fire i' th' blood. Be more abstenious" (*sic;* 4.1.51-53). In the masque's sudden disruption, these prohibitions are formally embodied, together serving to defer the closure of romance—the reproduction of noble lineage—to the arrival home. The play warns elsewhere of the danger of producing heirs in distant geographies in the context of a discussion of Claribel, Alonso's newly displaced daughter and, insofar as Ferdinand is believed to be dead by the newly arriving Neapolitans, his displaced heir as well. If there is a chance that she will produce an heir in Algeria—a possibility that "new-born chins" will become "rough and razorable" (2.1.249-50)—the play raises the possibility only to warn against it. Heirs born "Ten leagues beyond man's life" (l. 247), Antonio maintains, lose their connection to home by the sheer magnitude of space. In this play, reproducing abroad is a vexed and dangerous activity, and a problem that remains deferred and unresolved at the play's close.

By contrast, Fletcher and Massinger, in "rewriting" Shakespeare's play, take a hard look at the risks and rewards of reproducing abroad. Like Colt, their play acknowledges at every turn the vulnerability of blood abroad—the perception that noble blood might suffer debasement and that blood ties might be disjointed—if blood is not carefully tempered. Those who are distempered—and it is significant that the play's gallants are those who fit this description—are associated with genealogical erasure, with failures of reproduction. By contrast, those capable of continence and self-restraint—traits that the play assigns to the captain of a group of French pirates—accrue to themselves the language of nobility of blood. In looking to temperance as a safeguard against degeneration, the play produces a new narrative of blood. Rooted not in title, land, or wealth, blood is measured by temperance, which serves as its own sign of nobility, its own estate.

Tempering Passion

Both Shakespeare's play and that by Fletcher and Massinger follow Colt's narrative in foregrounding questions of appetite and distemperance, all structuring their narratives in uncannily similar ways around banquets and "hott" drinks and the excesses of passion surrounding them. In Shakespeare's play, however, differences of blood are carefully monitored, and Prospero's control of the climate, the external "tempest," is a figure for his control over the appetites of all the aristocrats on the island. He explicitly makes these connections when he asks Ariel, following the successful production of the storm and shipwreck: "Who was so firm, so constant, that this coil / Would not infect his reason?" (1.2.207–8). Here he suggests that producing such "infection," a passionate imbalance, was a central part of his intent in calling forth the storm. If Prospero uses his art to provoke a crisis of passion among the newly arriving Italian nobility—by toying with Sebastian's envy of the throne, Alonso's near-madness, and the group's collective hunger as they grasp at an illusory banquet—it is a temporary and controlled form of revenge that serves to remind the men of their nobility of blood and to reify its difference from base blood. By stoking the "fumes" of their base passions (5.1.67), he exacts revenge but also stages a purgation of the "foul and muddy" (5.1.82) qualities of the blood that they, in plotting his usurpation, had already allowed to invade "the reasonable [shores]" (5.1.81) of their "properly" noble minds. The intent would seem to be to spur them to moderate their blood, to purge it of the passions that signal its decline. Insofar as Alonso expresses his wish for "pardon" (5.1.119), while Antonio appears to remain hardened and unpurged, the play naturalizes his status as ruler. In moderating his passion, Alonso reclaims his powers as king, rule of self here imagined as the precondition to rule of others.

Indeed, we have good reason to follow the play's cues in reading Prospero's failing at home as a version of the passionate shipwreck that Alonso has submitted to while on the island. In recalling these originary events, he tells Miranda that "The government I cast upon my brother" (1.2.75), while he himself became "rapt in secret studies" (1.2.77). To the extent that his language signals someone in the grip of immoderate passions—the act of "casting" rule away suggesting impetuosity and the state of being "rapt" suggesting impassioned prostration—it describes a ruler who has violated the principle of noble blood and the temperate rule it ideally embodied. That Prospero has spent his years in exile attempting to correct the imbalances of such eruptions we learn from Miranda, who tells Ferdinand repeatedly that "My father's of a better nature, sir, / Than he appears by speech. This is unwonted / Which now came from him" (1.2.497-99). Later she will note how uncommon passionate behavior has been for him when she observes: "Never till this day / Saw I him touch'd with anger, so distemper'd" (4.1.144-45). But her words also suggest that maintaining a temperate condition—the act of stilling his "beating mind" (4.1.163)—is an ongoing struggle for him. Through countless acts of self-government, Prospero displays his blood in its properly elite form and establishes his claim to rule. As such, he comes to embody the freedom from passionate infection that he evokes among the island's newcomers. In allowing themselves to become subjected to such "madness" (5.1.116), these newcomers are made to embody their status as "subjects," as necessarily "thrown under" the care of a ruler like Prospero.[44]

In fact, Prospero demonstrates this principle of rule in carefully moderating the passions of the younger members of the nobility, including both Miranda and Ferdinand. From his daughter, he exacts temperate behavior when he receives her pity for the shipwreck victims with the rejoinder: "Be collected, / No more amazement. Tell your piteous heart / There's no harm done" (1.2.13-15). Similarly, he seeks to temper the grief Ferdinand feels in contemplating his father's likely death by instructing Ariel to orchestrate a "sweet air" that would "[allay]" the "fury" and "passion" that has erupted in the young prince (1.2.393-94). If he tempers these his subjects, he also seeks to undercut the authority of his rival, Sycorax, by describing her as ever in the grip of a "most unmitigable rage" (1.2.276). By emphasizing her subjection to passion, he defines her as unfit for rule.

If Prospero emphasizes his power to temper the passions of the nobility, he leaves the ship's servants—Stephano and Trinculo—to self-destruct by strategically placing "celestial liquor" (2.2.117) into their hands. By consuming what Colt calls hot drinks, they become enslaved to passion and quarrelsomeness, parodying their quest for upward mobility as emblematized by their desire to lord it over Caliban. Stephano's relationship to Caliban mocks the relationship of king to subject, not least in that Stephano moves to temper Caliban's supposed "fit" and "ague" (2.2.75, 93) as I have argued Prospero does for the noblemen. Stephano assumes this stance of paternal care when he concludes "I will give him some relief" (2.2.67-68), while taking steps to do so by dispensing wine. Clearly, the wine does for these men what Colt worried it not do to elite planters—drive them to passionate excess and distemperance. For Prospero, this is exactly as it should be for Stephano and his cohorts, their ill-governed passions being the sign he seeks to evoke of their base blood. He polices the divide separating gentle from base more overtly through his insistence that the courtiers' garments—the body's most visible document of rank—are refreshed and sustained under Ariel's diligent care, a point repeated in the opening act, first when Ariel indicates she has followed Prospero's orders precisely, and once again when Gonzalo wonders at their clothes' newly starched freshness (1.2.218-19; 2.1.62-65). Bolstering differences of blood rather than meditating on their undoing is Prospero's central concern.

Fletcher and Massinger's *Sea Voyage* is, then, less an iteration of *The Tempest,* as Restoration critics lamented, than a catalyzation of the tensions rippling beneath the earlier play's surface.[45] It systematically undoes all the safeguards to identity to which Prospero had carefully attended. In the first scene, the one that establishes clear connections to its Shakespearean antecedent, a ship of French pirates and planters try to fend off the attacks of a tempest, culminating in the captain's demands that the vessel be purged of all baggage. An early indicator of the play's interest in somatic matters, the scene develops correspondences between the surrounding storm and the men's rising passions. The ship itself assumes the quality of distemperance when they observe of the glutted vessel—"She reels like a drunkard" (1.1.13),[46] signaling the play's interest in gentle bodies grown distempered. In fact, the image of the impassioned body as ship on a stormy sea had become such a commonplace that in the year prior to the play's performance the English translation of *A Table of Human Passions* would be framed in precisely such terms: "For as that tempest is more dangerous that suffers not a ship to repaire to her haven . . . So most difficult are the minds stormes, that let a man to containe himselfe; nor suffer him to quiet and settle his disturbed reason."[47] Under the force of the Captain's orders, the ship's gallants are made to toss overboard all signs of their wealth and rising status; doublets, swords, crowns, double ruffs, as well as meats and

cakes all drop to the bottomless depths. If Prospero was eager to retain
these outward signs of rank, this play is just as eager to dispense with
them, forcing a confrontation with unaccommodated man, with little but,
in Tibalt's words, "thy skin whole" (1.3.34). By doing so, this play puts
gentle blood to the test, moving to define temperance as against land and
wealth as the real essence of gentle blood.

When the play opens degeneration, rather than temperance, is writ
large. And heated tempers are to blame. We learn, for instance, that the
events that immediately precede the play's actions involved the seizure of
a Portuguese plantation by a set of French planters. Based both on Andre
Thevet's account of a Portuguese crew shipwrecked off the coast of Brazil
and on Jean Ribault's French settlement in Florida in 1562, these events
resulted not in peace and plenty for the French planters but faction and
discord, the same passions of heat that Colt had observed a few years
after this play's performance in Barbados.[48] Leading to the demise of this
colony, those same passions threaten to erupt when members of that
earlier colony—led by the Frenchman Albert—set out to reconcile with
the other French faction but instead find themselves on a desert island
with no resources. Here unconstrained appetites threaten to produce self-
destruction for the group. Not only are they at each other's throats verbally,
but the one female planter, Aminta, finds herself literally "put to the knife"
before she is rescued. If Shakespeare's *Tempest* imagines a similar scene
of crisis in Sebastian and Antonio's temptation to kill the sleeping Alfonso,
The Sea Voyage has no magical medium of patriarchal law and order, such
as Ariel embodies, to effect stability. The distempered Frenchmen are left
to their own devices, or to those of the ship's captain, whose modulation
of his own desires prefigures his ability to temper theirs.

In fact, *The Sea Voyage* poses the possibility of undoing noble blood and
of genealogical failure in the context of plantation as the tragic possibility
that the romance has to resolve. As the play opens and the French planters
seek shelter during the storm on the deserted island, we hear a Portuguese
man and his nephew, Sebastian and Nicusa, members of the original
Portuguese colony shipwrecked years earlier on this island, reflecting on
how they have found themselves removed from history. They long for
a "little memory of what we were" (1.2.32), and reminisce about "our
kindreds," "our families," and "our fortunes" (1.2.35–36). The island has
removed them from history, from genealogy, from the monuments of blood.
The Frenchmen who arrive echo the question earlier put by Stephano

and Trinculo to Caliban (2.2.24–26, ll. 57–58, ll. 65–66), wondering if the Portuguese "islanders" are monsters or men. The French compare the islanders to shadows, sea-calves, and horses, and mock the possibility that they might once have been "a couple of courtiers" (1.3.102). If possessors of gentle blood, as they assure the Frenchmen, that status cannot be read from external signs of rank, since they lack the grooming, the wardrobe, and the well-fed bodies that would have made their status obvious at home. Later in the play, another group of Frenchmen will come into contact with these men and will repeat these questions, wondering if their "noble breedings" are legitimate or just something they "pretend to" (4.1.30). Gentleness, the play here suggests, must inhere in the blood, the body's tempered complexion must serve in and of itself as a "noble monument" (3.1.130).

That the French are in no way immune from a similar social failing is immediately brought to their attention by the Portuguese, who warn them to guard their appetites lest they suffer a similar fate. A group ravenous for gold and food, only the French leader Albert shows any signs of one who can rise above appetite. Where his French shipmates dream of surfeiting on medical by-products amid their hunger, Albert undergoes a purgation, his wounds are stitched, and his body is thus newly brought to curb. It is noteworthy that Aminta describes Albert's body as an altar of "staid temperance" (2.1.21–22). And yet we learn that this tempered posture is a new one for him. In recounting the events prior to the play, we hear that he had been led by a raging "heat" to seize as booty the woman, Aminta, who subsequently will help heal him. In traveling with him, she has transformed him from a youth in the "heat of blood," to a man of self-control who is capable of prescribing "laws to itself" (2.1.28–29).

In fact the power Aminta's cold kisses have to "allay [Albert's] fever" (4.3.234) explicitly suggests that the presence of a noble woman in the colonies actually could prevent degeneration. The unruly members of the French crew early seek to identify Aminta's presence on the ship as the real source of their troubles, blaming her for obstructing their pursuit of "happy places and most fertile islands" (3.3.83) in turning "the captain's mind" (3.3.85) to reconciling with her brother, Raymond. They also characterize her as a "leaky vessel," turning her into a metonymy for the ship and charging her with incontinence for reacting passionately to the storm's force: "Peace woman! / We ha' storms enough already—no more howling" (1.1.49–50). But her effect on Albert certainly neutralizes these charges.

In fact Albert attributes to her a process of physical regeneration. Though suffering physical hardship like the others stranded on this stark and barren island, he perceives his love for Aminta as a restorative: "I feel / New vigour in me, and a spirit that dares / More than a man" (2.1.74-76). Feeding on her love—"when I kiss these rubies, methinks / I'm at a banquet, a refreshing banquet" (2.1.38-39)—he gathers the strength to swim across the channel separating the two islands. He also steels himself against his hunger on her behalf. Though offered food upon his arrival to the fertile island (2.2.245-46), he honors his vow to Aminta that he will not "eat nor sleep" (2.1.86) till he returns. In the play's logic, gentle blood is a moral condition that is tightly bound to physical principles. Given the temptations to heat, passion, and distemper that the play associates with travel to hot lands, such blood is hardly something that can be presumed. Rather, it requires constant vigilance, countless efforts at restraint.

That Aminta's power involves not just "tempering" but "ennobling" Albert's blood is demonstrated by the way that his control of his body, and more specifically his ability to temper the heat associated with passion and desire, accrues the "metaphysical" force of a properly aristocratic ethos. Albert, that is, comes to embody the principle of noble hospitality. After discovering the abundance of the nearby island inhabited by women, for instance, Albert returns to his starving Frenchmen and distributes his newly found riches like a patron figured in a country-house poem.[49] Tending first to his lady—"some meat and sovereign drink to ease you" (3.3.163)—he turns immediately to satisfying the needs of the others: "Ye shall have meat, all of you" (l. 167). Even after he learns of the treacherous nature of their appetite, specifically their flirtation with cannibalism, he continues to distribute food. Because this act of distributing food is repeated in this scene, we have to assume this gesture that marks him as the noble patron is central. We observe him feeding them—"There, wretches, there." And see his bountifulness extend still further—"There's more bread"—and further still when he tells them, "There is drink too" (ll. 175, 177, 179). If Tibalt seeks to deny these men food on the principle that they are distemperate and deserve enforced restraint—"touch nothing but what's flung t'ye as if you / Were dogs" (ll. 173-74)—Albert reverses this pattern. In tending to their appetites, as he has tended to his own, he displays his nobility. It is clear that his blood has been restored to its nondegenerate form. His temperance marks him as a man worthy of his plantation, worthy, that is, of the plantation that the play's end celebrates as "[home]" (5.4.112).

The degeneracy of the other men, by contrast, is connected repeatedly to their respective violations of a landed, aristocratic ethos. Franville for one has joined the crew only after having sold his "lordship," leaving, in Tibalt's words, "no wood upon't to buoy it up" (1.1.135). Lamure, by contrast, is intent on purchasing land in the plantations with money "bred" usuriously, a history of living off of others that directly counters the landed ethos here being valued. Surely it is important that Fletcher's country patron, the earl of Huntingdon, explicitly embodied these ideal principles and that Fletcher's royal patron, King James I, was attempting to enforce such ideals as a corrective to absentee landlordism and rural unrest.[50] The two gallants evoke their failures at home, as abroad, when they reminisce about their distemperate habits of banqueting, where they have "lewdly at midnight / Flung away" their "healths" (3.1.30-31). Such behavior violates the decorum of an elite society, striking at its core values. They are parasites, men whose threat to Aminta's flesh—"we'll eat your ladyship" (3.1.128)—translates into a threat to nobility at large. If Albert's command that they "be better tempered" (1.3.62) goes unheeded by them, it is an oversight that seals their own demise. For the play will move to define such profligacy as the antithesis of generation itself.

In fact, only those who subscribe to the laws of temperance seem up to the task of reproduction at all. That seems to be why Fletcher and Massinger place an island nearby, which in addition to being fertile is inhabited by a colony of women, who, though bound by a vow of abstinence, find themselves in the grip of "youthful heats" (2.2.24). Just as their male counterparts long for "princely banquet[s]" and "dainty dishes" (3.1.49, 38), so this island's younger women dream of sexual satisfaction. As the two parties are brought together, the gallants pray for herbal aids to meet the requirements of copulation which they sense may be upon them. As such, their voracious appetites signal the failure of their reproductive ability, their impotency. By contrast, the other Frenchmen, those who have espoused continency in one form or another, "rise" to the challenge, Tibalt even refusing the power of antiaphrodisiacs to hold him back. In fact, in their view, mating with the women will promote continency, acting as a restorative purgative. In choosing the oldest woman as his own potential mate, Tibalt justifies his choice by saying, "The weather's hot, and men that have / Experience fear fevers. A temperate / Diet is the only physic" (3.1.321-23). Women, he urges, are the "diet" to end all fevers, the "physic" to cure all distempers. As such, the playwrights grant gentlewomen a central role in producing an uncorrupted version of elite blood within foreign climes and soils. If the play literally depicts Portuguese and French gentlewomen anchoring a planter class of men prone to physical and moral errancy, this representation functions analogously for English gentlewomen. Given their presence in the colonies, the reproduction of English blood, customs, and manners in lands far from England will prevail.

By affording women such an expansive role in plantations, Fletcher and Massinger do nothing less than rewrite the major colonialist theories inherited from an earlier generation. They not only revise Shakespeare's *Tempest* to qualify the role of a strong patriarch in preserving the bonds of blood abroad, but they reverse the gendering of degeneracy that had been so central to Spenser's Bower of Bliss.[51] Fletcher and Massinger give us two models of degeneracy. On the one hand, the play offers the Franvilles and the Lamures, willfully bent at home and willfully bent abroad. The degeneracy that they embody precludes place and locality. On the other hand, the figure of Albert serves as something of a shorthand for the widespread cultural assumption, most famously embodied by a writer like Spenser, that transplantation would produce degeneracy. Indeed, it seems Albert is the victim of a genealogical taint originating in the family's decision to transplant itself abroad. Although we know little of Albert's past, we do know that the initial act of plantation was carried out by his father, and that his father is therefore to blame for the original treachery of the colonists that consisted of the dispossession of a preceding Portuguese settlement. We also know that Albert and his cousin Raymond (brother to Aminta) were ensnared by this patriarchal pattern and fall into the trap of repeating it by sparring one with the other. In dramatizing Albert's ability to break the cycle of deeds produced by blood "enflamed," enacted as a pattern of ejecting first one planter then another, Fletcher and Massinger imagine degeneracy as reversible. If their play suggests that the colonies will pro-duce alterity, it refuses to define alterity as an intransigent condition. A compelling intervention in colonial theories, the play's resolution of the problem of colonial degeneracy seems also to have been short-lived on the stage.

I have already suggested some of the ways that Shakespeare's own play, written and first performed a decade earlier, guarded against the hard look at blood's alterity that Fletcher and Massinger willingly invite. On the other side of the temporal spectrum, a similar pattern emerges. In the post-Restoration period, when this play was revised by D'Urfey as *A*

Commonwealth of Women, many of the defining features of the Fletcher and Massinger collaboration outlined above were excised.[52] Indeed, this play can imagine no "Albert," no figure of degeneracy who must labor to effect temperance, as indicated by the wholesale removal of any character of this name. Our reviser instead is compelled to separate him out, to make two characters of the original Albert. Hence we get a good "Marine," who embodies all of Albert's finest qualities and is the object of Aminta's love, and we get a malign "LaMure," a character who absorbs the treacherous details of Albert's past, passionately seizing Aminta as a prisoner. D'Urfey's Marine never experiences the pangs of unruly passion that gripped Fletcher and Massinger's "Albert" to the point that he contemplated raping Aminta. Nor is D'Urfey's Marine visibly staged as undergoing purgation by his mistress, the scene where his injury requires bloodletting and resuturing at the hands of Aminta having been excised from this later play. In fact, if D'Urfey is not interested in imagining how Albert's passion might be reformed, neither is he interested in a sustained engagement with the threat plantations pose to social and physical identity. His play therefore seems to be less about transplantation than it is about celebrating "home," defined now not as a European polity (as in Naples or Milan) but a domestic unit. His heroine Aminta, though a Portuguese woman who is described as having been born in a colony, is raised "home" in England where she meets her love, Marine (20). That she loves this Englishman, as against the "French-firework" LaMure (17) who has captured her, indicates the proper orientation of her desire. In this play, the problem is not how to secure English blood against the threat of foreign places but how to secure the English patriarch at home. The failure here is disavowing patriarchy through self-exile. Fletcher and Massinger's wayward gentlemen-gallants, violators of a landed ethos, become in this play husbands who spurn their role within the English household. Here they swear to abandon England because they hate their wives and the way these wives lord it over them. They therefore vow "never to converse with," "kiss," or "remember" (27) them, willfully rejecting their children, as well, in urging that they too should "stay at home" (27). For them, home translates into a place for keeping "lent, and [chewing] the Cud" (27), a depraved posture that the play sets out to reform. Indeed, by the time these men have experienced enthrallment to the women's "commonwealth" abroad—a female community that we first observe singing songs of liberty, rather than hunting as in the earlier play—these husbands conclude: "few know the goodness of

Wives, till they want 'em. Ah would I were at home." Henceforth, they promise to live more soberly and to "sing Psalms" (100-1).

Transplantation, then, is imagined not as a heroic feat of self-rule that noble women enable but rather as cowardly resistance to rule of self, wife, and *domos*—that is, to life at home in England. Clearly invested with post-Restoration politics and the move to disavow Republican sentiments as unmanly and unpaternalistic, D'Urfey's play shifts Fletcher and Massinger's focus on mending injuries of blood abroad. Shakespeare had placed the heroic agency for this sort of project in the hands of a noble patriarch, one who had no less than magical resources at his disposal. He uses this magic to control the passions of those around him, naturalizing a social hierarchy by writing it on blood—on its physical properties, whether hot or moderate, impassioned or temperate. In controlling the passions of all who reside on the island, Prospero interpellates them as subjects who require his discipline to still their fits and passions. D'Urfey's English hero, by contrast, in seeking marriage to Aminta, pursues his destiny as patriarch, tending to his own ministate in guiding his wifely subject. Fletcher and Massinger imagine identity as structured along a different set of axes. For them, Englishness travels not exclusively through crown, land, or *domos*. It exists instead as a quality of the blood, inhering in the tempered blood that these playwrights equated with an aristocratic class: its men and women, and their capacity to govern self and community.[53]

Notes

1. In the early modern period, "hot waters" and "hot drinks" refer to spirituous liquors. *OED,* "hot water," sb. 2.

2. Sir Henry Colt, "The Voyage of Sir Henry Colt," *Colonising Expeditions to the West Indies and Guiana, 1623-1667,* ed. V. T. Harlow (London: Hakluyt Society, 1925), 54-102, esp. 66.

3. English plantation in Barbados began in 1627, alongside planting efforts in St. Christopher, Nevis, Antigua, and Montserrat, all of the Lesser Antilles; according to Richard S. Dunn, these were "the only successful English settlements between 1604 and 1640"; see his *Sugar and Slaves: The Rise of the Planter Class in the English West Indies, 1624-1713* (Chapel Hill, N.C.: University of North Carolina Press, 1972, rev. ed. 2000), 17. Dunn estimates that as many as thirty thousand people from the British Isles "went to the Caribbean to colonize during the reigns of James I and Charles I" (16). For a discussion of the "Barbados distemper" and the diseases associated with the hot climate, see his chapter "Death in the Tropics" (300-34).

4. Colt, 66.

5. Colt, 73.

6. Samuel Purchas, *Hakluytus Postumus: Or Purchas His Pilgrimes: Contayning a History of the World in Sea Voyages and Lande Travells by Englishmen and Others,* 20 vols. (Glasgow: James Maclehose and Sons, 1905-7), 19:222, qtd. in Gordon McMullan, *The Politics of Unease in the Plays of John Fletcher* (Amherst: University of Massachusetts Press, 1994), 212.

7. Early Americanists have been attentive to the discourse of degeneracy in the context of colonization for some time: see, for instance, John Canup, "Cotton Mather and 'Criolian Degeneracy,'" *Early American Literature* 24 (1989): 20-34; John Canup, *Out of the Wilderness: The Emergence of an American Identity in Colonial New England* (Middletown, Conn.: Wesleyan University Press, 1990); and Jim Egan, *Authorizing Experience: Refigurations of the Body Politic in Seventeenth-Century New England Writing* (Princeton: Princeton University Press, 1999), esp. chap. 1.

8. For comparative readings of these two plays, see McMullan, *Politics of Unease,* chap. 6; the introduction to *Three Renaissance Travel Plays,* ed. Anthony Parr (Manchester, U.K.: Manchester University Press, 1995), esp. 20-32; and Heidi Hutner, *Colonial Women: Race and Culture in Stuart Drama* (Oxford: Oxford University Press, 2001), chap. 1. In addition to the broadly allusive Atlantic references that I find in the genre of romance at large, a range of dramatic productions of this period were precise in identifying an Atlantic context. Chapman's 1613 *The Memorable Maske of the Two Honorable Houfes or Inns of Court; the Middle Temple, and Lyncolns Inne* was set in Virginia, for instance, and a now lost play on the Virginia massacre, called *A Tragedy of the Plantation of Virginia,* was staged at the Curtain about the same time that Fletcher and Massinger's *Sea Voyage* was being performed (see McMullan, 242).

9. Influential arguments to this effect have been made in Paul Brown, "'This Thing of Darkness I Acknowledge Mine': *The Tempest* and the Discourse of Colonialism," *Political Shakespeare: New Essays in Cultural Materialism,* ed. Jonathan Dollimore and Alan Sinfield (Manchester, U.K.: Manchester University Press, 1985), 48-71; Stephen Greenblatt, *Shakespearean Negotiations: The Circulation of Social Energy in Renaissance England* (Oxford, U.K.: Clarendon Press, 1988); and Meredith Skura, "Discourse and the Individual: The Case of Colonialism and *The Tempest,*" *Shakespeare Quarterly* 40 (1989): 42-69.

10. For an overview of such approaches, see *"The Tempest" and Its Travels,* ed. Peter Hulme and William H. Sherman (Philadelphia: University of Pennsylvania Press, 2000), especially the essays in part II on "European and Mediterranean Crossroads" (73-171). See also Richard Wilson, "Voyage to Tunis: New History and the Old World of *The Tempest,*" *ELH* 64 (1997): 333-57; and Jerry Brotton, "'This Tunis, sir, was Carthage': Contesting Colonialism in *The Tempest,*" *Post-colonial Shakespeares,* ed. Ania Loomba and Martin Orkin (London: Routledge, 1998): 23-42.

11. See, for instance, Barbara Fuchs, "Conquering Islands: Contextualizing *The Tempest,*" *Shakespeare Quarterly* 48 (1997): 45-62; and Dympna Callaghan, "Irish Memories in *The Tempest,*" *Shakespeare Without Women: Representing Gender and Race on the Renaissance Stage* (London: Routledge, 2000), 97-138.

12. See McMullan, 245.

13. For this category, see Roland Greene, "Island Logic," in Hulme and Sherman, 138-45, esp. 141.

14. Brotton, "Carthage and Tunis, *The Tempest* and Tapestries," in Hulme and Sherman, 137.

15. Citations of *The Tempest* follow *The Riverside Shakespeare,* ed. G. Blakemore Evans, 2nd ed. (New York: Houghton Mifflin, 1997), and will appear parenthetically in the text.

16. For these observations, I am very much indebted to McMullan, *The Politics of Unease,* esp. chaps. 2 and 6.

17. As quoted from the excerpts of Fynes Moryson's *An Itinerary* (1616) included in *Illustrations of Irish History and Topography, Mainly of the Seventeenth Century,* ed. C. Litton Falkiner (London: Longmans, Green, 1904), 214–325, esp. 310.

18. The body of literature excavating these connections is impressive; see, for instance, John Sutton, *Philosophy and Memory Traces: Descartes to Connectionism* (Cambridge: Cambridge University Press, 1998), esp. chap. 2; Mary Floyd-Wilson, *English Ethnicity and Race in Early Modern Drama* (Cambridge: Cambridge University Press, 2003); Roxann Wheeler, *The Complexion of Race: Categories of Difference in Eighteenth-Century British Culture* (Philadelphia: University of Pennsylvania Press, 2000); Joyce E. Chaplin, *Subject Matter: Technology, the Body, and Science on the Anglo-American Frontier, 1500–1676* (Cambridge: Harvard University Press, 2001).

Particular credit is due to Karen Ordahl Kupperman for opening this field of inquiry in two pioneering essays: "Fear of Hot Climates in the Anglo-American Colonial Experience," *William and Mary Quarterly* 41 (1984): 213–40; and "The Puzzle of the American Climate in the Early Colonial Period," *American Historical Review* 87 (1982), 1262–89. For a broad historical survey of how Western texts have seen culture as shaped by environment, see also Clarence J. Glacken, *Traces on the Rhodian Shore: Nature and Culture in Western Thought from Ancient Times to the End of the Eighteenth Century* (Berkeley: University of California Press, 1967).

19. Gail Kern Paster, *The Body Embarrassed: Drama and the Disciplines of Shame in Early Modern England* (Ithaca, N.Y.: Cornell University Press, 1993), 9; Sutton, 96.

20. Floyd-Wilson, esp. the introduction and chap. 1.

21. As quoted in Leonard Tennenhouse, *Power on Display: The Politics of Shakespeare's Genres* (New York: Methuen, 1986), 36.

22. Sir Thomas Elyot, *The Book Named the Governor* (1531), ed. Ernest Rhys (London: J. M. Dent, 1937), 17.

23. In fact, the *Oxford English Dictionary* reveals the extent to which "base" behavior was thought to be characteristic of the lower social ranks in that the term "villain," also spelled "villein," was in its earliest usage a term describing a lowborn "rustic" (sb. 1).

24. Elyot, *The Book Named the Governor,* 35. *The Governor* went through eight editions between 1531 and 1580, while *The Castel of Helth* (London, 1537) went through some sixteen editions between 1537 and 1610.

25. For connections between the language of temperance and colonialism, see David Read, *Temperate Conquests: Spenser and the Spanish New World* (Detroit, Mich.: Wayne State University Press, 2000). See also the discussion of the varied response of early modern writers to the Aristotelian ethic of moderation and temperance in Joshua Scodel, *Excess and the Mean in Early Modern English Literature* (Princeton and Oxford: Princeton University Press, 2002).

26. See, of course, Edmund Spenser, *The Faerie Queene,* ed. A. C. Hamilton, text. ed. Hiroshi Yamashita and Toshiyuki Suzuki (London: Longman, 2001), bk. II. For a sustained analysis of Spenser's use of the language of intemperance to justify conquest of the Irish, see Jean Feerick, "Spenser, Race, and Ire-land," *English Literary Renaissance* 32.1 (2002): 85-117.

27. For a reading of this virtue as embodied that anticipates my own, see Michael C. Schoenfeldt, "Fortifying Inwardness: Spenser's Castle of Moral Health," *Bodies and Selves in Early Modern England: Physiology and Inwardness in Spenser, Shakespeare, Herbert, and Milton* (Cambridge: Cambridge University Press, 1999), 40-73.

28. The words are those of John Ferne, *The Blazon of Gentrie* (1586), qtd. by Frank Whigham, *Ambition and Privilege: The Social Tropes of Elizabethan Courtesy Theory* (Berkeley: University of California Press, 1984), 83. See also the connections that Lee Patterson makes between servitude and Cain's incontinence, in "'No Man His Reson Herde': Peasant Consciousness, Chaucer's Miller, and the Structure of the *Canterbury Tales,*" *Literary Practice and Social Change in Britain, 1380-1530,* ed. Lee Patterson (Berkeley: University of California Press, 1990), 113-55.

29. Floyd-Wilson, chap. 2.

30. Colt, 66.

31. Colt, 65.

32. See, for instance, Floyd-Wilson's overview of how early modern writers understood climate's effect on the body's humors (chap. 1, esp. 35-36).

33. For a further discussion of the medical theories governing these choices, see Kupperman, "Fear of Hot Climates," 221-22.

34. Colt, 99-100 and 66.

35. Colt, 69.

36. Colt, 69 and 92.

37. Colt, 67.

38. Richard Ligon, *A True and Exact History of the Island of Barbados* (London, 1657), fol. 59. For further discussion of such physical shifts, see Chaplin, chap. 4.

39. Compellingly, in his *History of the Royal Society* (London, 1666) published in the period of the Restoration, Thomas Sprat would argue that England had all the conditions necessary for scientific inquiry, conditions produced specifically by England's environmental effect on the physiologies of her inhabitants: "So that even the position of our climate, the air, the influence of the heaven, the composition of the English blood; . . . render our Country, a Land of Experimentall Knowledge" (114), as quoted in Amy Boesky, *Founding Fictions: Utopias in Early Modern England* (Athens: University of Georgia Press), 81.

40. We learn, famously from John Smith, of the presence in the colony of one woman who was the desperate victim of cannibalism at the hands of her husband during a period of famine: "And amongst the rest, this was most lamentable, that one of our colony murdered his wife, ripped the child out of her womb and threw it in the river, and after chopped the mother in pieces and salted her for his food . . ."; see Philip L. Barbour, *Pocahontas and Her World* (Boston: Houghton Mifflin, 1970), 65. Karen Ordahl Kupperman notes that the second colony sent to Roanoke in 1587 consisted of families, rather than young men, but this colony famously failed to take root; see her *Indians and English: Facing Off in Early America*

(Ithaca, N.Y.: Cornell University Press, 2000), esp. 12. She describes the early Jamestown settlement as being "a relatively small company of young men under military leadership" (12). She notes further that the Plymouth Colony of 1620 and the Massachusetts Bay Colony of 1630 "began with families" (13), indicating a shift in colonial ideology for this later period.

41. *A Declaration of the State of the Colony and Affaires in Virginia. With the Names of the Adventurous, and Summes Adventured in that Action* (London, 1620), fols. 10 and 17.

42. *Declaration,* fols. 4 and 5.

43. For the council's early attempts to frame transplantation to Virginia as physically restorative, see Jean Feerick, "'A Nation . . . Now Degenerate': Shakespeare's *Cymbeline,* Nova Britannia, and the Role of Climate and Diet in Reproducing Races," *Early American Studies* 1.2 (2003): 30–71.

44. For this meaning of *subject,* see *OED,* v. 4, where it is defined as "To place *under* something or in a lower position; to make subjacent *to.*" I am grateful to Peter Stallybrass for this observation.

45. For Restoration responses to this play and to the Fletcher canon at large, see Lawrence B. Wallis, *Fletcher, Beaumont and Company: Entertainers to the Jacobean Gentry* (Morningside Heights, N.Y.: King's Crown Press, 1947). Pepys, for one, described *The Sea Voyage* as a "'mean' piece compared to Shakespeare's *The Tempest*" (27).

46. Citations of *The Sea Voyage* are to the text contained in Parr. Citations will appear parenthetically in the text.

47. Nicolas Coeffeteau, *A Table of Humane Passions. With Their Causes and Effects,* trans. Edw. Grimeston (London, 1621), sig. A3-4.

48. For further detail on these sources, see Parr, introduction, 23-24.

49. For Fletcher's poem to the countess of Huntington praising the estate at Ashby, see McMullan, 17-18.

50. For the earl of Huntingdon's role in quelling the civil unrest provoked by acts of enclosure, see McMullan, esp. chap. 2. For an elaboration of James's policies at this time, see Leah S. Marcus, *The Politics of Mirth: Jonson, Herrick, Milton, Marvell, and the Defense of Old Holiday Pastimes* (Chicago: University of Chicago Press, 1986), 19-20 and chap. 3.

51. For continuities of representation between Fletcher and Spenser, see James J. Yoch, "The Renaissance Dramatization of Temperance: The Italian Revival of Tragicomedy and *The Faithful Shepherdess,*" *Renaissance Tragicomedy: Explorations in Genre and Politics,* ed. Nancy Klein Maguire (New York: AMS Press, 1987), 114-37.

52. Thomas D'Urfey, *A Commonwealth of Women. A Play as it Is Acted at the Theatre Royal by Their Majesties Servants* (1685), ed. Edmund Goldsmid (Edinburgh, 1886). Citations will appear parenthetically in the text and refer to page numbers.

53. For a compelling discussion of the ways in which Restoration theater will rescript these associations, such that "expertise in the passions diffuses from elite skill to something all subjects are expected to understand in themselves," see Katherine Rowe, "Humoral Knowledge and Liberal Cognition in Davenant's *Macbeth,*" *Reading the Early Modern Passions: Essays in the Cultural History of Emotion,* ed. Gail Kern Paster, Katherine Rowe, and Mary Floyd-Wilson (Philadelphia: University of Pennsylvania Press, 2004), 169-91, esp. 178.

"Euery Soyle to Mee Is Naturall": Figuring Denization in William Haughton's English-men for My Money

ALAN STEWART

D URING THE PAST decade, William Haughton's London comedy *English-men for My Money: Or, A Pleasant Comedy Called, a Woman Will Haue Her Will* (ca. 1598), has received renewed critical attention.[1] Much of this interest has focused on its lead character, Pisaro, who has been variously identified as a Jew, of Jewish heritage, crypto-Jewish, Marrano, or New Christian.[2] That identification is usually based on a set of characteristics alluded to in passing: Pisaro plies "the sweete loude trade of *Vsurie*," as do his near contemporaries Christopher Marlowe's Barabbas and William Shakespeare's Shylock.[3] He describes his devious financial modus operandi as "*Iudas*-like," invoking what had become the eponym of anti-Christian Jewry. He is also casually insulted as "signor bottle-nose" (F2r),[4] his outsize "snoute" "[a]ble to shadow *Powles,* it is so great" (Bv), blotting out the legendarily visible beacon of London Christianity, St. Paul's. These features, identified as presumed tropes of the Elizabethan stage Jew, are seemingly reinforced by the geographical location of Pisaro's residence, mentioned not once but eight times, on or in Crutched Friars (the term can refer to both a house and a street),[5] since there is indeed some contemporary evidence that Crutched Friars was associated with a Jewish community.[6] Finally, Pisaro is Portuguese, like the notorious Dr. Roderigo Lopez, who in 1594 was tried and executed for conspiring to poison Queen Elizabeth and whose Judaism was later made much of by writers[7]—Andrew Gurr goes so far as to suggest that Pisaro was "modeled on Marlowe's Jew of

Malta with a touch of more local color from Dr. Lopez."[8] From these signs, Edmund Campos argues, "the play seems to treat [Pisaro] as a Crypto-Jew, for it is up to the audience to discover him through textual clues."[9]

This essay offers another approach that operates in complement to the textual clue hunt. It builds on work that has identified the crucial intersection between early modern humoral theories and understandings of geography, what Mary Floyd-Wilson has dubbed "geohumoralism."[10] It suggests that Pisaro can be best understood not directly or solely as a Jew, but rather through his interpellation in a set of figurative codes that fix the place of a character who fails to conform to the orthodox mappings of geohumoralism. For Pisaro, an immigrant living in London, is clearly not a product of his present location, nor is he a traveler from elsewhere who expects to return home. Instead, he is what the United States would now designate a "resident alien." As this reading will demonstrate, resident aliens pose a particular dilemma to theories of geohumoralism in the early modern period—but also provide answers to some problems in early modern comedy.

If we set to one side the identification of Pisaro as in some manner Jewish, how does the play lead us to understand him? He is identified in the dramatis personae, and self-identified in the opening monologue of the play, as "a Portingale" (Av, A2r), that is, an immigrant from Portugal, now residing in London and making his living as a merchant-usurer. A widower, he has three daughters of marriageable age, Laurentia, Marina, and Mathea, who have fallen in love with three English gentleman, Harvie, Heigham, and Walgrave. Like most young English gentlemen in Renaissance comic drama, Harvie, Heigham, and Walgrave are in severe financial difficulty and have been forced to borrow money from Pisaro by mortgaging their lands to him; the twist of the love plot is that if they succeed in marrying his daughters, they will be released from their debtors' bonds to him. Doubly horrified that he might lose his money and his daughters to "the loue of those, I most abhord; / Vnthrifts, Beggers" (A4r), Pisaro comes up with a scheme to marry his daughters to "three wealthy Marchants in the Towne, / All Strangers, and my very speciall friendes," an Italian, a Frenchman, and a Dutchman (Br). As Pisaro's choice of ideal sons-in-law suggests, the play turns on questions of Englishness, in relation both to the threat of the European suitors and to, more complicatedly, to Pisaro himself, as a Portingale in London.

While the opening speech manages to convey all this factual information, it is also saturated by metaphor:

How smugge this gray-eyde Morning seemes to bee,
A pleasant sight; but yet more pleasure haue I
To thinke vpon this moystning Southwest Winde,
That driues my laden Shippes from fertile *Spaine:*
But come what will, no Winde can come amisse,
For two and thirty Windes that rules the Seas,
And blowes about this ayerie Region;
Thirtie two Shippes haue I to equall them:
Whose wealthy fraughts doe make *Pisaro* rich:
Thus euery Soyle to mee is naturall:
Indeed by birth, I am a *Portingale,*
Who driuen by Westerne winds on *English* shore,
Heere liking of the soyle, I maried,
And haue Three Daughters: But impartiall Death
Long since, depriude mee of her dearest life:
Since whose discease, in *London* I haue dwelt:
And by the sweete loude trade of *Vsurie*
Letting for Interest, and on Morgages,
Doe I waxe rich, though many Gentlemen
By my extortion comes to miserie: (A2r)

The passage is driven by winds—the thirty-two winds corresponding to the thirty-two points of the compass and matched, since in Pisaro's world picture merchandise equals nature, by his thirty-two ships. This speech echoes the wind imagery of Marlowe's *Jew of Malta,* with which a bashaw replies to the governor of Malta's query, "What wind drives you thus into *Malta* rhode?": "The wind that bloweth all the world besides, / Desire of gold."[11] The linking of winds and financial success is reiterated throughout *English-men for My Money:* in one memorable comic sequence Pisaro is first informed by the merchant Towerson that "this iolly South-west wind with gentle blast, / Hath driuen home our long expected Shippes, / All laden with the wealth of ample Spaine" (B4r), only to be told by the Post that his ships were set on by Spanish galleys "by reason of the weathers calmnesse" (Cr)—the lack of wind. Finally the Italian Alvaro is able to reassure Pisaro that "dat after vn piculo battalion, for vn halfe howre de come a Winde fra de North, & de Sea go tumble here, & tumble dare, dat make de Gallies run away for feare be almost drowned" (C3r). Both Pisaro's self-portrait and the changing news of his fortunes vividly dramatize the nexus of natural phenomena and financial success implicit in "trade winds."

Perhaps more familiarly, Pisaro's monologue recalls the opening scene of *The Merchant of Venice,* in which Salarino quizzes Antonio on the cause of his "sadnes" and concludes "Your minde is tossing on the Ocean" propelled by winds that would make him ill: "My wind cooling my broth, / would blow me to an ague when I thought / what harme a winde too great might doe at sea."[12] But Pisaro's invocation of the winds is importantly different. For as those winds blew the "laden Shippes," the "wealthy fraughts," they also blow Pisaro himself, "driuen by Westerne winds on *English* shore." His very identification as a "Portingale" hints at this characteristic: "Portingale" is the standard sixteenth-century variant of "Portugal," but also one that, according to the *Oxford English Dictionary* (*OED*), may be constructed analogous to "nightingale," a bird carried by the wind,[13] and punningly also a "port-in-gale"—Pisaro, it seems, is welcome to any port in a storm.

From this opening statement on, Pisaro's status and by extension the comedy's plot are articulated through a repertoire of insistent metaphors. These metaphors—of various forms of plant importation, of plant grafting, and of foreign language acquisition—share one key feature: they all deal with crises in translation, of the wrench that occurs when a natural body is forced to deal with an alien environment. So much early modern discourse implies that the individual "body" should be understood as seen as continuous with and permeated by its "environment": as Mary Floyd-Wilson has argued in her recent study of ethnicity and race in early modern England, "Renaissance climate theory avers that a region's atmospheric temperature, moisture level, soil, and topography help fix an inhabitant's humoral complexion, coloration, and temperament."[14] This in turn has huge implications for peoples, even nations, to the extent that, in the period, "humoral theory is . . . the foundational knowledge for making ethnological distinctions." But, as Floyd-Wilson goes on to acknowledge, in making these distinctions, humoral theory operates in a sometimes strained conjunction with other factors: "Climate determines the color and temperament of general populations, but the transmission of traits also depends on the parents."[15] What then does it mean when this ambiguity is pushed to its limits, when an individual "body" is not contiguous with its "environment"?

This question was one that exercised early modern theorists, forcing them to consider the impact of both environmental and parental influences on the individual in situations where the individual had moved geographically from her or his natural environment. This was a matter of passing interest in temporary situations such as that of the traveler, who would move through different environments but ultimately come home;

but it acquired particular resonance in circumstances where a person had been permanently displaced from what might be understood as her or his "natural" habitat, and forced to make a home in a foreign one. As Jean Feerick has shown, a relocation of people could produce massive anxiety about "the humoral body's vulnerability to external forces like climate and diet," as when the "Old English" moved to Ireland only to become "all but indistinguishable from the Irish."[16] Conversely, writers such as the Spanish physician Juan Huarte suggested there was a "rooted quality" in people, which allows traits to pass from parent to child, whatever their location. While it was beyond argument that after long stretches of time, Huarte writes, people become "conformable to the countrey where they inhabited, to the meats which they fed vpon, to the waters which they dranke, & to the aire which they breathed,"[17] it was still the case that "once the environment has produced certain ingrained characteristics, generations of descendants are able to maintain and transmit these same traits even when residing outside their ancestral region."[18]

Perhaps the most familiar instance of this in English writings of the period is to be found in George Best's 1578 *A True Discourse,* as Best relates bemusedly how "an *Ethiopian* as blacke as a cole broughte into *Englande,*" married "a faire Englishe woman" and yet "begatte a Sonne in all respectes as blacke as the Father was, although *England* were his natiue Countrey, & an English woman his Mother." To Best this suggests that "this blacknesse procéedeth rather of some naturall infection of that man, which was so strong, that neyther *th*e nature of the Clime, neyther the good complexion of the Mother concurring, coulde any thing alter, and therefore we can not impute it to the nature of *th*e Clime." He concludes that "the most probable cause to my iudgemente is, that this blacknesse procéedeth of some naturall infection of the first inhabitants of that Countrey, and so all the whole progenie of them descended, are still polluted with the same blot of infection."[19] Although this example has deservedly received critical attention for its compelling articulation, in Kim Hall's words, of early modern "cultural anxieties—about complexion, miscegenation, control of women, and above all 'Englishness',"[20] its very insistence on the determining role of skin color may divert attention from those instances of relocation to England where "complexion" was *not* the crucial factor, but where cultural anxieties about marriage between English native and stranger,[21] control of women, and Englishness were nonetheless potent.

Pisaro inserts himself into this debate with his opening speech. In

the early modern period, England very clearly defined its native population against all "strangers" or aliens from overseas, and individual English
towns and cities defined their citizens against not only overseas strangers
but "foreigners" from other English provinces. But the reality of commercial life in England's more cosmopolitan ports, and an intermittent
influx of strangers, especially from Ireland, France, the Low Countries
and Iberia, had forced the state to reconsider whether it wanted all its
resident strangers—among them some of the most financially gifted of
England's population—to remain strangers. In response, it had developed
the possibility of "denization," or "endenization," a legal process whereby
a non-English-born stranger might achieve a status somewhere between
English and stranger, with certain privileges accruing. While a Portuguese
man in early modern England would normally be classed as a "stranger,"
the imagery Pisaro chooses to define himself—that of a wide-blown seed
rooting itself in English soil—identifies him firmly, I shall suggest, as a
"denizen."

For the most prominent early modern understanding of denization related not to humans, but to the importation of foreign plants to English soil,
such a denizen being, in the careful but torturous wording of the *OED,* "a
plant . . . believed to have been originally introduced by human agency
into a country or district, but which now maintains itself there as if native,
without the direct aid of man."[22] Michael Drayton, for example, eulogizing
Kent's flora in the eighteenth book of *Poly-olbion,* includes "The Peare-
maine, which to *France* long ere us was knowne, / Which carefull Frut'rers
now have denizen'd our owne,"[23] a line that echoes his historical account of
the defeat of the English at the Battle of Hastings in 1066 by "the Norman
powers, / Whose name and honors now are denizend for ours."[24] Barnaby
Googe, Englishing Conrad Heresbach's *Husbandry* in 1577, admits that
"though I haue dealt with many, both Graines, Plantes, and Trees, that are
yet strangers, and vnknowen vnto vs, I doo no whit doubt, but that with
good diligence and husbandry, they may in short time so bee denisend and
made acquainted with our soyle, as they wyl prosper as wel as the olde
inhabitantes."[25] He reminds his readers that even the supposedly "olde
inhabitantes" were once strange novelties:

It is not many ages agone, since both the Peache, the Pistace [pistachio], the Pine,
the Cypresse, the Walnut, the Almond, the Chery, the Figge, the Abricock [apricot],
the Muske Rose, and a great sort of others, both Trees and Plantes, being some

Perseans, some Scythians, some Armenians, some Italians, and some Frenche, all strangers and aleantes [aliens], were brought in as nouelties amongst vs, doo nowe most of them as well, yea and some of them better, being planted amongst vs in England, then yf they were at home.[26]

Despite this rosy picture of harmonious horticultural denization, the status and privileges of the human denizen were always in jeopardy.[27] The legal history of English denization dates back to the reign of Edward III when an act was passed distinguishing between natural born subjects and aliens, the latter of whom were forced to pay a double subsidy and higher import taxes. An alien could take on some of the privileges of a native subject through a parliamentary Act of Naturalization, or via a Letter of Denization acquired by royal grant, both in practice bought for hefty sums of money.[28] While the initial impetus for denization was clear enough, however, discussions of the process and uses of the word "denizen" in the period bear witness to considerable confusion. Etymologically, the term is said to derive from the Middle English "deinzein" [born within] in opposition to "for ein" [born without], and traditionally the term had simply meant a "native inhabitant." As every entry under "denisein" in the *Middle English Dictionary* testifies, a denizen was traditionally "(a) a legally established inhabitant or resident of a city or borough; a citizen as distinct from a nonresident Englishman or a foreigner; (b) a native or citizen of the realm of England; (c) a native; (d) a denizen of heaven." Indeed, the term "denisein" was emphatically used in contradistinction to "stranger": so a Privy Council proclamation of 1419 referred to "Marchauntes, densyns or straungers or bothe"; a 1429 entry in the *Rotuli parliamentorum* is directed to "Divers persones, as well Straungers as Denzens"; Bristol's Little Red Book of 1439 refers to "eny man of the same crafte, aswelle denisyens as foreyns or alyene, within the seide towne"; and so on. A 1450 entry in the *Rotuli parliamentorum* allows that strangers may *become* denizens by Letters Patent, referring to "any graunte made by us, by oure Letters Patentz or otherwise, to any persone or persones to be Deynseyn or Deynseyns within oure Realme of Englond."[29] But it is clear that by the late sixteenth century, it is only this group of people—strangers who have been granted denizen status—that continues to be known as "denizens." By then, as jurist Edward Coke explains, "many times . . . *denizen* is taken for an Alien borne, that is infranchised [that is, naturalized by Parliament] or denizated by Letters Patents."[30] So the term that etymologically meant "born within" now signaled the opposite: "born without but brought within." It is an anomaly that haunts representations of denizens in the period, and is played out figuratively in Haughton's play.

In practice as well as etymologically, the status of a denizen was always precarious, despite the legal definition. Although the act of being denizated should have made a stranger English, in reality, a denizen continued to be perceived as a form of stranger. The taxonomy employed by the compiler of *Profitable Instructions Describing What Speciall Observations Are to Be Taken by Trauellers in All Nations, States and Countries* (1633) is instructive. He suggests that the traveler should note the "Kinds and degrees" of people in each country, and divides them thus:

1 Natiues	1	Noble
	2	Not noble
2 Strangers	1	Denizens
	2	no denizens[31]

The denizen, although here clearly demarcated from the nondenizen, remains a stranger. It is clear from metaphorical uses of the term, moreover, that the "denizen" may have been popularly understood as a stranger who had somehow sneaked into the category of quasi-Englishman. In a 1609 sermon at Paul's Cross, George Benson rejoiced that "Happy are we . . . in whose land Popery is not infranchised and made free Denizen."[32]

Pisaro's real-life counterparts, the denizened Portingales of Elizabethan London, were subject to this same confusion, sometimes designated as "denizen" in subsidy rolls and parish registers, but nonetheless always placed in the lists of strangers. Take, for example, the most famous London Portingale, Dr. Roderigo Lopez. In 1567, living in the ward of Farringdon Without, "Doctor Lopus and his brother" Lewis were described as "Portingale" and "denizens." In the following year, in "Lyttell Saynt Bartholmewes," the list of strangers was headed by "Roger Lopus, doctor in phisick, a Portingale borne, and a denyson"; a note records that the doctor "goeth to the parishe church." According to a 1571 survey, at which time he was resident in St. Andrew's Parish, Holborn, "Doctour Lopus, Portingale, howsholder, denizen, came into this realme xij yeares past to get his lyvinge by physycke." In 1576, "Doctor Lopes" headed the list of strangers in "St Bartholomeues the Lesser," and was worth ten pounds a year in land, and twenty shillings a year in movable goods. By 1583, "Doctor Lopus," a "Portingaler" and "Physicion" was in Aldgate Ward.[33] Lopez's name is usually marked "denizen," to be sure, but nonetheless his presence on these lists designates him as first a "stranger," and then a "denizen." Similarly, Lopez's compatriot and fellow physician Dr. Hector Nuñez came to London as early as 1549, and achieved denizen status on June 4, 1579,[34] but despite this, he was still in 1582 being designated as a "stranger" in Tower Ward.[35]

To become "denizened" in Elizabethan England was thus to achieve a precarious status somewhere between native and stranger—and that precariousness was epitomized by the fate of a denizen's children in relation to inheritance (an issue that took on political significance in relation to the stranger-born Scots monarchs' claims to the English throne, and James I's later attempt to unite England and Scotland). As John Leslie puts it in 1569: "euery stranger and alien borne, maye haue and take inheritance as a purchasser. And if an alien do marrie a woman inheritable, the inheritance therby ys bothe in the alien, and also in his wife: And the alien therby a purchasser. No man dowbteth but that a denizen may purchasse landes to his owne vse, but to inherite landes as heire to any person with in the allegiance of Englande, he can not by any meanes."[36] In 1607, Francis Bacon introduces the issue of whether a denizen's children can inherit: "it [the Law] gives him [the denizen] power, to purchase Free-Hold, and Inheritance, to his Own use: And likewise, enables the Children, born after his Denization, to inherit. But yet, nevertheless, he cannot make Title, or convey Pedigree, from any Ancestour Paramount."[37] Also writing in the early seventeenth century, Edward Coke complicates this definition by distinguishing between those strangers naturalized by act of Parliament, and those made denizen by royal letters:

This Alien naturalized [by Parliament] to all intents and purposes, is as a naturall borne subiect, and differeth much from denization by Letters Patents, for if he had issue in England before his denization, that issue is not inheritable to his father: but if his father be naturalized by Parliament, such issue shall inherit. So if an issue of an Englishman be borne beyond Sea, if the issue be naturalized by Act of Parliament, he shall inherit his fathers lands; but if hee be made Denizen by Letters Patents, he shall not, and many other differences there bee betweene them.[38]

The battles that produced Coke's dictum (subtly but importantly different from Bacon's) were fought during the fourth parliament of Elizabeth's reign, responding to the significant influx of largely Huguenot refugees. At the more extreme end, the Lord Keeper Sir Nicholas Bacon demanded a "complete ouster of the French immigrants," charging that "if the ffrenche denizens hart continue naturally ffrenche and lovinge to his owne Cuntrye Then can he not Love our Cuntrye nor be meet to be amongest us, yf he be unnaturall and can find in his hart to hate his owne Cuntrye then will he not be trustie to our Cuntrye and so more unmeet to Lyve amongest us."[39] In Bacon's formulation, a denizen is de facto untrustworthy because he has already "unnaturall[y]" rejected his own country and can only be expected to do the same to his adopted country. While this demonization of the denizen always tacitly underlies most of the Elizabethan discussion on the issue, much of the parliamentary debate was more nuanced, focusing on the question of the status of children born on English soil whose parents were both born "strangers."[40] On February 21, 1576, it was proposed that such children "should pay subsidies and customes and in all other respects to be as straungers"; not coincidentally, on the same day, a bill was proposed for the "manumising" of the mirror image—children of Englishmen who by accident happened to be "borne beyond the seas," and who were therefore not English by a fluke of timing.[41] The attempt to penalize strangers' English-born children was intriguingly unpopular: it was rejected on March 3,[42] only to be reintroduced in a very stark form— "that the childrene of strangers should not be accompted English"—on January 24, 1581.[43] This bill argued that all strangers' children born since the first year of the present queen's reign—the eldest of whom would now be over twenty years old—should be "deemed as aliens." The debate that followed was lively. The bill was "impugned" as "being against charitie, against the lawe [of] nature, an imposition for the fathers' no offence." Interestingly, it was pointed out that the bill was "very perilous to all," since who was wholly English? It was "a thing that might be obiected to our children after two or three discentes [that is, generations] and call every man's enheritance in question." Most significantly, however, it could have detrimental commercial effects: "under pretense / of providing for the Queene's custome it would doe much harme."[44] The bill was sent to committee, and returned with a different caveat: that Englishness would remain only as long as the children remained "dwelling in England and continue their sole obedience to the Queene of England."[45] Ultimately, the debates were inconclusive, and old suspicions of denizens survived. Summing up the thinking in the first decade of the seventeenth century, Francis Bacon sounds remarkably similar, in content if not in tone, to his father forty years earlier: "[T]he Law, thinks not good, to make him [a denizen], in the same Degree, with a Subject born: Because he was once an Alien, and so mought once have been an Enemy. And *Nemo subitò fingitur:* Mens Affections, cannot be so setled, by any Benefit, as when from their Nativity, they are inbred, and inherent."[46] The contested position of the denizen, and especially the status of his children, provides one context for understanding Pisaro and the battle for his daughters in Haughton's play.

If the prevailing imagery of the play establishes Pisaro as a denizen, however, there is a secondary agricultural metaphor, closely related, that modifies that denizenship in a very specific manner. The image of the wind-blown seed that plants itself in foreign soil would have another connotation for its Elizabethan audience. As Moses foretells to the Israelites in Deuteronomy (chapter 28, verse 25), *"And* the Lord shal cause thee to fall before thine enemies: thou shalt come out one way against them, and shalt flee seuen ways before them, and shalt be scattered through all the kingdoms of the earth."[47] The Greek term in the final phrase is of course from the verb that gives us "diaspora"; medieval and early modern English translations of the passage use "dispersed" and "scattered," and those terms come to be intimately associated with the ancient Israelites and by extension contemporary Jews. In John Wyclif's translation of the Bible, Israel (in Jeremiah 50:17) "is a scaterid flok"; in the *Geneva Bible,* "Israél is like scattered shepe: the lyons haue dispersed them." When Henry Finch dedicates his *The Calling of the Iewes,* it is to "All the seed of Iacob, farre and wide dispersed."[48] In Marlowe's *Jew of Malta,* Barabbas, that repository of every Elizabethan cliché about Jews, pronounces, "They say we are a scatter'd nation."[49] And the figure gave rise to the myth of the Wandering Jew: as the alleged author of the 1640 *The Wandering-Jew, Telling Fortvnes to English-men,* the unlikely Gad Ben-arod, Ben Balaam, Ben-Ahimoth, Ben-Baal, Ben-Gog, Ben-Magog, puts it, "For a Jew to wander it is no wonder, because they are a scattered *Nation."*[50] For Haughton's first audience, that Jewish diaspora had become newly specific. As a Portingale in London, Pisaro is easily identifiable as a victim of the wave of emigration, most of it enforced by the threat of the Inquisition, from Iberia—first from Spain, then from Portugal.[51] Although the London "Portingale" community was relatively small—probably fewer than a hundred at any one time—it contained within its ranks a number of socially prominent men, such as the aforementioned physicians Dr. Hector Nuñez and Dr. Roderigo Lopez and the queen's grocer Dunstan Añes. By 1598, moreover, it seems to have been well known that Lopez had been born a Jew, and it may be that, in England as elsewhere, for some people the very term "Portingale" or "Portuguese" carried, or had begun tacitly to carry, the understanding of "exiled Jew."

But how might this affect his denizen status, if Pisaro is indeed being identified as a Jewish Portingale? For English commentators seeking to understand the meaning of God's creation, contemporary Jews posed a particular conundrum. As the minister Thomas Draxe puzzled through it in 1609, in a dedicatory epistle to Lucy, countess of Bedford, on the one hand, "we cannot but discerne & acknowledge that God hath most iustly reuenged himselfe vpon the Iewes & powred out his wrath vpon them to the vtmost." On the other hand, "it is a maruelous worke of God, & not without his mistery, that the Iewes (how soeuer wandring and dispersed in al countries almost,) should stil continue such a distinct and vnconfounded nation, so innumerable in multitude, and so constant in the keeping and obseruing of (as much as they possible may) their ancient lawes, rites, and ceremonies." The reason for this, Draxe concludes, is that God allowed the Jews to maintain their integrity in order that they might be converted to Christianity, "the conuersion of the nation of them is dayly expected"—"so great a multitude of them shalbe againe ingrafted into Christ and beleiue the gospel."[52]

The figure of being grafted into Christ, like the image of the diaspora, the dissemination of the wind-blown seed, is one of horticultural cross-fertilization. As Rebecca Bushnell has recently written, from the late six-teenth century, inspired by Continental works such as Giambattista Della Porta's *Magia naturalis* (1558) that recommended "copulation," or "fusion through grafting of disparate things on fertile ground," English gardeners embarked on "stunning experiments . . . for changing the scent, taste, and shape, and the very nature of all sorts of fruits and flowers," often through the use of the grafting of one plant onto another, a technique known for millennia.[53] In his *The English Husbandman,* Gervase Markham lauds the

effects, wonders, and strange issues which do proceede from many quaint motions and helpes in grafting, as thus: if you will have Peaches, Cherryes, Apples, Quinces, Medlars, Damson, or any Plumbe whatsoever to ripen early . . . you shall then graft them on the Mulberry stocke; . . . if you graft Apples, Peares or any fruit upon a Figge-tree stock, they will beare fruit without blooming; if you take an apple graft, a peare graft of like bignesse, and having cloven them, joyne them as one body in grafting, the fruit they bring forth will be halfe Apple and halfe Peare, and so likewise of all other fruits which are of contrary tastes and natures.[54]

As Bushnell notes, however, while Markham attests to "the belief that bringing any two disparate things in nature into close conjunction or 'copulation' will always result in something extraordinary,"[55] this copulation/grafting was by no means universally admired; in Shakespeare's history plays, for example, it figures easily as "a negative metaphor for the mixing of classes and for social transformation, whether the bastard scion is being grafted on a royal stock or a better plant on a wild one."[56]

However, grafting has another set of resonances that derive, like those of diaspora, from Scripture, and it is also to this that Draxe refers. His image is drawn directly from Paul's letter to the Romans, where he speaks of the possibility that those who are currently unbelievers may still be joined to the true, Christian church: "And thei also, if thei abide not stil in vnbelefe, shalbe graffed in: for God is able to graffe them in againe. For if thou wast cut out of the oliue tre, which was wilde by nature, and wast graffed contrary to nature in a right oliue tre, how muche more shal they that are by nature, be graffed in their owne oliue tre?" (Romans 11.24–25).[57] Despite's Paul's optimism, this grafting was by no means straightforward—and the problems are linked directly to Draxe's depiction of the Jews as "distinct and vnconfounded." As James Shapiro has shown, there is evidence that various early modern writers held "the belief that the Jews inherited distinctive personality traits" and "were thought to be constitutionally different from Christians."[58] He draws particular attention to the argument forwarded by English theologian Andrew Willet in 1590:[59]

If an Englishman should go to Spain, his heirs will be counted as Spaniards, though it is allowed that he himself does not lose his connection by blood. If a Scot should move from his kingdom and transport his household into France, his descendants would reek of French customs, no longer accustomed to Scottish ones. A Jew, though, whether he journeys into Spain, or France, or into whatever other place he goes to, declares himself to be not a Spaniard or a Frenchman, but a Jew.[60]

Willet prints a marginal note against the passage that again asserts the grafting metaphor: "Iudaei non inseruntur in gentium stirpem" ("Jews not grafted onto the stock of a people").[61] Here Willet is drawing on a notion shared by many sixteenth-century commentators, including the Frenchman Jean Bodin, whose 1566 *Methodvs, ad facilem historiarvm cognitionem* is often invoked as a classic text of sixteenth-century humoral theory.[62] Toward the end of his book, Bodin ponders the questions raised by contemporary minglings of discrete peoples ("the fusion of Circassians

with Egyptians, of Spanish with Americans, of Portuguese with Indians, . . .
the relationship of Goths and Vandals with Spanish and Africans"), and
notes that due to this fusing, "none can boast about the antiquity of their
origin and the great age of their race except the Jews,"[63] despite the fact that
they now "have scattered into Chaldea, Parthia, India, Gaul, Greece, Italy,
Spain, Germany and Africa."[64] The Jewish people, then, in Bodin's account,
are at once the most scattered, the most dispersed, the most migrated of
peoples—and at the same time, the people with the most integrity and
thus antiquity: "only the Jews excel all peoples in the certainty of their
antiquity."[65] But in order to achieve that excellence in antiquity, the Jews
have had to forbear from grafting. Although they are the most disseminated
of peoples, they cannot mingle with the peoples whose lands they come
to inhabit.

So how does Pisaro the ungraftable Jew square with Pisaro as grafted
denizen? I shall suggest in what follows that in creating a denizen who is
a member of the Portingale diaspora, Haughton tacitly draws on the belief
that Jews, despite their dissemination, cannot be grafted onto the stock
of the native peoples of their new lands. But whereas Bodin sees this as a
source of strength and integrity for the Jewish people, Haughton uses it to
suggest Pisaro's crucial weakness, and to bolster the strength and integrity
of the English.

The central plot of Haughton's play deals, in the broad pattern of Terentian
comedy, with the resolution of the obstacle in the path of a true love
match, the obstacle here being Pisaro.[66] But Pisaro's dilemma can also
profitably be examined alongside two other plays of the 1590s that feature
male Jewish leading characters both of whom, Barabbas in Marlowe's
Jew of Malta and Shylock in Shakespeare's *Merchant of Venice,* also
have daughters, respectively Abigail and Jessica. These daughters seem to
allow the possibility that a Jew's offspring can become Christian. Abigail
renounces her father and his religion explicitly by taking sanctuary in
a Christian convent. Jessica runs away with a Christian suitor, Lorenzo,
claiming that she will "Become a Christian and thy louing wife."[67] Although
one critic recently noted that these "Jewish daughters prove eminently
convertible,"[68] others have argued the plays consistently draw attention
to the problems inherent in such a conversion.[69] Haughton's play, I shall
suggest, significantly presents no such problems—Pisaro's daughters do
not convert, because they are already *English.*

At first glance, the play's logic would appear to be contained in its alternative title, *A Woman Will Haue Her Will*, at least in Pisaro's shoulder-shrugging characterization of events in the final scene: "Doe what we can, Women will haue their Will" (K4v).[70] In this reading, wily women carry the day—but this is to deny the complexity of what has gone before. As Moore points out at the close of the play, telling Pisaro to cease "to fret, / And fume, and storme" (a futile reenactment of the stormy Pisaro of the opening monologue),

> These gentlemen haue with your Daughters helpe,
> Outstript you in your subtile enterprises:
> And therefore, seeing they are well descended,
> Turne hate to loue, and let them haue their Loues. (K4v)

The play's happy ending, then, has the denizen's daughters happily married off to "well descended" Englishmen, the women's birth-Englishness, disputed because of their denizen father, now guaranteed as they are subsumed as wives of Englishmen, and future mothers of Englishmen. The Englishmen have outstripped Pisaro, "with your Daughters helpe": in other words, the battle that has been waged is not one between women and men, but one in which the denizen is pitched against the English, an alignment that relies on the Portingale's daughters seeing themselves as, and being seen as, English rather than Portuguese. This has caused no small confusion. The critic G. K. Hunter once sniffed disapprovingly that Pisaro's "three daughters are (illogically enough) totally English in outlook."[71] But this apparent illogic, I would argue, pierces to the heart not only of the play's comic structure, but also to its analysis of denization, and its depiction of this particular Portingale denizen. As Emma Smith has shown, the daughters' Englishness is played out comically in their resistance to the strangers' languages, which is in turn linked to their support for the mother tongue, which is of course their mother's tongue. "I haue so much *English* by the Mother," declares Matthea, "That no bace slauering *French* shall make me stoope" (G4v). The mother tongue, argues Smith, becomes "an image that shifts unsettlingly between the symbolic and the material. It is both a property of the country, the symbolic mother, and of the immediate, material parent."[72] In the question of language, we meet another important trope of denization. One of the most familiar forms of transition to Englishness comes in translation of classical or modern vernacular languages to English, a transition commonly known simply enough as "Englishing." But Thomas Wilson, Englishing *The Rule of Reason* in 1551, wrote to his readers that "my good will shall want no fauourers in that I haue first labored to bring so noble a mistresse, both of reason, and iudgeme*n*t, acquainted with so noble a cou*n*tre, & here to be made of a strau*n*ger a free denisen."[73] The metaphor was still potent in 1602, where the translator of Battista Guarini's *Il pastor fido* dedicated his version, claiming:

> Learned *Guarinies* first begotten frute
> I haue assum'd the courage to rebeare
> And him an English Denizen made here,
> Presenting him vnto the sonnes of Brute[74]

And yet, here as with its human counterpart, the denizened word can never be quite English as the English: when John Bridges defended the Church of England in its use of the word "elder" in opposition to "priest," since "the word *Prieste*, being deriued from the Gréeke, and ariued héere, is at the most but a frée denizen," whereas "elder" was "frée borne."[75] Thus the importation of foreign words into the English language is persistently, indeed banally, figured as the denization of strangers—and it's a denization that is always incomplete. Haughton's play accordingly dramatizes its denization issues through a battle of European vernaculars with English. The French, Dutch, and Italian suitors are portrayed as having broad, and broadly comic, foreign accents, which are mocked by Pisaro's man, the clown Frisco, even before their entrance: his characterization of the Frenchman he has been commissioned to find is "one that neuer washes his fingers, but lickes them cleane with kisses; a clipper of the Kings English: and to conclude, an eternall enemie to all good Language" (B2v).[76] Haughton frequently resorts to the easy humor of having his stranger characters speak in mock Dutch, Italian, and French; indeed, as Smith has noted, the Europeans "frequently speak in succession to heighten the comic effect":[77]

VANDA[LLE]: Gods sekerlin, dats vn-fra meskin, Monsieur *Delion* dare de Grote freister, dare wode ic zene, tis vn-fra Daughter, dar heb ic so long loude, dare Heb my desire so long gewest.
ALUA[RO]: Ah *Uenice, Roma, Italian, Frauncia, Anglitera,* nor all dis orbe can shew so much *belliza, veremante de secunda, Madona de granda bewtie.*
DELIO: Certes me dincke de mine depeteta de little Angloise, de me Matresse *Pisaro* is vn nette, vn becues, vn fra, et vn tendra Damosella. (Dr)

Unlike the stranger suitors, Pisaro seems very much at home in his adopted country, depicted as speaking fluent English—a sign, one might think, of successful grafting. But Pisaro has no intention of keeping his daughters English. The play's action begins with Pisaro's firing of the Englishman Anthony who has been hired to tutor his daughters, and Pisaro insists on "a *French-man* borne" rather than an Englishman to replace him, claiming the new teacher must speak French, Dutch, and Italian (A4r)—so that he might prepare the English denizen's English-speaking daughters to obey the language of their stranger husbands. Pisaro's daughters exhibit none of the contemporary enthusiasm of Englishwomen to master Continental tongues for reasons of religion, commerce, and recreation.[78] When the foreign suitors begin their courtship in their broken English, the daughters are figuratively and literally unmoved, and uncharacteristically silent: "What Stocks, what stones, what senceles Truncks be these?" exclaims Pisaro (A4v). Each daughter explicitly reacts against her stranger suitor's tongue, echoing Frisco's earlier, spirited parody of Continental languages (A4v). Marina declares, "I cannot tell what Language I should speake: / Yf I speake *English* (as I can none other) / They cannot vnderstand mee, nor my welcome" (Dr); Laurentia complains of her would-be lover's speech: "Shall I stay? till he belch into mine eares / Those rusticke Phrases, and those Dutch French tearmes, / Stammering halfe Sentences dogbolt Elloquence" (D3v); and when Mathea is challenged by her English suitor Walgrave, "But *Matt*, art thou so mad as to turne *French*?" she focuses her answer on the question of language: "Yes marry when two Sundayes come together; / Thinke you ile learne to speake this gibberidge, / Or the Pigges language?" (D2r).

The strangers' imperfect mastery of English is presented as an obstacle to marriage, as Laurentia tells the Dutch suitor Vandall: "If needes you marry with an *English* Lasse, / Woe her in *English,* or sheele call you Asse" (Ev, E2r). The possibility of any liaison between English and other languages is figured as dangerous and unhealthy: "Why," Matthea laughs, "if I fall sicke, / Theyle say, the *French* (*et-cetera*) infected me" her pun collapsing French language learning with infection by syphilis (as Juliet Fleming has noted, "then as now the French lesson was a euphemism for a visit to a prostitute");[79] Mattea's allusion is censored in the text, perhaps because it is spoken by a female character. The sisters remain adamant that they will not marry strangers, as Marina puts it:

> Yfayth sir no Ile first leape out at window
> Before *Marina* marry with a stranger . . .
> These horeson Canniballs, these *Philistines,*
> These tango mongos shall not rule Ore me,
> Ile haue my will and *Ned,* and Ile haue none. (Fv-F2r)

Pisaro's servant Frisco laments his errand to St. Paul's, London's very own Babel, to find such a man, figuring the outcome as a bestial multiple birth to the daughters: "Ah Gentlemen, doe not suffer a litter of Languages to spring vp amongst vs" (B2v). Later he expatiates on the possibility: "Oh the generation of Languages that our House will bring foorth: why euery Bedd will haue a proper speech to himselfe" (I3v). And when Mathea temporarily rebuffs her Walgrave, believing him to be French, Walgrave appeals to her fear of a possible stranger husband, invoking bestial and unnatural breeding,

> Harke you a word or two good Mistris *Matt,*
> Did you appoynt your Friends to meete you heere,
> And being come, tell vs of Whores in *Fraunce,*
> A *Spanish* Iennet, and an *English* Mare,
> A Mongrill, halfe a Dogge and halfe a Bitch;
> With Tran-dido, Dil-dido, and I know not what? . . .
> Youle change your *Ned,* to be a *Frenchmans* Trull? (G4v)

Although it is not mentioned, this denigrated hybridity is, of course, precisely what Pisaro's marriage to his English wife involved—and as the play progresses, it becomes increasingly obvious that such a marriage has compromised his paternity. Pisaro attempts to assert unwanted fatherly authority in the face of his daughters' "will" to marry their English lovers. As he tells the foreign merchants, "For you [I] bred them [his daughters], for you brought them vp" (D4v); "tis onely you / Shall crop the flower, that they esteeme so much" (D2r). Here, standard horticultural metaphors are employed to assert the father's natural right over his daughters. But the play's comedy insists that, ultimately, he must be foiled in his plans. The daughters alternately ignore and mock the suitors so that Pisaro cries out exasperatedly, "in whose Stable hast thou been brought vp" (Er), as if questioning their paternity. Pisaro here articulates the same confusion expressed by Hunter: why are the daughters of a Portingale so wilfully English?

The answer lies in Pisaro's vexed relation to his daughters and to English land. From their first appearance in the play's opening speech, the daughters are seen to be children not primarily of Pisaro's seed, but of the English land: "Heere liking of the soyle, I maried, / And haue Three Daughters: But impartiall Death / Long since, depriude mee of her dearest life" (A2r). While Pisaro is a wind-blown seed, England, and by extension his English wife, are emphatically "soyle." And yet Pisaro loses that "soyle" immediately—his anonymous wife is briefly uttered only as she dies[80]—and the play's plot is propelled by his desire to acquire it again. The English suitors are not simply in debt to Pisaro: specifically and crucially their *lands* are in hock to him: "three *English* Gentlemen," Pisaro explains, "Haue pawned to mee their Liuings and their Lands: / Each seuerall hoping, though their hopes are vaine, / By mariage of my Daughters, to possesse / Their patrimonies and their Landes againe" (A2r). The point is recognized and reiterated by other characters: Anthony points out to the sisters, "What though their Lands be mortgag'd to your Father / Yet may your Dowries redeeme that debt" (A3r), and warns the lovers that "all the loue [Pisaro] shewes, is for your Lands" (B2r); Walgrave asks sarcastically, "Will old *Pisaro* take me for his Sonne; / For I thanke God, he kindly takes our Landes" (Bv). To hammer home the point, when Pisaro hears that one of the English lovers, Harvie, is ill with a "suddaine mallady," "his health . . . vnrecouerable" (I4r), he breaks down, realizing that if Harvie dies his "Liuing mortgaged would be redeemed / For not these three months doth the Bond beare date." He weeps over lost land the way Shylock weeps over his lost daughter and ducats:[81] "Oh my sweete Lands, loose thee, nay loose my life: / . . . the Lands been mine *Pisaros* owne, / Mine, mine owne Land, mine owne Possession" (I4r-v).[82]

And yet these lands never are Pisaro's own, for he is unable to plant himself there permanently. Daughter Mathea makes this very clear, in a scene in which she berates what she mistakenly believes to be her French suitor:

> Heare you *Frenchman,* packe to your Whores in *Fraunce;*
> Though I am *Portingale* by the Fathers side,
> And therefore should be lustfull, wanton, light;
> Yet goodman Goosecap, I will let you know,
> That I haue so much *English* by the Mother,
> That no bace slauering *French* shall make me stoope: (G4v)

"English" here is defined in contradistinction to Pisaro, who is "lustfull, wanton, light," all terms that might be applied to his tendency to wind-borne dissemination. Pisaro acts out Andrew Willet's dictum: "Iudaei non inseruntur in gentium stirpem" ("Jews not grafted onto the stock of a people")[83]—despite his landfall in England, despite his marriage to English soil, despite his legal denizen status, Pisaro cannot graft himself onto English stock, and as a result, despite his best endeavors, his daughters are English and beyond his control.

Ultimately, of course, the obstacle to the happy ending is removed, after a series of comic maneuvers through which the daughters either marry, promise to marry, or sleep with their English sweethearts. Pisaro realizes that "I am vndone, a reprobate, a slaue; / A scorne, a laughter, and a iesting stocke" (K4r): he must pay back the Englishmen's debts in the form of dowries. But the play's ultimate end is not marriage, but the birth of children. As the lovers arrange their escape, Walgrave promises that "ere the morninge, to augment your ioyes, / Weele make you mothers of sixe goodly Boyes" (Hv), the three sets of male twins attesting to English virility. Heigham more circumspectly suggests that they "Promise them three good *Ned,* and say no more," but Walgrave maintains that "Ile get thre, and if I gette not foure," and even the hidden Pisaro has to admit admiringly, "Theres a sound Carde at Maw [that is, a strong trick in a card game], a lustie lad, / Your father thought him well, when one he had" (Hv). Walgrave's motive is made quite clear by the brutally explicit metaphor that soon follows:

> This workes like waxe, now ere to tomorrow day,
> If you two ply it but as well as I,
> Weele worke our landes out of *Pisaros* Daughters:
> And cansell all our bondes in their great Bellies,
> When the slaue knows it, how the Roge will curse. (Hv)

Sex with the Portingale's daughters is figured simultaneously as a cancellation of bonds with their father and the production of children to inherit their lands—the supposed *women's will* is ultimately only a guarantee that the Englishmen and their children will get the Portingale's money.

So while *English-men for My Money* may appear to play fast and loose with the hopes and fears roused by denization, its comic resolution comes down firmly on one side. Despite the insistence of Pisaro that "euery Soyle to mee is naturall" (A2r), the play allows that to be the case only to a point. Pisaro initially embodies the threat of denization—the stranger with perfect English who wants his English land, but who inevitably will want to transfer that wealth to strangers. This would seem to echo popular fears about granting full English status to children of denizens on the grounds that a denizen's heart is never truly won to his English sovereign, and a denizen's child will revert to his or her inner stranger, threatening the security and stability of English trade. But this denizen, because he bears the traces of a specific Jewish Portingale heritage, is unable to graft successfully, and so his daughters are shown as being perfectly, belligerently English—children of the maternal soil, not of the paternal seed. The play thus enacts a fantasy version of denization that allows the audience the vision of seeing the daughters of a denizen grow up to be sturdy, xenophobic English roses, fruits of English soil, the mother, and the mother tongue, in a blow against their alien paternity. And in the daughters' determination to *have their will,* to marry their English lovers, lies the guarantee for the ultimate victory for environment over blood, for soil over seed: that the grandchildren of this denizen-stranger will be multiple, male, and wholly, unchallengeably English.

Notes

I am grateful to participants at the Inhabiting the Body/Inhabiting the World conference at Chapel Hill and to Mary Floyd-Wilson and Garrett Sullivan for suggestions on earlier versions of this paper.

1. William Haughton, *English-men for My Money: Or, A Pleasant Comedy, Called, a Woman Will Haue Her Will* (London: W. White, 1616); further editions were printed in 1626 (London: John Norton for H. Perry) and 1631 (London: A. M[athewes] for R. Thrale). All references in the text are to the 1616 edition. The only critical edition is *William Haughton's Englishmen For My Money Or A Woman Will Have Her Will,* ed. Albert Croll Baugh (Ph.D, diss., University of Pennsylvania, 1917); an edition by Lloyd Kermode is forthcoming: *Three Renaissance Usury Plays: The Three Ladies of London, Englishmen for My Money, The Hog Hath Lost His Pearl* (Manchester: Manchester University Press [Revels Plays]). Recent criticism on the play includes A. J. Hoenselaars, *Images of Englishmen and Foreigners in the Drama of Shakespeare and His Contemporaries: A Study of Stage Characters and National Identity in English Renaissance Drama, 1558-1642* (Rutherford, N.J.: Fairleigh Dickinson University Press, 1992), 53–58; Lloyd Edward Kermode, "After Shylock: The 'Judaiser' in England," *Renaissance and Reformation/Renaissance et Réforme,* 20/4 (1996), 5–26; Emma Smith, " 'So Much English by the Mother': Gender, Foreigners, and the Mother Tongue in William Haughton's Englishmen for My Money," *MRDE* 13 (2001), 165–81; Edmund Valentine Campos, "Jews, Spaniards, and Portingales: Ambiguous Identities of Portuguese *Marranos* in Elizabethan England," *ELH* 69 (2002), 599–616; Jean Howard, "Staging Commercial London: The Royal Exchange" in *Theater of a City: The Places of London Comedy 1598-1642* (Philadelphia: University of Pennsylvania Press, 2006). I am grateful to Edmund Campos and Jean Howard for sharing their unpublished work with me.

2. Hoenselaars, *Images of Englishmen and Foreigners,* 55; Kermode, "After Shylock"; Peter Berek, "The Jew as Renaissance Man," *Renaissance Quarterly* 51 (1998), 128–62, at 157; Campos, "Jews, Spaniards, and Portingales"; see also Alan Stewart, "Portingale Women and Politics in Late Elizabethan London," *Women and Politics in Early Modern England, 1450-1700,* ed. James Daybell (Basingstoke, U.K.: Ashgate, 2004), 82–98. Earlier surveys of representations of Jews in English literature do not address the play: see Jacob Lopes Cardozo, *The Contemporary Jew in the Elizabethan Drama* (Amsterdam: H. J. Paris, 1925); Montagu Frank Modder, *The Jew in the Literature of England to the End of the 19th Century* (Philadelphia: Jewish Publication Society of America, 1939); Edgar Rosenberg, *From Shylock to Svengali: Jewish Stereotypes in English Fiction* (Stanford, Calif.: Stanford University Press, 1960); Harold Fisch, *Jerusalem and Albion: The Hebraic Factor in Seventeenth-Century Literature* (New York: Schocken Books, 1964); Harold Fisch, *The Dual Image: The Figure of the Jew in English and American Literature* (New York: Ktav Publishing House, 1971); and James Shapiro, *Shakespeare and the Jews* (New York: Columbia University Press, 1996).

3. Christopher Marlo[we], *The Famous Tragedy of the Rich Iew of Malta* (London: I.B. for Nicholas Vavasour, 1633); William Shakespeare, *The Most Excellent Historie of the Merchant of Uenice* (London: I.R. for Thomas Heyes, 1600).

4. It might be objected, however, that "bottle-nose" is also an epithet applied in the period by Ulpian Fulwell to the Devil ("my dame called thee bottle nosed knaue"), and John Harington writes of "a Blackamore" as "a Giptian . . . Blabber lipt, beetle browd, and bottle nozed, / Greasie and nastie, his apparell poore" (translating Ariosto's "uno Etiopo con naso e labri grossi"). See Fulwell, *A Pleasant Enterlude, Intituled, Like Will to Like, Quoth the Deuill to the Collier* . . . (London: Edward Allde, 1587), Aiijr; Harington, *Orlando Fvrioso in English Heroical Verse* (London: Richard Field, 1591), Iiv (43.128).

5. Haughton, *English-men,* Br, F3r, F3v, F4r, F4v, Gr, Gv, H3r.

6. In April 1613, the traveler Thomas Coryate witnessed a Jewish ritual circumcision in Galata, in "the house of a certaine *English* Iew, called Amis, borne in the *Crootched* Friers in *London,* who hath two sisters more of his owne Iewish Religion, Commorant in *Galata,* who were likewise borne in the same place." These London-born expatriate English siblings have been identified as Jacob, Rachel, and Elizabeth Añes, three children of Dunstan Añes, who did indeed live on Crutched Friars. "Master Coryats Constantinopolitan Observations abridged," in Samuel Purchas, ed., *Pvrchas His Pilgrimes. In Five Bookes* (London: William Stansby for Henrie Fetherstone, 1625), 8N6v–8Or (10.12.1824-25). The Añes family members are identified in Lucien Wolf, "Jews in Elizabethan England," *Transactions of the Jewish Historical Society* [hereafter *TJHSE*] 11 (1928), 1–91, at 14–16; E. R. Samuel, "Portuguese Jews in Jacobean London," *TJHSE* 18 (1958), 171–230, at 179 and 179 n.1; Edgar Samuel, "Añes, Dunstan," *Oxford Dictionary of National Biography.*

7. On Lopez, see recently David S. Katz, *The Jews in the History of England 1485-1850* (Oxford, U.K.: Clarendon Press, 1994); Dominic Green, *The Double Life of Doctor Lopez: Spies, Shakespeare and the Plot to Poison Elizabeth I* (London: Century, 2003); Edgar Samuel, "Lopez, Roderigo," *Oxford DNB;* Alan Stewart, *Killing Dr. Lopez: Shylock and the Portingales of Elizabethan London* (forthcoming).

8. Andrew Gurr, "Intertextuality at Windsor," *Shakespeare Quarterly* 38 (1987): 189–200, 195.

9. Campos, "Jews, Spaniards, and Portingales," 610. For an alternative view, see Gilbert R. Davis, "The Characterization of Mamon in Jack Drum's Entertainment," *English Language Notes* 3 (1965), 23, which argues against Pisaro's Jewishness pointing out that his religion is never explicitly stated.

10. See especially Mary Floyd-Wilson, *English Ethnicity and Race in Early Modern Drama* (Cambridge: Cambridge University Press, 2003), 2.

11. Marlowe, *Iew of Malta*, F4v–Gr.

12. Shakespeare, *Merchant of Uenice,* A2r. As Gail Kern Paster has recently pointed out, for the early moderns as for the ancient Greeks, "the wind had an emotional component and an urgent meaning largely unknown and phenomenologically unrecoverable to us," citing the opinion of the Dominican Nicolas Coeffeteau, writing in the early seventeenth century, "that as there foure chiefe winds which excite diuers stormes, be it at land or sea; so there are foure principall Passions which trouble our Soules, and which stir vp diuers tempests by their irregular motions." Paster, *Humoring the Body: Emotions and the Shakespearean Stage* (Chicago: University of Chicago Press, 2004), 8–9, citing Nicolas Coeffeteau, *A Table of Humane Passions,* trans. Edward Grimeston (London: Nicholas Okes, 1621), C4r.

13. *OED,* s.v. "Portingale."

14. Mary Floyd-Wilson, "Transmigrations: Crossing Regional and Gender Boundaries in *Antony and Cleopatra,*" in *Enacting Gender on the English Renaissance Stage,* ed. Viviana Comensoli and Anne Russell (Urbana: University of Illinois Press, 1999), 73–96, at 74.

15. Floyd-Wilson, *English Ethnicity and Race,* 1, 9.

16. Jean Feerick, "Spenser, Race, and Ire-land," *English Literary Renaissance* 32 (2002), 85–117, at 94–95.

17. Juan Huarte, *Examen de Ingenios. The Examination of Mens Wits,* trans. R[ichard] C[arew] (London: Richard Watkins, 1594), O ijr.

18. Floyd-Wilson, *English Ethnicity,* 9.

19. George Best, *A Trve Discovrse of the Late Voyages of Discouerie, for the Finding of a Passage to Cathaya, by the Northweast, Vnder the Conduct of Martin Frobisher Generall* (London: Henry Byneman, 1578), f.iij.r–v.

20. Kim F. Hall, *Things of Darkness: Economies of Race and Gender in Early Modern England* (Ithaca, N.Y., and London: Cornell University Press, 1995), 11–13, at 11; see also Ania Loomba, *Shakespeare, Race, and Colonialism* (Oxford: Oxford University Press, 2002), 54–55; Floyd-Wilson, *English Ethnicity,* 8–9.

21. I am here avoiding the use of the word "miscegenation," a mid-nineteenth-century term that was first defined as "The theory of the blending of the races applied to the American White Man and Negro," and therefore builds on later, and specifically American, notions of race. See *OED,* s.v. miscegenation, 1.

22. *OED,* s.v. denizen, n. 2c.

23. Michael Drayton, *Poly-olbion* (London: M. Lownes, I. Browne, I. Helme and I. Busbie, 1612), Cc5v.

24. Drayton, *Poly-olbion,* Aa2r.

25. Barnabe Googe, "The Epistle to the Reader," in his trans., Conrad Heresbach, *Fovre Bookes of Husbandry* (London: Richard Watkins, 1577), (iij)r–v.

26. Googe, "Epistle," (iij)v.

27. Although there is a good deal of work on stranger communities in London, the specific status of denizens has yet to be fully addressed. See William Page, ed., *Letters of Denization and Acts of Naturalization for Aliens in England, 1509-1603* (Lymington: Huguenot Society [vol. 8], 1893); Irene Scouloudi, *Returns of Strangers in the Metropolis 1593, 1627, 1635, 1639. A Study of an Active Minority* (London: Huguenot Society of London [Quarto Series, vol. LVII], 1985); Steve Rappaport, *Worlds Within Worlds: Structures of Life in Sixteenth-Century London* (Cambridge: Cambridge University Press, 1989), 54-60; Ian W. Archer, *The Pursuit of Stability: Social Relations in Elizabethan London* (Cambridge: Cambridge University Press, 1991), 131-39; Laura Hunt Yungblut, *Strangers Settled Here Amongst Us: Policies, Perceptions and the Presence of Aliens in Elizabethan England* (London and New York: Routledge, 1996).

28. Page, *Letters of Denization*, i.

29. All references to the *Middle English Dictionary*, s.v. "denisein."

30. Edward Coke, *The First Part of the Institvtes of the Lawes of England. Or, A Commentarie vpon Littleton, not the Name of a Lawyer Onely, but of the Law It Selfe* (London: Societie of Stationers, 1628), Kkr.

31. *Profitable Instructions Describing What Speciall Obseruations Are to Be Taken by Trauellers in All Nations, States and Countries* (London: Beniamin Fisher, 1633), B4v-B5r.

32. George Benson, *A Sermon Preached at Paules Crosse the Seauenth of May, M.DC.IX* (London: H. L[ownes] for Richard Moore, 1609), Fr.

33. *Returns of Aliens Dwelling in the City and Suburbs of London from the Reign of Henry VIII. to that of James I,* ed. R.E.G. Kirk and Ernest F. Kirk, 4 parts (Aberdeen: Huguenot Society of London,1900-8), 1: 365, 3:342, 2:10, 2:172, 2:319.

34. Charles Meyers, "Debt in Elizabethan England: The Adventures of Dr. Hector Nunez, Physician and Merchant," *TJHSE* 34 (1994-96), 125-40, at 129, citing National Archives, Kew, C[hancery] 66/1176 M. 23 Patent Roll 21 Elizabeth 1579 Part 2, June 4, 1579. See also Edgar Samuel, "Nunes, Hector (1520-1591)," *Oxford DNB*. Nunez's belated denization came after a 1576 appeal to the Commissioners for Spanish Causes for the restitution of goods held in Spain in which it was decided that, although he was not a natural born subject, his long sojourn in England granted him a quasi-English status. Page, *Letters of Denization*, ii.

35. Kirk and Kirk, *Returns of Aliens*, 2: 255, 258, 324.

36. John Leslie, *A Defence of the Honour of the Right Highe, Mightye and Noble Princesse Marie Quene of Scotlande* (London: Ptolemé and Nicephore Lycosthenes [Rheims: J. Foigny], 1569), Iv-ijr.

37. Francis Bacon, "A Speech in Parliament Touching the Naturalization of the Scots Nation," *Resuscitatio,* ed. William Rawley (London: Sarah Griffin for William Lee, 1657), Dr-v.

38. Coke, *First Part of the Institvtes,* Kkr.

39. Sir Nicholas Bacon, speech in Parliament, 1576. British Library Additional MS 33271, f. 16r-v, qtd. in Yungblut, *Strangers Settled Here Amongst Us,* 36.

40. For these parliamentary debates, see *Proceedings in the Parliaments of Elizabeth I,* ed. T. E. Hartley, 3 vols. (Leicester: Leicester University Press, 1981-95); *Journal of the House of Commons* (n.p.: n.pub, n.d.), vol. 1.

41. Hartley, *Proceedings,* 1:481-82.

42. Hartley, *Proceedings,* 1: 486. The *Commons' Journal* (1: 110) suggests it was "committeed" rather than "rejected."

43. Hartley, *Proceedings,* 1: 527.

44. Hartley, *Proceedings,* 1: 528 (January 27, 1581).

45. Hartley, *Proceedings,* 1: 531, 532 (February 3 and 4, 1581). But the Commons were still not happy with the bill, and it was "againe committed to certeine committees," before returning in mid-February, "reformed in diverse points," given a fourth reading, passed and sent to the Lords, where it was "not liked of." Hartley, *Proceedings,* 1: 533, 537, and Commons' Journal 1: 127 (February 8 and 17, 1581).

46. Bacon, "Speech in Parliament," Dv.

47. *The Geneva Bible: A Facsimile of the 1560 Edition,* intro. Lloyd E. Berry (Madison: University of Wisconsin Press, 1969), A.i.r. The Vulgate reads "Tradat te Dominus corruentem ante hostes tuos; per unam viam egrediaris contra eos, et per septem fugias, et dispergaris per omnia regna terræ." *Biblia Sacra juxta vulgatam Clementinam divisionibus, summariis et concordantiis ornate* (Rome, Tournai, and Paris: typis Societatis S. Joannis Evang., 1947), 191.

48. [Henry Finch], *The Calling of the Iewes. A Present to Ivdah and the Children of Israel that Ioyned with Him, and to Ioseph (the Valiant Tribe of Ephraim) and All the House of Israel that Ioyned with Him . . .* (London: William Bladen, 1621), Ar.

49. Marlowe, *Iew of Malta,* B3r.

50. *The Wandering-Jew, Telling Fortvnes to English-men* (London, 1640). The *STC* classifies this text under "God, Arod" (STC 11512), A3r.

51. Campos notes that Haughton's play "affirms the implicit equation between Portuguese and Jewish identities." "Jews, Spaniards, and Portingales," 610.

52. Thomas Draxe, *The Worldes Resvrrection, or The Generall Calling of the Iewes, A Familiar Commentary vpon the Eleuenth Chapter of Saint Paul to the Romaines* (London: G. Eld for Robert Boulton and Iohn Wright, 1609), ¶2v.

53. Rebecca Bushnell, *Green Desire: Imagining Early Modern Gardens* (Ithaca, N.Y., and London: Cornell University Press, 2003), 142, 141. I am grateful to Vin Nardizzi (Duke) for pointing me toward Bushnell's work. See also Conway Zirkle, *The Beginnings of Plant Hybridization* (Philadelphia: University of Pennsylvania Press, 1935), 82–85.

54. Gervase Markham, *The English Husbandman* (London, 1613; rpt. New York: Garland, 1982), second book, p. 35, cit. Bushnell, *Green Desire,* 144. See also Wendy Wall, "Renaissance National Husbandry: Gervase Markham and the Publication of England," *Sixteenth Century Journal* 27 (1996), 767–85.

55. Bushnell, *Green Desire,* 144.

56. Bushnell, *Green Desire,*149. Bushnell cites uses in *Henry V* (3.5.3–6); *Richard III* (3.7.125–27); *2 Henry VI* (3.3); and *The Winter's Tale* (4.48–49, 89–97).

57. *Geneva Bible* (1560), TT.ii.v.

58. Shapiro, *Shakespeare and the Jews,* 36.

59. Shapiro, *Shakespeare and the Jews,* 167–70.

60. [Andrew Willet], *De vniuersali et novissima Ivdæorum vocatione, secundum Apertissimam Divi Pauli prophetiam, in vltimis hisce diebus præstanda Liber vnus* (Cambridge:

Ex officina Johannis Legati, 1590), G2v: "Si Anglus Hispaniam petierit, eius hæredes Hispanorum loco censebuntur, licet ipse cognationem non amittat: Si Scotus res suas deportet & transvehat in Galliam, eius posteritas Gallicos mores redolebit, Scoticis non amplius assueta. Iudæus tamen siue Hispaniam, siue Galliam itinere petierit, siue in quamcunque aliam regionem proficiscatur, non Hispanum aut Gallum, sed Iudæum se profitetur."

    61. [Willet], *De vniuersali et novissima Ivdæorum vocatione,* G2v, marginal note.

    62. Jean Bodin, *Methodvs, ad facilem historiarvm cognitionem* (Paris: apud Martinum Iuuenem, 1566).

    63. "Quid commemorem id quod incredibile posteritati videbitur, Circassiorum cum Ægyptiis, Hispanorum cum Americis, Lusitanorum cum Indis? Gothorum & Vandalorum cum Hispanis & Afris cognationem? ex his ergo intelligitur omnes homines tùm peragrationibus, tùm etiam coloniarum multitudine ac frequentia, tùm bellis & seruitute iampridem ita confusos, vt nulli de originis antiquitate ac vetustate, preter Hebræos, gloriari possint." Bodin, *Methodvs,* Kk iiijv–Llr; trans. Beatrice Reynolds as *Method for the Easy Comprehension of History* (New York: Columbia University Press, 1945), 362.

    64. "Quòd hæc vna gens his quoque temporibus in Caldæa, Parthia, India, Gallia, Græcia, Italia, Hispania, Germania, Africa, dispersa videatur." Bodin, *Methodvs,* Kk iiij r–v); trans. Reynolds, 362.

    65. "Igitur soli Hebræi generis antiquitate certissima populis omnibus præstant," Bodin, *Methodus,* Ll ijr; trans. Reynolds, 364.

    66. See Joel B. Altman, "Terence and the Mimesis of Wit," *The Tudor Play of Mind: Rhetorical Inquiry and the Development of Elizabethan Drama* (Berkeley: University of California Press, 1978), 130–47.

    67. Shakespeare, *Merchant of Uenice,* C4r.

    68. Campos, "Jews, Spaniards, and Portingales," 612.

    69. See for example Mary Janell Metzger, " 'Now by My Hood, a Gentle and No Jew': Jessica, *The Merchant of Venice,* and the Discourse of Early Modern English Identity," *PMLA* 113 (1998), 52–63; James Shapiro, "Jessica's Daughters," Shakespeare's Birthday Lecture, Folger Institute, 2001 (unpublished); Janet Adelman, "Her Father's Blood: Race, Conversion, and Nation in *The Merchant of Venice,*" *Representations* 81 (2003), 4–30.

    70. Earlier, Anthony twice uses the phrase: "For sooner may one day the Sea lie still, / Then once restraine a Woman of her will"; "Women & Maydes will alwayes haue their will" (I2r).

    71. G. K. Hunter, "Elizabethans and Foreigners," in *Shakespeare in His Own Age,* ed. Allardyce Nicoll, *Shakespeare Survey 17* (1964), 37–52, at 43.

    72. Smith, " 'So Much English,' " 175.

    73. Thomas Wilson, *The Rule of Reason, Conteinyng the Arte of Logique* (London: Richard Grafton, 1551), A.iv.r–v.

    74. Anon., dedicatory poem to Sir Edward Dymock, in his trans., *Il Pastor Fido: Or The Faithfull Shepheard. Translated out of Italian into English* (London: Simon Waterson, 1601), title page verso.

    75. John Bridges, *A Defence of the Gouernment Established in the Church of Englande for Ecclesiasticall Matters* (London: Iohn Windet [and T. Orwin] for Thomas Chard, 1587), P8v.

76. For a survey of stage characters speaking in broken English, see Wilson O. Clough, "The Broken English of Foreign Characters of the Elizabethan Stage," *Philological Quarterly* 12 (1933), 255-68.

77. Smith, "'So Much English,'" 172.

78. Juliet Fleming, "The French Garden: An Introduction to Women's French," *ELH* 56 (1989), 19-51.

79. Fleming, "The French Garden," 32.

80. Pisaro later revives her memory when attempting to seduce "Susan" (who is in fact Walgrave in female disguise): "I tell thee Mouse, I knew a Wench as nice: / Well, shee's at rest poore soule, I meane my Wife, / That thought (alas good heart) Loue as a toy, / Vntill (well, that time is gon and past away) / But why speake I of this . . ." (I2v).

81. Shakespeare, *The Merchant of Uenice*, D3r.

82. I am grateful to Naftali Balanson for pointing out the importance of this passage.

83. [Willet], *De vniuersali et novissima Ivdæorum vocatione,* G2v, marginal note.

The Actor's Inhibition: Early Modern Acting and the Rhetoric of Restraint

PAUL MENZER

> The strength of every thing, is exercised by *Opposition:* We see not the violence of a River till it meet with a Bridge; and the force of the Wind sheweth it self most, when it is most resisted: So the power of the *Will* is most seene, in repairing the breaches, and setling the mutinies, wherewith untamed *Affections* disquiet the peace of mans nature; since *excesse* and disorder in things otherwise of so great *use,* requireth amendment, not extirpation; and we make straight a crooked thing, we doe not breake it.
>
> —Edward Reynolds,
> *A Treatise of the Passions and Faculties of the Soule of Man*

SOMETIME IN 1595 the Lord Chamberlain's Men cast a player as "Tybalt" in the play of *Romeo and Juliet* by William Shakespeare. Shortly thereafter, the bookkeeper issued him a side that required him at one point to say, "Patience perforce with wilful choler meeting / Makes my flesh tremble in their different greeting" (1.5.86–88).[1] We can never know what England's first Tybalt planned to do at this line. We can never know, that is, the extent to which the body of this early modern subject did or did not tremble on the theater's broad stage. We can only know that the script invited the player to signify a violent interior event through the mildest of exterior shows.

From the evidence of dramatic texts, early English players often asked their audience to understand that physical stasis was not incompatible with great feeling. Nor, from the evidence of contemporary rhetorical manuals, courtesy books, "passion" literature, and quasi-medical treatises, was such an idea limited to the stage, for an ethics of salutary moderation dominates these various discourses. Nevertheless, many scholars imagine that the early modern stage hosted extremely kinetic performances of passion. Peter Thomson has written of the English stage that, "the idea that the human body might remain comparatively still while the passions race is fairly new to England."[2] Elsewhere, Erika Fischer-Lichte has aligned the stage with an Eliasian process in which decorum has progressively civilized the body, a process in which early modern actors play an early and demonstrative role. To accommodate the Eliasian tenor to the stage, however, Fischer-Lichte ignores considerable evidence (and vast diversities of performance modes) to aver that for the last four hundred years the European theater has moved toward ever more civilized bodily habits.[3] Yet physical stasis was quite clearly part of the early English stage's performance technology.

For early English actors, the point of physical restraint was less to civilize behavior than to signify a legible passionate experience, one that an audience could dependably "read." To start to understand how such a technique might work onstage, we should replace common diagnostic terms—such as "natural" and "artificial"—with descriptive ones, "stillness" and "motion." The terms "natural" and "artificial" provide no traction on what "Tybalt" did when he deliberately trembled his flesh. To talk about acting in terms of "artificial" versus "natural" is to pursue an infinite regression—the explanation of one phenomenon by contrast with an earlier phenomenon that will in turn require the same type of explanation.[4] "Stilllness" and "motion," at the least, offer intelligible coordinates as we graph the elusive bodies of early English players. Ultimately, scripted enjoinders to suppress the body may reveal far more about acting and actors than staged calls for "naturalism"—such as Hamlet's famous but ultimately elusive notion that, ideally, acting should mirror nature.

I employ "stillness" and "motion" in the most basic kinetic sense of a body at rest and a body in motion. I intend therefore a more limited meaning than P. A. Skantze, who, in *Stillness in Motion in the Seventeenth-Century Theatre,* evaluates categories of the stable and the ephemeral across seventeenth-century culture, ranging well beyond bodily stasis.[5] "Stillness" refers here as precisely as possible to scripted occasions on which actors self-consciously acknowledge their own or another's static exterior. "Motion" accompanies "stillness" because players so frequently contrast that exterior stasis with highly charged interiors, thereby *producing* an effect of a turbulent but necessarily unseen passionate inner life.

This dialectic of stillness and motion was readily available in the period's preoccupation with passionate restraint. Shakespeare and his contemporaries inhabited a culture—rather, it inhabited them—that retailed a regimen of moderation through its edifying literature and elsewhere. Emotional regulation was more than just a matter of politesse, however; failure to master the self was a matter of life and death. ("If you go on thus, you will kill yourself," says Antonio to the angry Leonato in *Much Ado About Nothing* [5.1.1].) Crucially, this regimen idealized the *mastery,* not the defeat, of passion. Such a regimen enabled a language of affect in which the lack of discernable passion could denote not dispassion but precisely the opposite. Literary and cultural scripts that idealized a suppressed—but not absent—passion provided early modern players with an efficient means to relay a powerful affective experience with little evident effort. Greedily appropriative, the stage translated the language of passionate moderation into performative terms.

This language—both rhetorical and somatic—proved highly tractable, and playwrights deployed it to a number of ends. For one thing, the language of physical temperance helped authenticate the bodies of the actors. By scripting the restraint of internal perturbation, playwrights could code the lack of evident passion as passion itself. In doing so, the stage infused stillness with significance, whereby to do nothing was to do something indeed. While it has been routinely suggested that seventeenth-century English actors naturalized the habits of their rude progenitors, I would argue instead that the stage grew increasingly self-conscious about the expressive divorce between interior and exterior. Moments of scripted static were strategic interventions by playwrights concerned by the problem of showing "that within." Confronted by the impossibility of surpassing shows, the stage discovered an articulate stasis, deploying a rhetoric of restraint fully elaborated in the period's edifying literature.

In other words, scripted stillness allowed actors to escape the innate problem of representation, what we might call the "players' paradox": the minute an external feature is understood to signify a certain way, it can be easily feigned and condemned as "artificial," thus ensuring an accelerated obsolescence of the "natural." Yesterday's convention is today's cliché. What can look, from the vantage of four hundred years, very much like indices of an evolving, "natural" playing style are in fact deployments of a dialectic that produced exterior symptoms of the player's interior by drawing attention to the player's relative restraint. Furthermore, as this essay argues, a passion moderated did not signify a moderate passion, but precisely the opposite. In strictly utilitarian terms, scripted restraint provided players an efficient means to represent a passion genuine, powerful, and, above all, legible.

Nevertheless, emotional display—or the opportunity for it—was not entirely banished from the stage; nor was it understood to be axiomatically inauthentic. In fact, an emphasis on passionate suppression might seem to create opportunities where a character's failure to control himself denotes the extreme volatility of his grief, joy, anguish, or fear. After all, early moderns like Thomas Wright repeatedly stressed the overwhelming power of passions. The "most part of men," he writes, "graunt them whatsoeuer they demand."[6] In short, idealizing restraint does not alone inauthenticate display (though as in any dialectical economy, the terms redefine one another). Curiously, though, early modern plays do not privilege passionate release as a way of knowing another.[7] Rather, in a culture invested in emotional maintenance, the indecorously mobile character—whether weeping, ranting, or stamping—is taken to be fraudulent, possibly deranged, and certainly at risk. In all cases, emotive display ruffles the "self-sameness" or "manly constancy" prized by humanist thought.[8] Passionate exhibition therefore risks more than just inauthenticity. The external manifestation of interior events falls within a range of habits condemned as insalubrious, illegible, and possibly insane. In pragmatic theatrical terms, external manifestations of passion do not reliably register *particular* emotional experiences. Rather, playwrights produce legible passion by stabilizing the actor and instructing the audience how to read stasis. Within the dialectic of restraint, then, the ideal staged passion is literally *obscene* (literal in that "obscene" derives from *obscaenus*, "offstage"),[9] a force defined by absence whose legibility evaporates upon exposure. The language of emotional maintenance is therefore not just a means to produce authenticity onstage. By relocating ideal passion as an unseen spectacle, scripted suppression inscribes the players' static bodies as sites and sources of closure and disclosure, legible vessels of secrecy and revelation. Finally, if acting is understood to be an art of inhibition as much as exhibition, we can renovate our understanding of the English Renaissance's representation of the passionate experience.

I. The Player's Paradox

This essay is chiefly concerned with the representation of passionate suppression, namely its emergence as an early English performance technology. This concern does not preempt, however, the cultural work such simulations of passionate restraint could effect. More than merely mimetic, the stage surely joined schools of dance and fence, liturgical and ceremonial processions, the graphic arts, and other nonliterary forms in broadcasting a somatic decorum to early modern subjects. Moreover, the ethical utility of these broadcasts was a subject of much contemporary comment.[10]

The pedagogical—or at least citational—sway manifested by the staging of emotional suppression cannot be ignored, though this essay's primary warrant is the mimetic use of the static body. By rendering literary and cultural scripts into performative ones, the stage, wittingly or not, helped circulate, reinforce, and popularize ideas of passionate maintenance.

Neither does the present argument attempt to displace recent work that suggests early modern passion was less a proprietary or internal experience than an intersubjective or transactional one. In fact, stage representations of passionate restraint relied on the "dense cultural and social context"[11] in which Gail Kern Paster embeds early modern emotional life. Inhibited acting may relocate legible passion as necessarily unseen, but to do so it must rescript the way theater audiences established credible onstage behavior. That rescripting, in turn, relies upon the kind of "emotional scripts" that inform a culture's understanding and expectation of the ways bodies register meaning.[12] In other words, far from proprietary, representations of passion are creative collaborations among playwright, player, and audience. Thus, like many recent critics, I am specifically interested in the language of passionate representation. Strictly speaking, however, I am concerned here with the way language, audience, and the players' bodies labored together to represent authentic and legible passion onstage. The particular means by which a player's body might have inhabited the language of passionate restraint is the focus of what follows.

As stated earlier, passionate exhibition was understood to threaten the constancy and "self-sameness" expected of early modern men, in particular. Acting threatens this "self-sameness" too, of course, since it demands protean flexibility of players—the precise opposite of constancy.[13] Passionate exhibition, therefore, attracts the very dubiety that attends on playing. When characters condemn, critique, or question overt expression, they give voice to a kind of antitheatrical prejudice, deploying the attack so frequently used against them and defusing it through a strategy of triangulation. The stage appropriates the language of its critics to legitimize its own practice.

For instance, by the 1600s playwrights can assert the idea that the most authentic expressionistic habits were those least "player-like." Somatically, this notion threatens to undo itself because it enforces an accelerated supersession of acting style lest expressionistic modes grow too conventional, hence too self-evidently mimetic, and thus too "player-like."

Rhetorically, however, the overdoing actor provides an ever-shifting—and hypothetical—performative standard against which the restrained actor defines himself. Intra-dramatic acting critiques therefore build into a play a hedge against cliché. For example, in John Marston's *Antonio's Revenge,* a boy player refuses to make a show of his grief, dismissing physical habits conventionally associated with great passion: "would'st have me . . . / Stampe, curse, weepe, rage, & then my bosom strike? / Away, tis apish action, player-like."[14] Marston's player here does not distinguish between good and bad acting; showing his grief would simply look like acting, period. As a means to establish authenticity, the straw man of an "apish" player is a blunt but effective tool.

The crux for actors then as now is that bodily eloquence has to be both unique *and* conventional. Paul Cefalu phrased the equation in economic terms in a recent essay:

What domesticates Ophelia's behavior and makes it interpretable is the common recognition that her behavior, call it x, functions to vent a certain passion, call it y . . . based on a common understanding of the way x and y relate and on the function they serve.[15]

The very fact that a "common understanding of the way x and y relate" exists simultaneously enables communication and subverts it. Since there is a common understanding—what the theater calls "convention"—*x* is easily feigned and undermines the authenticity of *y.* As Hamlet recognizes, for "trappings" to lucidly "show" (sighs, tears, dejected visages), they must access a shared lexicon of comprehensible physical habits. Those physical habits are easily understood but are therefore easily feigned. The search for bodily eloquence that is simultaneously authentic *and* fully comprehensible is a semiotic nightmare.

This paradox requires a subtle solution, not the blind alley of a simultaneously unique and conventional bodily art, but a somatic and verbal rhetoric that can reliably articulate internal conditions. In fact, the period's dramatic and nondramatic literature *does* sustain a belief in an authentic bodily voice, but it is a voice that, by definition, cannot be staged because it would not dependably signify. Inevitably, players must rely on physical expression to register meaning; they must rely, that is, on Richard II's "external manner[s]" of "unseen grief" or joy or anger (4.1.285, 87). By virtue of their conventionality, however, these external manners can be aped, which erodes authenticity. Therefore, a truly authentic display must be *un*conventional but, by virtue of being so, risks incoherence. A staged display of unconventional authenticity would produce little more than Hamlet's inexplicable dumb show. Reliably articulate physical behavior may be unfeigned, but it cannot be unfeignable.

In their important work on the early modern body, Joseph Roach and Michael Schoenfeldt imagine a lucid discourse of the interior manifested verbally or physically. In the *Player's Passion,* Roach suggests that the player's purpose was to raise a passion but hold it in check through craft, transforming unruly affection into coherent spectacle. Like Roach, Michael Schoenfeldt, whose work analyzes emancipatory repression in the period, calls our attention "to a cogent and flexible discourse that possessed the remarkable ability to render inwardness tangible."[16] While I share Roach's and Schoenfeldt's emphasis on the productive restraint of the body, the interior/exterior relationship behind their arguments depends on a notion of cause and effect where bodies reliably register meaning. The stage continuously troubles this reliability, however, because scripted calls for restraint appear precisely when passionate clarity is most in question. Such critiques point not to the body's articulation of the interior, but to its expressive limits and fraudulent capacities.

In fact, early modern play texts frequently trouble the very notion of a tangible inwardness. Hamlet's renowned skepticism toward demonstration— "seems, madam?"—undermines the notion that the body reliably provides outward and visible signs of an inward and hidden life. When Hamlet describes the player "forc[ing] his soul so to his whole conceit" (2.2.530) and thereby producing tears, a distracted aspect, and a suitable function, Roach notes that Shakespeare details a biological process in which marshaled pneuma literally and appropriately animates the First Player's frame.[17] Hamlet's assessment of the player is, however, bracketed with wariness. In the buried tautology that opens Hamlet's review—"Is it not monstrous . . . ?"—Shakespeare dilates the Latinate root, *monstrare*—"to show"—to point up the player's hideous demonstrativeness. (Hamlet is also disgusted with his own lack of passion, though he seems simultaneously dubious about the possibility of representational sincerity.) As Patricia Parker has observed, "monstrous" in early modern texts crosses barriers of domestic and exotic and shares the language of "opening, uncovering or bringing to light something at the same time characterized as 'monstrous' or 'obscene.' "[18] By exposing his grief, the player unfolds the closed secrets of the interior, a literal staging of an obscene spectacle. Hamlet's review of the player may indeed verge on wonder, but it is also tinged with voyeuristic disgust at the player's self-exposure.

For Hamlet, revelation is suspect for the very fact that it is revelatory. Significantly, Shakespeare links monstrous exhibition with meretricious feigning, a position highly skeptical of the uninhibited body. Following Hamlet's critique, a vision of excessive solubility—a torrent of tears, a rush of "horrid speech"—first excites then embarrasses Hamlet. (In this respect, he seconds Polonius: "Look whe'er he has not turned his colour, and has tears in 's eyes. Prithee, no more" [ll. 499–500].) In fact, Hamlet closes in disgust at his own expressiveness, where, "like a whore," he "unpacks" his heart with words. The comparison challenges the authenticity of exposure qua exposure. The player's volubility surely builds into *Hamlet* an histrionic metric against which restraint can be measured.

Katharine Eisaman Maus finds such skepticism toward the body's expressive means prevalent in English Renaissance drama. Maus writes that such skepticism produced a suspicion of the body's expressive abilities, as evidenced in *Hamlet,* where the prince's dilemma is less that his sighs and suits do not denote him truly but that they might not: "Even reliable indicators or symptoms of his distress become suspect, simply because they are defined as indicators and symptoms."[19] W. B. Worthen describes the viral effect of that skepticism, the way suspicion infects the play's evaluation of performance: "Hamlet's alienation . . . challenges the value both of sincere action and of dramatic performance. Since no act can be unequivocally expressive, all acts are to Hamlet perniciously 'histrionic.' "[20]

For an art that depends on the derivable meanings of external habits, the unreliability of "indicators or symptoms" of distress or grief or joy or fear constitutes a genuine crisis. As Michael Schoenfeldt has it, " . . . the real mystery is not to announce that one has 'that within that passeth show,' but rather to try to manifest what is within through whatever resources one's culture makes available."[21] Indeed, if there were "chronic doubts about the adequacy of what can be seen" on the Elizabethan and Jacobean stage, the solution was not to develop a more "sophisticated" relationship between x and y.[22] The solution was to find other resources available in the culture, in this case a rhetoric of restraint.[23] (John Marston's boy player self-consciously emphasizes his reticence against an extreme of demonstration that he *could* but does not enact.)

Playwrights responded to the problem of authenticity on two broad fronts. First, players and playwrights retailed the artificial/natural binary to authenticate their own playing, deploying it to legitimize contemporary playing styles. Second—the focus of what follows—they found in the culture's emphasis on repression a useful language of restraint and adapted that rhetoric to the purposes of playing. This language of repression proved particularly amenable to a stage suspicious of demonstration, for it coded physical stillness rather than physical action with literal significance.

II. The Rhetoric of Restraint

In early modern rhetorical manuals, courtesy books, and quasi-medical treatises, a prevailing conversation addressed the proper synchronization of exterior exhibition and interior passion. Throughout this literature, writers promoted the training of the body in methods of passionate expression and detailed a regimen whereby the subject could harness his passions to his purpose. The survey that follows does not pretend to be comprehensive. Rather, I present a range of examples to point up how this literature put a premium on suppression. The ethics of moderation here surveyed presented an answer to the paradox outlined above because restraint could signify not that the passion was weak but precisely the opposite. Such an ethic also helps to explain the stage's dubiety toward passion that evades control and, important for the purposes of representation, troubles the relationship between sign (external manner) and signified (internal event). Theatrically speaking, passionate release seems to paraphrase general lunacy rather than precisely denote a particular emotional experience.

Collectively, the authors discussed below urge passionate maintenance and stillness for the purposes of health, decorum, and constancy. Importantly, these writers urge the maintenance not the elimination of the passions. As Richard Strier has recently reminded us, "both the humanist and the Reformation traditions provided powerful defenses of the validity and even the desirability of ordinary human emotions and passions."[24] Certainly, then, an actor who stood stock still onstage could represent a healthy, decorous, and controlled character, the paragon of passionate self-mastery. But dramatic fiction demands more than just salubrious moderation from its characters. In fact early modern drama occasionally verges into modes of passionate vaudeville, where an Olivia can fall instantly in love or Leontes into a jealous fit. How does the stage discriminate between the static but passionate subject and Lear's "men of stone" (5.3.250), who remain stoically unmoved in the face of disaster? How does the stage produce legible, passionate stasis?

By drawing attention to the suppression (or its failure) of passionate exhibition, early modern play scripts shared in a discourse of moderation to represent the *physiomachia* of bodies on the brink of giving passion the reins—Reynolds's "opposition"—thereby producing fictive symptoms of suppressed interiors on the surface of the players' bodies. With minute or no visible gestures, players could signify great passion. Tybalt, we recall, silenced by Juliet's father, vibrates with rage at Romeo's intrusion of the Capulet fete: "Patience perforce with wilful choler meeting / Makes my flesh tremble in their different greeting" (1.5.86-87). Joseph Roach might note that, "the actors/orators of the seventeenth century sought to acquire inhibitions" and convert it into passionate expression.[25] Yet whether the actor playing Tybalt *actually* mustered his choler and then suppressed it— as Roach would argue—is unknowable. (Given the period's emphasis on the dangers of liberated passion, actually generating choler would surely qualify as hazardous duty.) In any event, Shakespeare invites his Tybalt to tremble, rather than "rage, weep, or strike his breast," which deploys a rhetoric of repression that signifies a body under siege from within, coding minute movement with significant meaning. Similarly, in the throes of *tremor cordis,* Leontes's heart may "dance" but the body of the player need not because the audience understood that coronary turmoil could and should be suppressed, though with great difficulty (1.2.133-35). (In fact, the assumed difficulty of suppressing great emotion *enhanced* a character's somatic strife.) Therefore, without ever having to employ physical gestures that risked inauthenticity or illegibility, players could signify through their stillness an intensely coiled passionate interior, which they interpret for the audience. This move helps assuage prevailing skepticism about the legitimacy of exhibition through a particularly efficient performance technology. At moments of emotional intensity onstage, players could represent bodies on the verge of giving way before a passionate revolt without ever having to do so.

To signify powerful emotion through static frames, players and playwrights depended upon an audience that understood the terms of emotional maintenance. In fact, the early modern period produced a glut of "passion" literature, which—like the period's playwrights—worried about the expression and modulation of internal perturbation. In his *Treatise of the Passions and Faculties of the Soule of Man,* Edward Reynolds pilots a middle passage between extremes of tempest and calm:

As in the Wind or Seas, (to which two, Passions are commonly compar'd) a middle temper betweene a quiet Calme and a violent Tempest, is most serviceable for the passage betweene Countreyes; so the agitations of Passion, as long as they serve onely to drive forward, but not to drowne Vertue; as long as they keepe their dependence on Reason, and run onely in that Channell wherewith they are thereby bounded, are of excellent service, in all the travaile of mans life, and such as without which, the growth, successe, and dispatch of Vertue would be much impaired.[26]

As Reynolds signals, the passions were "commonly compar'd" with the wind and seas. But Reynolds does not despair in the face of heavy weather. He insists that, "the toughest, and most unbended Natures by early and prudent discipline may be much Rectified,"[27] and he recommends "three meanes. Education, Custome, and Occasion."[28] Importantly, Reynolds argues for the proper "agitation" (not elimination or expression) of passion. In other words, physical stasis need not signify calm; instead, it could signify the labor necessitated by the proper management of passion.

While Reynolds's "Education, Custome, and Occasion" promote the acquisition of physical habits to calm the roughest tempest, John Bulwer describes a dynamic interplay of natural and learned gesture that work together to produce graceful expression:

There are two kinds of action . . . : one, that Nature by passion and ratiocination teacheth; the other, which is acquired by Art. An Oratour is to observe both the Naturall and the Artificiall; yet so, that he adde a certain kinde of art to the Naturall motion.[29]

Bulwer here reveals the codependent relationship of the "Naturall and the Artificiall," coding one as volition and the other as acquisition. However, Bulwer does not seem to be thinking in binary terms any more than Reynolds. The "two kinds of action" work in tandem—temperately, smoothly—to produce a seamless effect. They are not coincident but coordinate. The artful action is, in this regime, no less authentic than the natural, for the two work in concert.

Hamlet's disgust for the uninhibited body prevails in the period's nondramatic literature as well. Unchecked nature can be monstrous. Lacking Reynolds's "Custome" or Bulwer's "Art," the body may incline to reveal itself

too readily, as Francis Bacon describes in his *Advancement of Learning.*
Here, Bacon evacuates the space between being and seeming:

For the Lyneaments of the bodie doe disclose the disposition and inclination of the
minde in generall; but the Motions of the countenance and parts, doe not onely so,
but doe further disclose the present humour and state of the mind & will.[30]

Bacon's confidence follows a Galenic physiology wherein an image in the
soul generates bodily response. Unguarded, unmodulated, the body will
speak, though the language may not be intelligible. Against such a notion,
Robert Burton posits a complex network of checks and balances whereby
the body suppresses its more telling impulses:

This moving faculty is the other power of the sensitive soul, which causeth all those
inward and outward animal motions in the body. It is divided into two faculties, the
power of appetite, and of moving from place to place. This of appetite is threefold,
so some will have it; natural, as it signifies any such inclination, as of a stone to fall
downward, and such actions as retention, expulsion, which depend not on sense,
but are vegetal, as the appetite of meat and drink, hunger and thirst. Sensitive is
common to men and brutes. Voluntary, the third, or intellective, which commands
the other two in men, and is a curb unto them, or at least should be, but for the
most part is captivated and overruled by them.[31]

The classifying system is—typically for Burton—bewildering, and the passage seems to forget where it began. Nevertheless, Burton's point is similar
to Reynolds's in that the "intellective" faculty should command the natural
and vegetal ones, even if Reynolds himself ultimately doubts its ability
to do so. Mastering one's passionate nature does not, therefore, denote
the *absence* of passion but, paradoxically, its presence. Inhibition can be
exhibition.

Other discourses of physical culture challenge Bacon's unmediated relation between sign—the body's lineaments—and signified—the mind's
humor, and they promote methods to shore up Burton's intellective faculty. For instance, behavioral manuals patrolled the body's expressive life,
urging both graceful expression and artful repression. By this means, as
Susanne Scholz has outlined, conduct books translated self-expression into
"techniques of the self and body practices. Besides opening up a gap for self-
consciousness in the most immediate sense of the word, this performative
remodeling of the body entailed a domestication of affective impulses
which were accorded the status of 'nature' to be disciplined by 'culture.' "[32]

This project often aimed to construct bodies in ways that would distinguish the subject's class or national origin. Erasmus describes a range of bodily tics that will signify the agent's provenance:

It is also all of the carte to shake the head and cast the busshe, to coughe without a cause, to hem or reyche . . . to scrubbe or rubbe thy necke, shrugge or wrygge thy shoulders, as we se in many Italians.[33]

The decorous Englishman, Erasmus implies, should suppress such urges and thereby distinguish himself from the more demonstrative Italian.[34] In fact, the "cult of decorum," as Keith Thomas calls it, was part of a widespread effort to "develop new standards of bodily control and social decorum," a movement that coded a range of behaviors in specifically class and gendered ways. A 1649 account reports that those "most apt to laughter" were "children, women and the common people."[35] Giovanni della Casa's *Galatea* plots the body's physical coordinates in familiar terms:

For albeit, the power of Nature be greate: yet is she many tymes maistered and corrected by custome: But we must in tyme begin to encounter and beate her downe, before she get to muche strength and hardiness.[36]

These accounts all depict an essentialized body, one that may *want* to laugh, to shrug, to "caste the busshe." Applying to "custome," the pedagogical thrust of these treatises urges the reader to "beate . . . downe" the body's impulse to tell.

These generically various treatises portray a physical culture of the English Renaissance that stressed stillness or suppression, not to the exclusion but to the management of passion. Hugh Rhodes's hectoring volume of proscriptions, *The Boke of Nurture,* tells young boys to "Hold still thy hands, move not thy feete" when speaking, or, even harder one imagines, "Keepe still thy hands and feete" when eating. Stretching, leaning, head wagging, and scratching are also ruled out of bounds.[37] Richard Brathwait, whose *The English Gentleman* makes a near fetish of moderation, cites in particular the gentlemanly control of great emotion, in this case joy: "Sure I am, there is nothing that tasteth more of true wisdome, than to temper our desire in effects of joy. . . . [T]hese passions rather become women than men, *who should themselves be still,* but especially when they feele any such conceit undermining them" (emphasis added).[38] Hamlet's grief seems "unmanly" to Claudius not merely because of its durability, it seems, but also because it is so showy. As one instance of the way a player could make use of this notion, Othello "prattle[s] out of fashion" at seeing Desdemona safely embarked. His garrulity finds its indecorous counterpoint in the physical impact it has on the Moor: "It stops me here, it is too much joy" (2.1.203, 194). His susceptibility to an "undermining" conceit may, in Brathwait's terms, effeminize him and embarrass the onstage audience, but the actor may nevertheless signify his great joy with little noticeable exertion.

While this emphasis on mastery may read as neo-stoicism—enjoinders to lead a dispassionate life—Edward Reynolds insisted otherwise. He reminded his readers of Christ's passionate career. "There is more honour," Reynolds wrote, "in having *Affections* subdued, than in having none at all."[39] As Gail Kern Paster reminds us, the perfect temperance of Christ meant that immoderate passion—though not the passions themselves—is a sign of "human sinfulness . . . an instrument of excess and indecency."[40] Brathwait too diverts from the stoics in this regard, citing the positive moderation—not elimination—of passion:

Passions rise up in a drunken man, like a Swarme of Bees buzzing on every side. Which passions are not such as are prevented by reason, and directed by vertue; for these are not altogether to be extinguished, as the Stoicks supposed, but to be provoked as movers of vertue, as Plutarch teacheth.[41]

The distinction between stoicism and stillness is an important one, for bodily control can signify not the absence of passion but its mastery. Brathwait's martial metaphors reveal the internal combat that rages beneath the composed gentleman, praising those "ever readiest to enter lists with their owne passions, that if any either exceed or come short of this meane, they may so square and hammer it til it be reduced to a proposed meane."[42] Though the body may seem still, at a stable "meane," it may yet contain a roiling storm of passion.

A body in which custom fails to counter passion may not just be indecorous or effeminate or sinful, it may be a risk. Discipline and self-regulation were part of a medical as well as behavioral philosophy in the English Renaissance. As has been amply demonstrated, early modern medicine promoted, above all, equipoise. The humoral hegemony in early England may be overstated, but both learned and lay medical practitioners continued to consider health care a matter of balancing hot and cold, dry and moist, even if they did not subscribe to humoral theory per se.[43] Within this paradigm, good health depended on a tenuous equilibrium. The role of medicine was to maintain the balance and restore it when disturbed. The famous opening definition of the *Canon of Avicenna* described medicine as the "science by which the dispositions of the human body are known so that whatever is necessary is removed or healed by it, in order that health should be preserved."[44] Robert Burton put the matter more bluntly: "Physic . . . is naught else but addition and subtraction."[45] One medical historian cites the astonishing pharmacopeia of tonics, toxins, purgatives, and herbs medicos applied to the English alimentary tract: "analgesics, anesthetics, emetics, purgatives, diuretics, narcotics, cathartics, febrifugues, contraceptives, and abortifacients" were available to stabilize the unbalanced Englishman and -woman.[46] If internal agents failed, invasive techniques were at hand: "Cauteries or searing with hot irons, combustions, borings, lancings . . . plasters to raise blisters, and eating medicines of pitch, mustard-seed and the like."[47] John Harington's *Englishman's Doctor,* a verse translation of the *Salernitan Regimen Sanitatis Salernitanum,* dispensed seven hundred lines of tin-eared advice on purgatives and emetics to restore the English equipoise.[48] John Donne's dour description of the state of health in the seventeenth century summarized the glum anxiety such a system provoked: "There is no health; physicians say that we / At best, enjoy but a neutrality."[49]

To separate physiology, decorum, and medicine, however, is to splinter the synthesis of those categories in the early modern period, as the regime of moderation or "neutrality" cuts across modern disciplines. The ethical goal of this material is to produce a body that may modulate, moderate, and manage its passionate life for the sake of health and decorum. Yet nowhere does this premium on suppression propose that passion be eliminated. Most important, the physical exhibition of passion does not alone denote its authenticity; it denotes the failure of the manager's regulatory system. The most "authentic" passion is then not necessarily that which escapes the body's control. In fact, failure of the regulatory system does not denote a particularly strong passion but, as with Lear, an infirmity in the subject. Inhibited passion may be every bit as strong, every bit as "authentic" as the exhibited.

In what follows, I maintain that this ethic was particularly congenial to the player because within this mind-set, to "seem" to do nothing was to "be" doing quite a bit. Indeed, failure in Brathwait's passionate lists would not denote the depth of the human emotion, but the sinfulness or errancy of the human emoter. By urging the suppression of rising passions, early modern conduct books, physiological briefs, and oratorical handbooks offered to players and playwrights a satisfying answer to the crisis of representation: a signifying restraint. Moreover, the tremulous relationship between passion and its restraint gave players and playwrights a way of thinking through the body about secrecy and revelation.

III. Telling Bodies

Scripted suppression defines credible passion as that which cannot be shown or seen; literally *obscene,* it should be kept offstage or kept inside. Unrestrained, exposed passion is an embarrassment, the province of women, children, frauds, lunatics, and sinners. ("Thus do men from children nothing differ" says the frustrated Antonio to Leonato, who insists on the exceptionalism of his anger.) Dramatic occasions of great emotion simultaneously become occasions where the credibility of representation is itself challenged.

In other words, scripted suppression is more than just theatrically efficient; it is central to a particular dramatic and theatrical occasion, one on which the representation of passion is itself relocated. In fact, playwrights script physical restraint *precisely* in terms that pressure the legitimacy of overt expression. On one hand, due to the cultural investment in restraint, somatic exhibition symptomizes mental derangement, fraudulence, or error. More crucially, however, self-conscious restraint among characters rescripts the way an audience establishes credible onstage behavior. In a complex transaction, audiences are asked to consider not just what the players are doing but what they are not. For example, in the instance from *Much Ado* quoted earlier, Antonio tells the distraught Leonato, "If you go on thus, you will kill yourself" (5.1.1). The two have just come onstage; "thus" signifies the offstage, *obscene* spectacle of Leonato's unchecked anger. The moment is both pertinently dramatic and impertinently metadramatic. Dramatically, Leonato experiences life-threatening anger (which the audience must verify by its absence). Metadramatically, "If you go on thus" may winkingly witness the fact that the two players have just stepped from the tiring house. "If you go on[stage] thus"—in a fulminating rage— "you will kill yourself." In several representative plays by Shakespeare and his contemporaries, we can see the adoption of this dynamic: suppressed passion authenticates and makes legible the bodies of the players while resituating the place of passion as necessarily undiscovered.

We can recall here that Bacon's notion of disclosing lineaments helped produce this dialectic, whereby inhibition acquires signifying power. In *The Winter's Tale,* for instance, Leontes describes the body's involuntary expressions and insists that the body's inner voice will give its tongue the lie.

> Praise her but for this her without-door form—
> Which on my faith deserves high speech—and straight
> The shrug, the "hum" or "ha," these petty brands
> That calumny doth use . . .
> . . . these shrugs, these "hum's" and "ha's,"
> When you have said she's goodly, come between
> Ere you can say she's honest.
> (2.1.71–78)

The mental image of Hermione's "infidelity" will excite the animal spirits—in Galen's terms—and force Leontes's courtiers to mutter in a speechless dialect. Such moments retail a subversive but "natural" somatic voice that in Burton's terms will evade the voluntary or "intellective" faculty. The shrugs and the quasi-verbal "hum's and ha's" disclose Burton's "present humour and state of the mind and will." Players, however, cannot rely upon the "natural" or "vegetal" voices to reliably register meaning, because "hum's" and "ha's" do not signify in reliably coherent ways.

Elsewhere, Baconian confidence confronts Shakespearean skepticism toward bodily eloquence, a skepticism that disturbs any simple relationship between the interior and the exterior. Othello explicitly recognizes the way the closed interior may expose itself. Responding to Iago's cat-and-mouse queries about Cassio, he confesses that

> these stops of thine fright me the more;
> For such things in a false disloyal knave
> Are tricks of custom, but in a man that's just,
> They're close dilations, working from the heart
> That passions cannot rule.
> (3.3.125–29)

Dilations "from the heart" can evade passionate arrest. While Reynolds and others assert that "custome" can check the effects of emotional turmoil, Othello frets that "custom" may also produce their burlesque. In fact, "custom" here seems nearly synonymous with "convention." The paradox of authenticity—phrased succinctly by Othello—frightens the Moor, but he naively implies a discernible difference between real and feigned "stops," though they appear identical. Othello does not answer the question of how one determines authenticity, however; he invites it. The moment suggests that even the body's closest dilations may be faked (or, dangerously, that even repression itself could be faked), which undermines the legitimacy of expressive behavior.

The language of restraint, however, helps ameliorate the problem of fraudulence that *Othello* presents. We are not asked, like Othello, to distinguish between real and feigned behavior. We are asked instead to distrust exhibition *because* it is exhibition, or, to be more precise, to distinguish between and qualify certain kinds of passionate exhibition and inhibition. In fact, plays repeatedly condemn passionate exhibition (though not expression, of which inhibition is a kind), and not only do they question its authenticity, but they argue for its repression. In some cases, the external expression of an internal condition is not just potentially inauthentic, but possibly insane and certainly unhealthy. For however authentic this interior voice may be, the immoderate articulation thereof can verge into symptomatic lunacy.

Such is the case in *Hamlet,* where the prince's watchers read his indecorous mobility as a symptom of his madness. Authenticity is not explicitly at stake here, however; no one suspects that Hamlet is faking it. Madness, in fact, actually offers an opportunity for an "authentic"—but illegible—display because carefully scripted suppression authenticates its own failure. Following Hamlet's nunnery rant, Ophelia characterizes his transformation in terms that indicate an undermined body: "That unmatch'd form and feature of blown youth / Blasted with ecstasy" (3.1.159–60). To be *ecstatic* in these terms points to the overthrow of "sovereign reason" (l. 156) by the body, which is "put out of place," as the word's etymology discloses.[50] Claudius also diagnoses Hamlet's madness as an interior disruption of bodily comportment: "This something-settled matter in his heart, / . . . puts him thus / From the fashion of himself" (3.1.172–75). Robert Weimann's term "contrariety" for such deformative moments in *Hamlet* captures the physical strife when the interior evades control:

Play, especially its bodily and laughable underside, could exceed or subvert the discursive and behavioral constraints in the disciplining, unifying rules of humanist composition. Thus, these play-ful figures of deformation were anything but mere comic relief; in their contrarious function, they underlined, even helped unleash, moments of crisis and revelation.[51]

Hamlet is not mad because his heart is unsettled; he is mad because he cannot contain himself, ironically authenticating what we know to be a mere show of madness.

Hamlet's behavioral career charts the paradox of passionate display. Sighs, suits, and a "dejected havior" are too conventional to denote truly, but knocking knees, piteous looks, and finding one's way without eyes are too *un*conventional to signify dependably (2.1.85–110). Conventional behavior can seem insincere, but a unique expressive vocabulary founders into incoherency. After all, Hamlet's ecstasy strikes no one as inauthentic (except Marcellus, Horatio, and the audience, who know better). Rather, the crisis in *Hamlet* is legibility. The prince's observers may agree that he is mad, but no one can agree on the *particular* passion Hamlet's derangement signifies. Love for Ophelia, grief at Old Hamlet's death, anger at his mother's "oer hasty marriage"? To put this another way, madness is not an emotion; it is a confusion.[52] Hamlet's disheveled clothes, his shake of Ophelia's arm, his odd postures—these behaviors can relay a variety of different and conflicting things: love, grief, anger. Hamlet's visit to Ophelia's closet is little more indeed than an "inexplicable dumb show."

To be strictly taxonomical, on metadramatic occasions, display looks fraudulent; dramatically, it just looks plain weird. It is not surprising that fraudulence and derangement look alike onstage, however, because both divorce sign (behavior) from signified (emotion). Within Weimann's "unifying rules of humanist composition," then, physical exhibition of the interior is hardly the player's purpose. To the contrary, physical or gestural demonstration of the interior condition denoted, at best, an immoderate but imprecise distress, as in *Henry VIII,* where Norfolk observes of Cardinal Wolsey:

> Some strange commotion
> Is in his brain: he bites his lip, and starts,
> Stops on a sudden, looks upon the ground,
> Then lays his finger on his temple, straight
> Springs out into fast gait, then stops again,
> Strikes his breast hard, and anon he casts
> His eyes against the moon. In most strange postures
> We have seen him set himself.
> (3.2.112–19)

Like Hamlet's deformations, Wolsey's "strange postures" denote some "strange commotion" in the minister, though Norfolk cannot determine

what precisely it portends. Revealingly, the passage also recalls Buckingham's description of the "deep tragedian" in *Richard III:* "I can . . .
tremble and start at wagging of a straw, / Speak, and look back, and pry
on every side" (3.5.5-7). Both descriptions disturb the dialectical goal of
early modern ethics, which was a stillness that represented moderation. Of
course, Buckingham is faking it; Wolsey is not. One moment is explicitly
metadramatic; the other is not. One moment is inauthentic; the other is
illegible. The point here is that the idealization of somatic stasis codes both
exhibitions as dubious. Hamlet and Wolsey are estranged from their usual
selves, just as Buckingham is not himself in playing the deep tragedian.

In the teeth of an unproductive paradox, then—reliable signifiers are
easily forged; unique ones are incoherent—the stage elaborated a more
useful one: one way to appear passionate is not to appear passionate. As
we saw in the preceding section, reigned passion may be just as strong
as that which has slipped the bit. In John Webster's *Duchess of Malfi,* the
Cardinal first chides Ferdinand for his intemperance then counsels him
to amend it, drawing attention to his own self-control: "I can be angry /
Without this rupture. There is not in nature / A thing that makes man so
deformed, so beastly, / As doth intemperate anger. . . . Come, put yourself
/ In tune" (2.5.56-63).[53] (As before, the emphasis is on the deformative
quality of intemperance.) Ferdinand replies with what could serve as the
actor's axiom: "I will only study to seem / The thing I am not" (ll. 63-
64). The distinction is slight but significant: The Cardinal does not tell his
brother not to be angry, or even to *pretend* not to be angry. He tells him to
tune his discord. Ferdinand takes his brother's advice. He will "seem" calm
and temperate; he will "be" passionately angry. This move authenticates
that which the audience cannot see and invalidates what they can. In this
case, inauthenticity produces authenticity, a reverse spin on the players'
paradox.

The exchange brilliantly frames the complex question of how audiences
onstage and offstage establish authentic and legible behavior. As with
Hamlet, no onstage auditor doubts the sincerity of Ferdinand's anger.
In both cases expression is read as authentic but deformative registers
of internal events. Like Hamlet's ecstasy, however, Ferdinand's "beastly"
anger represents a falling off from the idealized control (as the Cardinal
boasts, "I can be angry / Without this rupture"). In both dramatic situations
transformative passion draws acute attention to subjects bent on secrecy.
Therefore, Hamlet and Ferdinand deploy the dialectic of restraint to come

at a similar problem from opposite ends: Hamlet obscures his true intent by pretending that his passionate restraint has failed; Ferdinand obscures himself from others by rallying those same defenses. That is, Hamlet *depends* upon the illegibility of deformative passion while Ferdinand cannot risk the attention it draws. So the *character* of Ferdinand is urged to hide his passions while the *actor* represents them by staging their repression. The audience to both spectacles is asked to privilege a truth that runs counter to what they see.

With the body's authentic voice established by means of its restraint, intra-dramatic acting critiques draw from the Reynoldian language of bodily admonishment, which urges repression, not expression, of the inner storm. Hamlet, after all, is training the First Player how to moderate "the very torrent, tempest, and . . . whirlwind of [his] passion" (3.2.5–6). Don't eliminate; harness. As Edward Reynolds pointed out, the meteorological imagery would have been familiar to Shakespeare's audience. Following Hamlet's stab-in-the-dark at Polonius, Gertrude describes the prince as "mad as the sea and wind when both contend" (4.1.6). Here, it is not the tempest but the failure to control it that denotes lunacy (or bad acting). Such moments onstage represent Bulwer's dynamic interaction between the interior and exterior, a physiological model in which the body is given to unruly spasms of passion, which can, which must, be controlled through physical rigor for the sake of health and legibility.

Hamlet's "Advice to the Players" should therefore be considered a slight but significant misnomer. Hamlet does not advise the player; he trains him to control his body. "Speak the speech, I pray you, as I pronounced it to you, trippingly on the tongue," Hamlet says, emphasizing the physical disposition of tongue and lip.[54] Do not "mouth it." Furthermore, he urges the player to "acquire" (a Bulwerian stress on artful acquisition, not internal volition) and "beget" a temperance that will give his passion smoothness. As with the Cardinal and Ferdinand, Hamlet does not censure passion. His prescriptions strive to modulate, not eliminate, the player's passion. Do not saw the air, "thus," but use all "smoothly." Without such modulation, the passion goes to "tatters," an unseemly rent that threatens seamless representation. The entire scene demonstrates a training program by which "nature" is to be manufactured, not by "mirroring" offstage behaviors but by a practiced regulation of the interior, a subject-object relationship that disrupts any simple notion that the exterior frame will reliably register the interior event. Hamlet's "advice" echoes a peculiarly early modern understanding of moderated passion, the appropriate excitement, direction, moderation, and repression of which produces the appropriate body.

The chimera of the "natural" and "artificial" binary seems to linger at such moments. But when players recite scripted condemnations of other actors, they draw attention not to the relative naturalism of their own bodies but to their practice of artful suppression. As quoted earlier, in John Marston's *Antonio's Revenge,* a boy player takes a characteristic swipe at actors who would—as *Hamlet's* First Player does—express himself:

> would'st have me turn rank mad,
> Or wring my face with mimic action;
> Stampe, curse, weepe, rage, & then my bosom strike?
> Away, tis apish action, player-like.[55]

The criticism is of actors who would express their anger through conventional—and therefore feignable and therefore suspect—signifiers. "Player-like" behavior is that which seeks a gestural outlet for extreme passion. Rather than introduce an alternative language of authentic gesture—that an audience must still "read," that therefore must be simultaneously unique *and* conventional—the speaker here draws attention to his comparative reticence, which does not invalidate the authenticity of his passion but rather produces it.

Recalling Hamlet's assessment of the First Player, we can see that those actors who find exterior shows for interior passion are not the most praised but the most suspect. For example, in Chapman's *The Widow's Tears* from 1605, a player responds to his fellow's demonstration of grief: "This straine of mourning with Sepulcher, like an over-doing actor, affects grosly, and is indeede so farr forct from the life, that it bewraies it selfe to be altogether artificiall" (4.1).[56] On one hand, the "over-doing actor" is a straw man who points up the relative restraint of the speaker. On the other, what betrays his mourning to be "altogether artificiall" is not the manner of his exhibition but that he is exhibiting at all. Playwrights can invoke a range of habits and mannerisms deemed demonstratively extreme for being demonstrative, which therefore read as feigned or "player-like."

If there was an acting innovation in the early seventeenth century, it is this signifying inhibition. Richard Gloucester, although he is lying, emphasizes his sincerity when he proudly catalogues the conventions of loyalty he refuses to perform: "Because I cannot flatter and look fair, / Smile in men's faces, smooth, deceive, and cog, / Duck with French nods and apish courtesy, I must be held a rancorous enemy" (1.3.47-50). Here, he invokes his restraint to authenticate his behavior. In the same year that William Shakespeare died, Nathan Field's *Amends for Ladies* could feature a servant, Ingen, who complains that his mistress doubts his love because he does not exhibit the conventional symptoms of desire: "cause I doe not weepe, / Lay mine arms ore my heart, and weare no garters, / Walke with mine eyes in my hat, sigh, and make faces" (1.1).[57] While rehearsing Hamlet's dilemma—the only way to show love or loyalty is to employ indicators that could be fake—the lover's complaint here asserts the authenticity of his love when he refuses to give it physical expression. This not an index of realism, or naturalism, or formalism, nor does it point to "realistic characterization" or even to the inhabitation of character. It is, rather, a rhetoric of restraint that scripts legitimacy onto the body of the actor.

IV. Personation

It has become a nearly unshakeable position among scholars of early English drama that the age witnessed an unprecedented sophistication of acting style. "The fiercer formalists have recanted," Peter Holland writes, and scholars of all stripes seem to agree that whatever the English Renaissance player actually did onstage, it was sophisticated, it was realistic, it was, above all, natural.[58] Andrew Gurr maintains, in a representative quote, that the period witnessed the dawn of realistic "characterization."[59] We err, however, if we assume that acting circa 1600 became more "naturalistic" compared to older bombastic styles. It is an easy mistake to make, however, for the period's players and playwrights worked hard to produce precisely that impression.

Critical emphasis on the maturation of early English playing has led not only to temporal chauvinism but misunderstandings about the way actors represented the passionate life onstage. For instance, Ramie Targoff forges an alliance of devotional and theatrical practice upon a familiar misunderstanding of acting. Considering the "emblematic" playing of the medieval theater, she writes, "[o]n the sixteenth-century stage, by contrast, the player strove to assume his role as convincingly as possible."[60] Targoff's position assumes a "connectedness of external practice and internal will"[61] and echoes a Baconian confidence that the "lyneaments of the bodie doe disclose the disposition and inclination of the minde in generall."

The argument is representative in its Baconian reading of "personation"—the modish noun for acting than came into vogue circa 1600.
Targoff's argument depends for its efficacy on a confidence in "external
practice" that the period's playwrights seemed not to share:

> *Hamlet* . . . firmly aligns devotional with theatrical performance: in both instances,
> performance ultimately privileges an outwardly convincing appearance over a
> potentially hypocritical inwardness . . . [and] testifies at once to the difficulty of
> conjoining the theatrical and the sincere, and to the sheer will of the spectator,
> nonetheless, to believe what he or she sees.[62]

Indeed, conceptions of interior sincerity and exterior theatricality are
similar on the stage as in the nave, but I would argue contrarily that early
modern theatrical performance ultimately casts doubt upon "outwardness"
and requires the spectator to believe in what he or she *cannot* see.[63]
An inhibited playing style ultimately recognizes the difficulty in staging
"outwardly convincing appearances" and discards external demonstration
as a reliable register of legible meaning.

A focus on the actor's inhibition can help us better understand the ways-
of-knowing privileged by the period's players and playwrights. The stage
labored to produce authentic bodily expressions of interior states, unique
expressions that would at the same time dependably convey meaning to an
audience. Against the impossibility of such a thing, the stage developed a
kind of signifying nothing. By rejecting and policing histrionics, actors
produce an affect of "genuine" behavior. The interior cannot be both
conventionally and authentically displayed, so do nothing and code it
as something instead. In doing so, players and playwrights joined the
conversation about the body by broadcasting somatic self-consciousness
to playgoers and dilated the dilemma of representing authentic passions
through habitual expression. For the purposes of the player, it is immaterial
whether the internal "torrent, tempest . . . whirlwind" is real or feigned
because the moderation signifies its presence. To act well is to perform a
scripted stasis, a peculiar algebra where the absence of x equals y. If real
and feigned behaviors are ultimately indistinguishable, then to stage the
body's suppression of passion may ultimately be the only way to reveal it.

Finally, dramatic occasions that skeptically assess the body's outward
and visible signs—be they scripted suppressions or intra-dramatic acting
critiques—need not be isolated as charming but discrete data on the art
of playing. Rather, such moments participate in a prevalent discourse that

assesses and addresses the body's signifying play. Such moments, which give voice to what Thomas Wright called the "eloque[n]ce of the bodei,"[64] take part in a sustained conversation among early moderns about how meaning was lived in, on, and through the body. Between the players and those who watch, the passionate life becomes a transactional exchange, the theater an arena where a community works to forge a legible lexicon of articulate and authentic selfhood. An articulate stillness was evidently among the particular somatic dialects spoken by the period's players and understood by their audience.

Notes

1. Quotations from Shakespeare are from *The Norton Shakespeare,* ed. Stephen Greenblatt, Walter Cohen, Jean E. Howard, and Katharine Eisaman Maus (New York: W.W. Norton and Company, 1997).

2. *Shakespeare's Theatre,* 2nd ed. (London: Routledge and Kegan Paul, 1983), 125.

3. "Theatre and the Civilizing Process: An Approach to the History of Acting," in *Interpreting the Theatrical Past: Essays in the Historiography of Performance,* ed. Thomas Postlewait and Bruce A. McConachie (Iowa City: University of Iowa Press, 1989), 19–36, esp. 23. To cite but one of many pertinent examples to the contrary, it was David Garrick's hyperkineticism that struck both his critics and his acolytes. Theophilus Cibber complained of Garrick's "pert vivacity" (quoted in George Winchester Stone Jr. and George M. Kahrl, *David Garrick: A Critical Biography* [Carbondale: Southern Illinois University Press, 1979], 505). Richard Cumberland praised "little Garrick" as "young and light and alive in every muscle and feature." Cumberland in particular casts Garrick's muscular acting as a reformation of a stolidly stentorian mode suited more to the "senate than the stage"; " . . . old things were done away with and a new order at once brought forward, bright and luminous, and clearly destined to dispel the barbarisms and bigotry of a tasteless age, too long attached to the . . . illusions of imposing declamation" (*The Memoirs of Richard Cumberland,* ed. Richard J. Dircks [New York: AMS Press, 2002], 49). Innovations in acting are always cast as reformations, but whatever David Garrick was doing with his body, he seems not to have repressed his "sensual nature."

4. I have made the argument about the "infinite regress" at length in "That Old Saw: Early Modern Acting and the Infinite Regress," *Shakespeare Bulletin* 22 (2004): 27–44.

5. New York: Routledge, 2003.

6. *The Passions of the Minde in Generall,* ed. Thomas Sloan (1604; Urbana: University of Illinois Press, 1971), 10.

7. Jane Tylus has recently written that one of the "principal legacies of fifteenth-century Italian humanism was its emphasis on visibility as a mode of knowing" but that a play like *Hamlet* "stages the difficulty of bringing together, on the one hand, humanism's faith in the necessity of rendering 'visible,' and on the other, the potentially violent and often grotesque manner in which the hidden is brought to light" (" 'Par Accident': The Public Work of the Early

Modern Theatre," in *Reading the Early Modern Passions: Essays in the Cultural History of Emotion*, ed. Gail Kern Paster, Katherine Rowe, and Mary Floyd-Wilson [Philadelphia: University of Pennsylvania Press, 2004], 253–71, esp. 256, 270–71).

8. *Humoring the Body: Emotions and the Shakespearean Stage* (Chicago: University of Chicago Press, 2004), 22.

9. According to the *Oxford English Dictionary*, the Latin grammarian Varo suggested a "derivation from *scaena*," which the editors call a "folk etymology." The antique meaning of "scene" is the "stage of a Greek or Roman theater, including the platform on which the actors stood, and the structure which formed the background" (I.1).

10. See, for instance, Timothy Murray's *Theatrical Legitimation: Allegories of Genius in Seventeenth-Century England and France* (Oxford: Oxford University Press, 1987).

11. Paster, 8.

12. I am using "transactional" in the social rather than the material sense here. For illuminating work on materially transactional passions, see Paster (44–50) and Mary Floyd-Wilson's "English Mettle," in *Reading the Early Modern Passions*, 130–46. I am indebted to the introduction of that collection for a clearer understanding of Anna Wierzbicka's "Emotion, Language, and Cultural Scripts," in *Emotion and Culture: Empirical Studies of Mutual Influence*, ed. Shinobu Kitayama and Hazel Rose Markus (Washington, D.C.: American Psychological Association, 1994).

13. Jonas Barish's work details the particular nervousness prompted by the protean flexibility of actors in *The Antitheatrical Prejudice* (Berkeley: University of California Press, 1981).

14. Act 1, scene 5. *The Plays of John Marston*, ed. Harvey Wood, 3 vols. (Edinburgh: Oliver and Boyd, 1934–39), vol. 1.

15. "'Damnéd Custom . . . Habits Devil': Shakespeare's *Hamlet*, Anti-Dualism, and the Early Modern Philosophy of Mind," *English Literary History* 67.2 (2000), 399–431, esp. 426.

16. *Bodies and Selves in Early Modern England: Physiology and Inwardness in Spenser, Shakespeare, Herbert, and Milton* (Cambridge: Cambridge University Press, 1999), 38; Joseph P. Roach, *The Player's Passion: Studies in the Science of Acting* (Newark: University of Delaware Press, 1985), 40.

17. Roach, 27, 45.

18. Patricia Parker, "Fantasies of 'Race' and 'Gender': Arica, *Othello* and Bringing to Light," in *Shakespeare's Tragedies*, ed. Susan Zimmerman (New York: St. Martin's Press, 1998), 167–93.

19. Katharine Eisaman Maus, *Inwardness and Theater in the English Renaissance* (Chicago: University of Chicago Press, 1995), 1.

20. *The Idea of the Actor: Drama and the Ethics of Performance* (Princeton: Princeton University Press, 1984), 27. Worthen reads Hamlet's "monstrous" as an allusion to the long history of antitheatrical prejudice.

21. Schoenfeldt, 2.

22. Maus, 210.

23. Not all cultural resources are textual, of course. Somatic information is and was available everywhere from lived experience. Though far more difficult to trace—as it leaves no residue—models of bodily behavior circulated throughout early modern culture through imitation and replication.

24. "Against the Rule of Reason: Praise of Passion from Petrarch to Luther to Shakespeare to Herbert," in *Reading the Early Modern Passion,* 23–42, esp. 32.

25. Roach, 52.

26. Reynolds, 60.

27. Ibid., 11.

28. Ibid., 10.

29. John Bulwer, *Chirologia, or the Natural Language of the Hand* (London, 1644), 132.

30. *The Two Bookes of the Proficience and Advancement of Learning* (New York, Da Capo Press, 1970), 37.

31. Robert Burton, *Anatomy of Melancholy,* ed. Hobrook Jackson (New York: New York Review Books, 2001), 160.

32. *Body Narratives: Writing the Nation and Fashioning the Subject in Early Modern England* (New York: St. Martin's Press, 2000), 16.

33. Quoted in Scholz, 19.

34. English reticence and Italian demonstrativeness was not universally assumed, however. See Mary Floyd-Wilson's *English Ethnicity and Race in Early Modern Drama* (Cambridge: Cambridge University Press, 2003).

35. Keith Thomas, "The Place of Laughter in Tudor and Stuart England," *TLS* 21, Jan. 1977, 77–81.

36. Giovanni della Casa's *Galatea,* in a 1576 English translation by Robert Peterson, 97–98.

37. Hugh Rhodes, *The Boke of Nurture,* ed. Frederick J. Furnivall (John Childs and son, 1857), 17, 20–22.

38. Richard Brathwait, *The English Gentleman* (London, 1630; Amsterdam: Theatrum Orbis Terrarum, Ltd., 1975): 222.

39. Reynolds, 48. See also Strier (cited above) and the introduction to *Reading the Early Modern Passions* (12) as well as Paster, *Humoring the Body,* esp. 1–3. Lily Campbell writes, "the Stoic attitude toward passion, that of complete rejection, met an objection in Christian teaching; it was pointed out that the passions could not be evil in themselves since the Scriptures attributed certain passions to Christ and to God himself" (*Shakespeare's Tragic Heroes: Slaves of Passion* [Cambridge: Cambridge University Press, 1930], 70).

40. Paster, 1.

41. Brathwait, 78.

42. Ibid., 311.

43. Galen did not go unchallenged by the early moderns. Describing the impotence of medicine in the face of plague, Thomas Nashe wrote that "Galen might go shoe the gander for any good he could do" (*The Works of Thomas Nashe,* ed. R. B. McKerrow, 5 vols. [Oxford: Basil Blackwell, 1958], 2:230); responding to the same plague, Thomas Dekker noted that "Galen could do no more than Sir Giles Goosecap" (*Plague Pamphlets of Thomas Dekker* [London: Oxford University Press, 1925], 36). Paracelsus, typically, was the most combative towards Galen: "My shoelaces are more learned than your Galen . . ." (*Paracelsus, Selected Writings,* ed. Jolande Jacobi, trans. Norbert Guterman [London: Routledge and Kegan Paul, 1951], 80). On the literary response to dwindling Galenism, see Herbert Silvette, *The Doctor on the Stage: Medicine and Medical Men in Seventeenth Century England,* ed. Francelia Butler (Knoxville: University of Tennessee Press, 1967).

44. *Liber Canonis* (Venice, 1507; facs. Repr. Hildesheim, 1964), Book 1, fen. 1, doctrinal 1, chap. 1, fol. Tr.

45. Burton, 21.

46. Roy Porter, *Disease, Medicine, and Society in England, 1550-1860* (Basingstoke, U.K.: Macmillan, 1987), 35.

47. Robert Burton, *The Anatomy of Melancholy,* 3 vols. (London: J. M. Dent and Sons, 1932), 2:235.

48. *The School of Salernum; Regimen sanitatis Salernitatum* (New York: A. M. Kelley, 1970).

49. Ll. 91-92, "The Anatomy of the World" in *John Donne: The Complete English Poems,* ed. A. J. Smith (London: Penguin Books, 1966).

50. The *OED* describes "ecstacy" as "the state of being 'beside oneself,' thrown into a frenzy . . ." (1).

51 *Author's Pen and Actor's Voice: Playing and Writing in Shakespeare's Theatre* (Cambridge: Cambridge University Press, 2000), 175.

52. To be sure, faked madness is doubly confusing. Perhaps the ontological riddle of inauthentic madness (which, as I have argued here, always courts inauthenticity) helps explain why audiences have traditionally questioned Hamlet's sanity despite being explicitly told by the character that he's going to don madness like a costume.

53. Quotes from *Duchess of Malfi* refer to *English Renaissance Drama: A Norton Anthology,* ed. David Bevington, Lars Engle, Katharine Eisaman Maus, and Eric Rasmussen (New York: W. W. Norton, 2002).

54. Roach makes a similar point about the lips and tongue, 32-33.

55. Act 1, scene 5. *The Plays of John Marston,* ed. Harvey Wood, 3 vols. (Edinburgh: Oliver and Boyd, 1934-1939), vol. 1.

56. Quotes from *The Widow's Tears* refer to *Drama of the English Renaissance II: The Stuart Period,* ed. Russell A. Fraser and Norman Rabkin (New Jersey: Simon and Schuster, 1976).

57. Nathan Field, *Amends for Ladies. With the Humour of Roring* (London: 1633), Huntington Photostat Facsimile.

58. Peter Holland, "*Hamlet* and the Art of Acting," *Drama and the Actor, Themes in Drama 6,* ed. James Redmond (Cambridge: Cambridge University Press, 1984), 39-61, esp. 61.

59. *The Shakespearean Stage: 1574-1642,* 3rd ed. (Cambridge: Cambridge University Press, 1994), 100. The standard argument is rehearsed well by Michael Hattaway in *Elizabethan Popular Theatre: Plays in Performance* (London: Routledge and Kegan Paul, 1982), 72-78. See also B. L. Joseph, *Elizabethan Acting* (London: Geoffrey Cumberlege, 1951); G. Blakemore Evans, *Elizabethan-Jacobean Drama: The Theatre in Its Time* (New York: New Amsterdam, 1988), 82-92; G. B. Harrison, *Elizabethan Plays and Players* (Ann Arbor: University of Michigan Press, 1956); M. C. Bradbrook, *The Rise of the Common Player: A Study of Actor and Society in Shakespeare's England* (Cambridge: Harvard University Press, 1962); and *Themes and Conventions of Elizabethan Tragedy* (Cambridge: Cambridge University Press, 1935). See also arguments for a "presentational" style in J. L. Styan's *Shakespeare's Stagecraft* (Cambridge: Cambridge University Press, 1967), 45; Bernard Beckerman

uses the term "ceremonial" for early English acting style in *Shakespeare at the Globe* (New York: Macmillan, 1962), 129.

60. *Common Prayer: The Language of Public Devotion in Early Modern England* (Chicago: University of Chicago Press, 2001), 51.

61. Targoff, "The Performance of Prayer: Sincerity and Theatricality in Early Modern England," *Representations,* 60 (1997): 49–69, esp. 50.

62. Ibid., 65.

63. Targoff argues elsewhere, however, that theologians programmatically deployed common prayer to instill a devotional decorum that worshipers could dependably imitate and reproduce (genuflecting, folding hands in prayer, heart thumping, blessing). Whereas the church invoked Aristotle's belief that physical expression could induce interior change, actors struggled to find legible modes by which the body can eloquently express an authentic interiority. Churchmen were interested in authenticity too, of course. While theologians admitted that outward decorum could be feigned, they invoked Aristotle's belief that even feigned behavior could induce sincerity in the subject (while humanists from Sidney to Heywood believed that even feigned behavior could induce sincerity in the audience). See her *Common Prayer.*

64. *The Passions of the Minde in Generall* (1604; Urbana: University of Illinois Press, 1971), 176.

Understanding in the
Elizabethan Theaters

WILLIAM N. WEST

Why, stand-under and under-stand is all one.
>   —Launce, *Two Gentlemen of Verona*

I N THE AUTUMN of 1599, Thomas Platter, a Swiss medical student on
a tour of Europe, went to see a play about Julius Caesar at one of
London's playhouses. Another day he saw a play in which suitors from
several countries wooed a young woman (the English suitor ran off with
her, Platter notes plaintively, after the victorious German suitor got drunk
and fell asleep). He seems to have been as intrigued by the layout of the
playhouses as by the performances:

The places [*örter,* sc., where comedies are performed] are built so that they play
on a raised platform, and everyone can see everything well. But there are different
galleries and places (*gäng unndt ständt*), where one sits more pleasantly and
better and also for that reason pays more. For whoever cares to stand below (*unden
stehn*) pays just one English penny, but if he wishes to sit, somebody lets him in
another door, and he pays another penny, but if he desires to sit on cushions in the
most pleasant place, where he not only sees everything well, but can also be seen,
then he pays yet another English penny at another door.[1]

The playhouses and in particular the arrangements for their audiences
were frequently as compelling to foreign visitors as anything that went on
inside them. Samuel Kiechel, a German visitor of 1584, was so interested in
these "peculiar houses" that he didn't even describe the plays he saw, and
Johannes deWitt, a Dutch traveler who sketched the earliest extant interior
view of an outdoor theater in 1596, labels the places and entrances of the

113

audience as scrupulously as those of the stage.[2] For many early theatergoers, and not only non-English ones, the theater was not exclusively or even primarily concerned with drama. Instead, it was a complex environment with its own temporality, offering multiple experiential levels and diverse events, which one absorbed and which absorbed one in return.

Above all, theaters demanded and supported novel modes of apprehension and interaction in audiences, actors, and playwrights alike. Platter spoke no English and so may not have been able to understand what he saw; he was more interested in the graceful ("zierlich") dancing that followed each performance and in physical comedy ("the servant threw his shoe at his master's head") than in plot. But Platter probably didn't understand the play in another sense; judging from his description of the levels of seating, he seems to have paid the extra pennies to sit above, where he could both see and be seen. Standing in the yard below him, their heads level with the raised stage, would have been the playgoers who had paid just one penny and entered just one door.[3] While these people are called many things—some specifically referring to their placement, like "groundlings" (*Hamlet* 3.2.11; 1600), others more general like the "multitude," the "common people," or just "the people"—the most common contemporary term for them is *understanders* or *understanding men*.[4] These words almost inevitably suggest the joke that the understanders are the least understanding men in the theater; along with their location standing below the stage, what characterizes them is their *lack* of understanding. For instance, when the Citizen interrupts the Prologue in *The Knight of the Burning Pestle* (1607), asking why they need new plays when there are already so many good ones, the Prologue observes sarcastically, "You seeme to bee an understanding man" (Ind. 23); the Induction to Ben Jonson's *Bartholomew Fair* (1614) nods toward the "understanding Gentlemen o' the ground" (Ind. 49f.), whose experiences of the real Bartholomew Fair may leave them disappointed with Jonson's theatrical representation of it.[5] In these representations, the understanders are those most fully absorbed into the environment of the theater, not set above it to see and be seen but immersed in it indistinctly. As a description of bodies rather than minds, *understanders* (as the word literally implies) are those who are physically subjected to the stage rather than intellectually independent of it.[6]

In this picture, instead of what demands thought and judgment, the understanders prefer fare like clowning, jigs, and sword fights. The Prologue of Fletcher and Shakespeare's *Henry VIII* (1613) predicts that the play-wrights' decision to present a drama "Sad, high, and working, full of state and woe" (3) rather than "a merry, bawdy play" offering "A noise of targets" and "a fellow / In a long motley coat guarded with yellow" (14–16) "Will leave us never an understanding friend" (22). The "gentle hearers" (17) are addressed for their interest in the play's truth (9, 18; similarly, 21, 27) and its accurate representations; the understanders are left the physical "show / As fool and fight is" (18f.), clowning and fencing.[7] James Shirley's prologue to *The Doubtful Heir* (1653; performed c. 1640) makes it clear that his play, especially now that the theaters have been closed and it is in print, offers little for the understanders' tastes. His vocabulary is virtually unchanged from that of *Henry VIII,* forty years earlier:

> Our Author did not calculate this Play
> For this Meridian . . .
> No shews, no dance, and what you most delight in,
> Grave understanders, here's no target fighting
> Upon the stage, all work for Cutlers barr'd,
> No bawdery, nor no Ballets. . . .
> No clown, no squibs, no Devil in't (2f., 7–10, 13)[8]

The Prologue makes it clear from its negative description that what the preferred spectacles of the understanders share is their refusal of the proper intellectual and cognitive functions of a "high, and working" play (*Henry VIII,* 3) and their replacement by "work" (*Doubtful Heir,* 9): performances that foreground physicality and exertion and minimize intellectual comprehension, interpretation, even meaning—the "inexplicable dumb shows and noise" of *Hamlet.*

The understanders' activity was characterized by its corporeality and noise, things falling below the level of speech and reason. We hear that the understanders do not quietly stand by and watch—during the show they crack nuts, as Shirley's prologue goes on to lament ("You squirrels that want nuts, what will you do / Pray do not crack the benches, . . ." ll. 14f.), and fizz open bottles of ale.[9] They decide as a body rather than judging as individuals. Editions of John Fletcher's *The Faithful Shepherdess* (1610Q; 1647F) include a poem by Francis Beaumont complaining of how their judgment is grounded physically rather than rationally, in their neighbor's response:

> One company knowing they judgement lacke,
> Ground their beliefe on the next man in blacke:
> Others, on him that makes signes, and is mute,
> Some like as he does in the fairest sute,
> He as his mistres doth, and she by chance.[10]

They talk back to the performers.[11] They smell.[12] In *Jack Drum's Entertainment* (1600) Marston praises the audience of Paul's, an indoor venue, because there "A man shall not be choakte / With the stench of Garlicke, not be pasted / To the barmy Jacket of a Beer-Brewer."[13] Thomas Dekker warns playgoing gallants in *The Gull's Horn-Book* (1606) of "the garlicke mouthd stinkards" and "the Breath of the great *Beast*" that they will encounter, and regrets that "your Stinkard has the selfe same libertie to be there in his Tobacco-Fumes, which your sweet Courtier hath."[14] Webster admits that *The White Devil* (1612) is "no true Drammaticke Poem," but blames the conditions in the theater; if one wrote "the most sententious Tragedy that ever was written . . . the breath that comes from the uncapable multitude, is able to poison it."[15] This physical reek, like their place in the yard, their position on their feet in it, their love of mindless clowning and violence, and their equivocal title, is another manifestation of the understanders' corporeality.[16] The almost automatic doubling and splitting of the word's meaning raises the question of why it was felt to be so apt for these playgoers in the pit. In the vocabulary of early modern playgoing, what exactly did *understanding* stand for?

The ambivalence of understanding between physical and cognitive meanings, in fact, often motivates its use.[17] Viola's answer to Toby Belch in *Twelfth Night* (1601) is a typical example: "My legs do better understand me, sir, than I understand what you mean by bidding me taste my legs" (3.1.79f.). The *Oxford English Dictionary*'s earliest citation of the word *understander* similarly opposes bodily understanding and rusticity to cognitive understanding: in *Philotimus* (1583), the Inns of Court student Brian Melbancke recalls that in Erasmus's *Encomium Moriae*, Folly "leuieth her army of huge boisterous hobs, wel beseming for their understanders to bee the offspringe of Giauntes."[18] As in Viola's quip, this mob's organ of understanding is their legs rather than their heads. In a surprising inversion of the expected relation of literal and metaphorical meaning, the physical, literal sense of *understanding* seems here—and generally—to depend on its metaphorical, cognitive meaning. That is to say, in its cognitive sense, "understanding" frequently occurs alone; the physical sense, on the other hand, almost always appears when the cognitive sense is stated or implied, even if that sense is then discarded. A play on the word from *Two Gentlemen of Verona* (c. 1590) shows both the division and the entailment of physical and cognitive meanings:

SPEED: What an ass art thou! I understand thee not.
LAUNCE: What a block art thou, that thou canst not! My staff understands me.
SPEED: What thou say'st?
LAUNCE: Ay, and what I do too. Look thee, I'll but lean, and my staff understands me.
SPEED: It stands under thee indeed.
LAUNCE: Why, stand-under and under-stand is all one.
(2.5.24–33)

The staff, Launce assures Speed, understands him both in language and as a body, whether he *says* or *does*. But Launce is the clown; if under-stand and stand-under is all one to him, it is partly because for him, the difference between mind and body is never clear or complete, as his comic bits show—conflating Speed's lack of understanding with the understanding staff that he resembles as another "block," trading places with his dog Crab to save it from whipping, or puzzling with his props over how to represent his leaving home.[19] The point in such uses of *understand* is that the pun is empty—Launce's understanding is not understanding at all.

Or is it? A poem of the 1580s by the Scottish John Stewart of Baldynneis advises "lerne to understand./ Stand quhair ₃e vill, firm be ₃our under stand."[20] As in *Twelfth Night* or *Two Gentlemen of Verona,* the two senses of the word are set against one another. Unlike the plays, though, the poem hints that physical understanding might be a kind of real understanding, either enabling a cognitive understanding or perhaps not wholly distinct from it. To understand cognitively, in Stewart's poem, is to be aware of what you stand under and what stands under you. In some cases, in particular in regard to physical properties, a bodily understanding was acknowledged to judge better than its intellectual counterpart. In the first book of *The Laws of Ecclesiastical Polity* (1593), Richard Hooker observes that while philosophers know the nature of fire and of gold, an ordinary artisan, knowing neither, can gauge by common sense and his senses how to purify them, and that "this is a great deal more easy for common sense to discern, than for any man by skill and learning to determine."[21] While reason allows one to articulate the laws that order the world, it is not necessary to articulate them in order to obey them and to work within them; the world can also be understood differently and in some ways more fully.

The double framing of the term *understanding* as ambiguously cognitive and corporeal precedes the establishment of the theaters and persists through the decades that follow their closing. Nor is it confined to theatrical contexts. One crux of the Reformation was the question of what sort of understanding was necessary for salvation—what languages and rituals were suited for liturgy, and to what extent they needed to be intellectually understood or merely corporeally performed to function, with Protestantism usually assumed to take the side of cognition rather than practice.[22] Thomas Cranmer's prologue to the English Bible of 1540 acknowledges the difficulties the Bible presents to understanding and concludes that since its aim is that its "speciall entent and purpose myght be understanded and perceaved of euery reader," it must be written in a language that every person understands.[23] The Preface to the *Book of Common Prayer* (1552) objects to services conducted in Latin, "whiche thei [the congregation] understoode not, so that thei have heard with their eares onely, and their hartes, spirite, and mynd, haue not been edified therby" (a.ir). It offers itself as an alternative that is, in both language and structure, "plain and easie to be understanden" (a.iv).[24] The twenty-fourth of the *Thirty-Nine Articles* (1571) reiterates the centrality of cognitive understanding to Anglicanism when it rejects a liturgy performed in "a tongue not understood of the people."[25]

Most religious examples focus narrowly on linguistic comprehension and only secondarily on the hermeneutic problems that texts pose. But there are suggestions of the corporeal countermeaning of understanding as well, especially in this hermeneutic dimension. The sense of understanding in the *Thirty-Nine Articles* seems exclusively linguistic, especially if we compare it to the Latin versions of 1552 and of 1562, which prohibit, respectively, *lingua populo ignota* and *lingua populo non intellecta*.[26] But in Cranmer's prologue to the Bible, "perceived" may also have a physical meaning, since he assures his readers that even if the sense is unclear to them, merely reading or hearing the words of the Bible allows for a kind of understanding (+iiir). Here perception and hermeneutics seem allied against the middle term of literal signification. In a conversation with her almoner, Mary Tudor, having been told that she should not pray during the Latin Mass, wondered

In my God, I can nat se what we shall do at the masse, if we pray nat.
Ye shall thynke to the mystery of the masse and shall herken the wordes that the
preest say.
Yee, and what shall they do which understande it nat.
They shall behold, and shall here, and thynke, and by that shall they understande.[27]

Here *understanding* means something like it does in Cranmer's qualifica-
tion, watching and attending to something as a means of comprehending
it. The conversation insists, as does Cranmer, that this too is right understanding. In his *Waie to Wealth* (1550), Robert Crowley argues that the
attentive listening of a churchgoer will produce a Pentecostal effect even
if the words of the sermon are garbled or inaudible:

For thy sake God shall make thy curate (that otherwise wold mumble in the mouth
& dround his words) to speake out plainly, or else he shall geve the[e] such a gift
that thou shalt understande him plainely. . . . For he that coulde make the Hebrue
tonge (which sowndeth far otherwise then other tonges do) sownd al maner of
languages, to everie man his owne language, can also make thine owne language
sownde plaine unto the[e].[28]

Both Mary's almoner and Crowley—one Catholic, one Protestant—recognize an understanding that is not strictly cognitive. In each case, understanding is something other than merely intellectual comprehension or
at least comes from processes not exclusively mental; it follows bodily
presence or a corporeal encounter rather than proceeding from intellectual
communication. This corporeal sense of understanding persists through
the period of public theaters. In *Leviathan* (1651), Thomas Hobbes generally uses "understanding" in the cognitive sense, but introduces the term
as something that is primarily sensual and corporeal:

The Imagination that is raysed in man (or any other creature indued with the
faculty of imagining) by words, or other voluntary signes, is that we generally call
Understanding; and is common to Man and Beast. For a dogge by custome will
understand the call, or the rating of his Master.

Human beings, according to Hobbes, are capable of a further sort of
understanding based on language, but understanding begins in a physical
response to the corporeality of sound or gesture rather than to their
meaning.[29]

   In the sixteenth and early seventeenth centuries, then, there were two
competing meanings for *understanding*—the cognitive one more familiar

to us and its parodic, corporeal opposite: usually represented as derivative of or falling off from the cognitive meaning; based on the encounter of bodies with each other, spatial positioning, and physical sensation; and often associated specifically with the theater. This second sense made a claim of its own for a different sort of comprehension that was not intellectual and absolute but materially and temporally determined—*savoir* as opposed to *connaître,* or *Kennen* as opposed to *Wissen.* This second meaning, however comically it might be advanced, could also call on privileged vocabularies, like the half-serious recollections of scholastic Latin calques of "understanding" like *substantia* or *supposition.*[30] It is thus not really possible to say outside of a given instance what *understand* means and whether cognition or corporeality is intended. It is on these tensions that the peculiarly theatrical meaning—or let us say usage—of *understander* is constructed.

The peculiar arrangement of the Elizabethan outdoor theater, with its understanding listeners above and its incapable understanders below, was a physical site where the problem of the relation (or disjunction) of cognition and corporeality could be immediately and concretely explored. The use of *understander* as a technical term of theater in the first fifteen years of the seventeenth century can virtually be traced to the works of Ben Jonson, the sharpest critic of the audience of his time and its most acute, who most fully reveals and exploits the word's two-edgedness. For Jonson, understand and stand-under is not all one, and the need to distinguish between understanders and understanders acquires new urgency. Understanding is what is most betrayed by an audience of mere understanders, who passively absorb what is set before them and look only for physical action. In *Every Man out of His Humour* (1599), Jonson's critic-spokesman Asper decides that the play he is about to stage should please "attentive auditors, / Such as will ioyne their profit with their pleasure, / And come to feed their understanding parts" (Ind. 201–3); to do this, Asper will "speake away my spirit into ayre" (205), dissolving his physical presence into language.[31] But the precise location of those "understanding parts" in the mind or the body is open to doubt, which Jonson makes more palpable by specifying that understanding parts, like stomachs, must be fed. While the importance of the distinction between the thinking, attentive auditor and the reactive, corporeal understander is ultimately reinforced here—as in the Prologue in *Knight of the Burning Pestle,* it is clear that Asper (and Jonson) hopes for an audience that understands cognitively—the possibility that the understanders of the body may also have a way to understand is raised. It appears as well in the Induction to *Bartholomew Fair* mentioned earlier, which suggests that the understanders will object to the play on the basis of their "experience" of the fair (Ind. 30; 6: 14); they understand what a more elite viewer "do's not know" (Ind. 11f.; 6: 13).

Jonson has other terms for contrasting good and bad audiences, although the poles between which he evaluates them remain knowledge or ignorance. He distinguishes adept audiences that attend to his language from ignorant ones swept away by (usually Inigo Jones's) "Mighty Showes."[32] In his masque *Pleasure Reconciled to Virtue* (1618), he admonishes his dancers not to "perplex men, unto gaze," but to perform so that "men may read each act you doo" (263–66).[33] But Jonson's cultivation of the ambivalence of the particular term *understanding* is clear in the prefaces that he writes for individual plays in his Folio *Works* (1616). The Folio is virtually an essay in the subtle shifts that are possible between understanders, understanding readers, and Jonson's ideal audience of knowing, like-minded critics. In the dedication to the Inns of Court that prefaces the Folio edition of *Every Man out of His Humor,* Jonson suggests the problem of interpreting *understanding:* "I Understand you, Gentlemen, not your houses: and a worthy succession of you, to all time, as being borne the Iudges of these studies."[34] Jonson's preference for the intellectual understander is complicated by his assertion that he himself "understand[s]" the scholars of the Inns as individuals, "Gentlemen" and "Examples of living," rather than in their official identity as scholars and students of the law, "great Names in learning." Their future public careers as judges in court are prefigured in their supposedly private ability to judge Jonson's plays. Jonson's understanding of them in his Folio, then, mirrors their understanding of his plays.[35] But this kind of understanding as instinctive recognition comes close to dispensing with the rules that characterize the critic; Jonson and his gentlemen almost judge by feel.

The folio dedication "To the Reader" of *The Alchemist* plays further on the possibilities subsumed in *understanding.* For this play, Jonson addresses specifically readers, but aspires to something better: "If thou beest more, thou art an Understander, and then I trust thee."[36] Jonson's naming recalls the (generally negative) sense of *understander* associated with theaters and the original, unthinking theatrical audience from which he seems to try to protect his work—also because this play more than almost any other that Jonson wrote relies on the physical execution of its actors in timing and disguise. While hardly a target fight, *The Alchemist* does show the corporeally experimental being mistaken for the mental. Jonson's professed goal is to write plays for readers rather than (physical?) understanders, but the goal of the reader is to become a (cognitive?) understander. The pun here comes alive in linking the two kinds of understanding. The understander offers a model as well as a warning for the reader.

Much later, in *The New Inn* (1629; pub. 1631), Jonson allowed theatrical understanding a more positive sense than he had previously. In the bitter "Dedication to the Reader," Jonson complains that the performance was spoiled by its audience—not, however, the ignorant crowd but the fashionable gallants, who sought to "possesse the Stage, against the Play. . . . And by their confidence of rising between the Actes, in oblique lines, make *affidavit* to the whole house, of their not understanding one Scene" (10-13).[37] Standing is once again the sign of the lack of understanding, but here Jonson prefers the reader's "rustick candor" (l. 18) (in which the reader also resembles a theatrical understander) to the "pride, and solemn ignorance" (ll. 18-19) of the fashionable spectator. What might have been the crowd's deplorable rusticity is revealed as a more decorous understanding of how to attend a play than that shown by the gallants who abuse their freedom to judge it. In *Bartholomew Fair* (performed 1614), the division of the crowd into "the said *Spectators,* and *Hearers,* as well the curious and envious, as the favoring and iudicious, as also the grounded Iudgements and understandings" (Ind. 74-76) suggests that the last group is a category that somehow falls outside any attempt to locate it, and Jonson mocks those who "will swear *Ieronimo,* or *Andronicus* are the best playes, yet" (Ind. 106-7). But he also has grudging admiration for a consistency of taste "whose Judgement shewes it is constant, and hath stood still, these five and twentie, or thirtie years," especially when compared in retrospect with those of the gallants of *The New Inn:* "Though it be an *Ignorance,* it is a vertuous and stay'd ignorance; and next to *truth,* a confirm'd errour does well; such a one, the *Author* knowes where to find him" (Ind. 109-12).[38] "Stood still" is both "not moved" and "continually occupied the standing section," and so the last sentence can be read literally: the author can find him standing in the yard—location, location, location.[39] A similar nostalgia for the understander's taste can be seen in Philip Massinger's dedicatory reflections on *The Roman Actor* (1626; printed 1629), which contrasts his own printed play rather wistfully with the "Iigges, and ribaldrie" that it replaces. John Ford contributes a poem that concludes by likening the cognition of the reader to the embodiment of the understander or actor: "Hee may become an Actor that but Reades."[40] I conflate the actor and the understander here, because the understander in part signifies a common interest of producer and consumer in the theater that is dissolved by conceiving of the audience's role as critical, adversarial, and cognitive rather than receptive and corporeal.[41]

Many other writers that followed Jonson in his interests in print and authorial property also refer to their understanders, usually picking up only the more obvious side of the problem: that cognitive understanding is what is most desirable in an audience and that it is opposed to the practice of physical understanding. In the isolation of the printed folio as a medium for a drama that is read rather than performed, the understander in the theater could be completely replaced by the understander of the book who silently pondered the page.[42] In his dedicatory poem to Fletcher's *The Faithful Shepherdess,* Beaumont sneers at the illiterate, incompetent first audience of theatrical understanders: "Your censurers must have the quallitie/ Of reading, which I am affraid is more/ Then halfe your shreudest judges had before" (44-46).[43] In print, presumably, Fletcher can expect a better understanding. In Beaumont and Fletcher's *The Fair Maid of the Inn* (performed 1626), the Prologue opposes "true sence" of cognitive understanding to the "idle custome" of the physical understanders:

> Plays have their fates, not as in their true sence
> They're understood, but as the influence
> Of idle custome madly workes upon
> The drosse of many-tongu'd opinion.
> (1-4)[44]

The crowd relies on both unarticulated habit and mindless gossip—action without talk and talk without reflection—to make sense of a play, rather than uncovering its "true sence" in, one supposes, private judgment. The prologue to "The great Variety of Readers" that Heminge and Condell write for Shakespeare's posthumous Folio (1623) warns that, after having read Shakespeare "againe, and againe," "if then you doe not like him, surely you are in some manifest danger, not to understand him."[45] What exactly, though, are Heminge and Condell asserting about the relation between the feeling of liking Shakespeare and cognitively understanding him? If you do not like Shakespeare, is that because you have not understood him, or must you like him in order to understand him? Which state produces the other? In this folio, the literate judges of printed drama and Jonsonian critics of performance can be overruled by the massed opinions of the understanders: "And though you be a Magistrate of wit, and sit on the stage at *Black-Friers,* or the *Cock-pit,* to arraigne Playes dailie, know, these Plays have had their triall alreadie, and stood out all Appeales. . . ."[46] How these plays "stood out" is a reminder that the understanders who first approved these plays in the outdoor theaters have passed a judgment that the contemporary magistrates of wit cannot with all their reasons revoke.

There is always more to the joke, then, than that the understanders are the ones who do not understand, the ones who exchange location for comprehension. But though Jonson and his followers resolutely decide in favor of cognition (although not always without regrets), not every audience privileged it. The long tradition of "fool and fight" at the Red Bull and other London playhouses, the success of English actors in central Europe, even the enjoyment that Platter apparently got from seeing plays, suggest that for many audiences physical understanding was a sufficient reward for playgoing.[47] Fynes Moryson describes the English actors wandering on the continent during the 1590s as "pronowncing peeces and Patches of English playes, which my selfe and some English men there present could not heare without greate werysomenes."[48] But this does not seem to have concerned the rest of their audiences, who were content with different forms of understanding. Elsewhere Moryson notes that despite what he saw as the players' mediocrity, "the Germans, not understanding a word they sayde, both men and women, flocked wonderfully to see theire gesture and Action, rather than heare them, speaking English which they understand not."[49] In light of Moryson's observations, Webster's damning preface to *The White Devil,* in which he notes "that it wanted (that which is the onely grace and setting out of a Tragedy) a full and understanding Auditory" ("To the Reader," 1:107) seems less straightforward. Is Webster's complaint that his audience was too dull to get his play? Certainly this is what many of the dedicatory poems imply. Or was the problem that because "it was acted in so dull a time of winter, presented in so open and blacke a Theater," there were not enough understanders in the playhouse to give his drama life?[50]

From these accounts it might be possible to invert the negative evaluation placed on corporeal understanding by Jonson and others. But to do this would cede the comprehension of plays solely to cognition and privilege

instead something like bodily pleasure. The enjoyment of physical pleasures like laughing, drinking, being in a crowd, shouting, is not something
to dismiss, especially not only because they have left fewer traces than
the more austere pleasures of criticism. But to recover the range of understanders in these theaters, it is not enough to invert the values of these
pleasures; they must also be transvalued, remastered so that physical understanding appears to us as a kind of what we call understanding and not
just as an alternative to it. There are hints of a transvalued understanding—a
corporeal grasp of something that eludes cognitive understanding—even in
Jonson. Another more complicated version emerges outside the sphere of
performance altogether, especially in works of nondramatic poetry. Many
of these texts, like the dedication of Jonson's *Alchemist,* hint that to be
a reader is not yet to be an understander, while to be an understander
still suggests the corporeal encounter of the theater. Jonson, again at the
forefront of interrogating understanding, calls his *Epigrams* (1616) "my
theatre" and invites William Herbert, the dedicatee, to enter it without
fear of scandal, exactly like a playgoer.[51] The first poem of the epigrams,
a couplet "To the Reader," continues this theatrical image by asking for
understanding:

> Pray thee, take care, that tak'st my booke in hand,
> To reade it well: that is, to understand.

If in printed collections of plays the judicious reader was often contrasted
to the ignorant understander, here, as in the dedication to *The Alchemist,*
the understander is relocated above the reader; here the reader is associated with physicality and the quasi-theatrical understander with thought.
John Donne's *Poems* (1633) is prefaced with a notice "The Printer to the
Understanders" that begins "For this time I must speake only to you: at
another, *Readers* may perchance serve my turne"; reversing this notion,
John Taylor's misogynist tract *A Juniper Lecture* (1639) is offered "To
as many as can Read, (though but reasonably) it makes no great matter
whether they can understand or no."[52] One could read Donne or Taylor or
other contemporary writers who address understanders as not referring
to the theater at all, least of all to its unthinking groundlings. But Jonson
had made it clear that he found some sort of continuity from (corporeal)
understander to reader to (cognitive) understander. In the wake of Jonson's
influential folio, though, and the word's theatrical history by the 1630s, the

form *understander* in particular seems necessarily to demand a double sense and raise the question of cognition and embodiment.

The corporeal side of understanding is brought out in Phineas Fletcher's allegory *The Purple Island* (1633), in which the body's structure is recast as an island paradise. The preface "To the Readers" states,

He that would learne *Theologie,* must first studie *Autologie.* The way to God is by our selves: it is a blinde and dirty way; it hath many windings, and is easie to be lost: This Poem will make thee understand that way; and therefore my desire is, that thou maist understand this Poem.[53]

Both preface and poem explicitly associate the cognitive dimension of understanding with the corporeal; the path to the spiritual knowledge of theology is (quite literally, in Fletcher's poem) through the body considered as the location of the self, autology. The preface ends, "I invite all sorts to be readers; all readers to be understanders; all understanders to be happie." In other words, it makes the relation between understanders and critics, or readers and understanders, not oppositional, but developmental and transformative—by understanding one's self in one's physicality, one becomes a reader; by being a reader one becomes, again, an understander. Understanding is knowing your position in every sense—physically as a body, politically in relation to others, spiritually with regard to God. These printed works that elevate and seek to develop understanding and the tradition of denigrating the theater's understanders are linked. The ignorant understander of the theater, reconceived through the printed book, becomes the ground of the cognitive understander.

The most profound transformation of the understander occurs not within the front matter of these works but in the poems themselves. As its preface explains, Fletcher's allegory of the body is the means by which the self is taught to recognize first its identity and subsequently God's majesty. George Herbert's "Prayer [1]" (1633) deepens this sense of the richness of a physical understanding as opposed to the purely intellectual one championed in the printed dramatic texts. Herbert's poem is a string of brilliant metaphors for the encounter that is prayer:

> Prayer the Church's banquet, Angels' age,
> God's breath in man returning to his birth,
> The soul in paraphrase, heart in pilgrimage,
> The Christian plummet sounding heav'n and earth;

Engine against th'Almighty, sinners' tower,
Reversed thunder, Christ-side-piercing spear.
(1–6)[54]

It ends quietly, with "Church-bells beyond the stars heard, the soul's blood, / The land of spices; something understood" (13f.). But if prayer is "something understood," who is doing the understanding? The poem provides two answers, which correspond to the two sorts of understander that appear in the theaters. The poem's initial metaphors meditate on the human activity that goes into prayer and how it may be imagined as an attempt to reach beyond the human—and beyond human thought—to an encounter with God. The poem's last two words can be read as suddenly reversing the perspective from human to divine: the prayer is "something understood" by God, however mysteriously. Or not—"something understood" may be the final description of prayer as work rather than resolving it from a divine perspective which knows its meanings, intentions, or effects. What is understood is what is set under all other human experience as its support. God understands prayer, but prayer understands, like Launce's staff, human experience. Here this barely articulable corporeality seems to rate higher than any cognition of its meaning. The heft of the poem's metaphors is not less but more real than what prayer communicates. All this suggests that a positively transvalued corporeal sense of *understanding*—of the body as a real means of knowing, not merely its parody—was available by the 1630s—but outside of drama. But why outside it?

Further complicating this question, *understanding* and the *understander* do not only participate in an equivocal structure that classifies audiences. Understanding has a history as well as a structure. My title specifies "Elizabethan theaters" as sites for understanding, but my examples of specifically theatrical understanding are drawn almost exclusively from the Jacobean and Caroline theaters looking backward.[55] Firmly negative or equivocally positive, the term understander is invariably associated with loyalty to an outmoded dramaturgy—clowning, target fights, jigs, dumb shows—and the understanders are belatedly attributed to Elizabethan theaters by playwrights who set themselves above them and are as conscious of their work in print as onstage. By the time the joke is in its widest circulation, there are far fewer real understanders left, the outdoor amphitheaters being gradually replaced by indoor private theaters, where all the viewers had seats.[56] Shirley's definitive description of understanders in *The Doubtful Heir* was originally presented in such a private playhouse lacking understanders altogether and was published a decade after theaters had been closed. The understander is most visible in retrospect, in printed collections of plays like those of Jonson or Beaumont and Fletcher, and to that extent seems to be a creature of print—as its necessary opposite— as much as or more than the memory of another mode of playgoing.[57] Understanding apparently only finds a voice in the words of its opponents, who systematically devalue the inarticulate experience of the onlooker in the crowd in favor of that of the critic, who judges as well as watches.

Is it possible to construct a sense of the understanders of the theater when they do not speak for themselves, and when we hear of them only from their opponents? Is there a counterdiscourse that we could uncover, recover, or imagine, for a positive understanding—even if we must speak it on behalf of the understanders rather than hear it directly from them? For we would expect them to be inarticulate, if neither passive nor unengaged, not because they could not say what they felt, but because, from their description, they would not have wished to; the modes associated with them are receptivity, participation, physicality, community, all opposed to the distinctions and self-promotion that are the province of the critic. The distinction that is made by the writers who reject (or, more complexly, long for as foregone) the understanders is between those who want theater to be translated into a code of some kind—a message, a valuable lesson, decorous personation, adherence to classical rules—and those for whom tarrying in the presence of performance is enough. And of course we will hear more from the first kind of understanders, who seek above all to distinguish themselves, than from the second. But if this is so, how can the experience of understanding be recovered and revalued outside of either dismissal or nostalgia?[58] Who speaks for the understander, and how can one prevent this recovery, like Jonson's, from being merely nostalgic?

Jonson's appraisal of understanding in *The New Inn* drove him away from the stage altogether to the ideal theater of the book.[59] The definition in print of understanding tends finally toward not only the mental but the private, as opposed to corporeal and corporate. So another important question remains—is the corporeal sense of understanding ever positively valued, or only derided? Much earlier, roughly contemporary with Jonson's use of the term in a particularly theatrical sense in *Every Man out of His Humor* (1599), John Marston, one of Jonson's opponents in the Poets' War, had taken a very different attitude toward the loss of physical understanding that accompanied a play's translation into print. Before *The Malcontent* (printed 1604), Marston complains

I would faine leave the paper; onely one thing afflicts me, to thinke that Scenes invented, meerely to be spoken, should be inforcively published to be read . . . the unhansome shape which this trifle in reading presents, may be pardoned, for the pleasure it once afforded you, when it was presented with the soule of lively action.[60]

The printed edition of *The Fawn* (1606) begins with a similar warning that "*Comedies* are writ to be spoken, not read: Remember the life of these things consists in action." Such assertions are less frequent than claims for the discriminating viewer, but even Webster notes of *The Devil's Law-Case* (printed 1623) that "A great part of the grace of this (I confesse) lay in Action."[61] Such remarks differ from the conventional blaming of the ignorant audience (whether specifically understanders or not) for a play's failures. Marston's point is just the opposite—that a play is not a poem designed to be read and appraised from a cool distance, but an encounter; that it is not, recalling the distinction between understandings made by Hobbes, exhausted in its meaning but also possesses a phenomenology of poses, gestures, sounds.[62] On this phenomenology, in our terms, rather than on signs privileged by Jonson, the understanders focused their attention. A play's essence is that its audience encounters it. In bringing it to the page, something literally vital is lost—not only the "fond and frivolous Jestures" that were excluded from Marlowe's *Tamburlaine* by the printer as unsuitable for "Gentlemen Readers," although "gaped at" by "fondlings," but the structurally mandated responsiveness of the understanders to those gestures.[63] In keeping with his investment in physicality of the theatrical event, Marston is also one of the playwrights who comments most insistently on the smell of the crowd.

It is possible to reconstruct from Marston a positively valorized dramaturgy of the corporeal understander—not merely a use of physicality in performance, which must always have been a feature of drama, from the jigs and forgotten hobbyhorses through the stalking heroes of Marlowe and the squeaking boys feared by Cleopatra, but a dramaturgy exploring the phenomenology of action and work, their impact as undefined materiality neither determined nor depleted by interpretation.[64] This physicality that *supports* (or understands) but does not *include* interpretation is one source of the tangible anxiety in antitheatrical writings that reject the argument that theater can educate and focus on its physical form as inherently corrupting.[65] Taking over the title of Marston's 1599 play for his antitheatrical compendium *Histrio-mastix* (1633), William Prynne stresses theater as an experience outside of its content by insisting that the Old Testament patriarchs were never "so much as once *experimentally* acquainted with" plays.[66] But Richard Baker, answering Prynne in *Theatrum Redivivum* (1662, written by 1643), sees the same physicality as the basis of theater's value. He explains that the comparison between sermons and plays is inapt because "we see *Plays* but as a *bodily recreation.*"[67] The didactic power of the sermon is limited to its disembodied cognition; it "may teach us to know our selves, but it cannot shew us to see our selves" (133). Plays on the other hand have a different force, based not on cognition but on embodiment and sense: "neither is the Understanding it self so much wrought upon by that we read, as by what we hear, and see; and this makes *Plays* to be of far more use, and profit" than texts (136). The "Understanding" Baker cites is nominally the process of cognition, but in his description it takes shape from the corporeal pressures around it. This physicalized understanding in some ways is more profound, and certainly different, from the one that grasps only meaning, as Baker argues in discussing ancient opposition to a play by Euripides that included a scandalizing speech by the villain: "For the speech (saith [Euripides]) was but to shew the Spectatours their own Errour; but the event in Fact, was to shew them, the Truth it self" (42), not the speech as its meaning but in its context. Baker is not consistent in pursuing this alternate power of physical understanding in theater—he goes on to discount the actor as a picture until he speaks and as a story afterward, and therefore in either case harmless—but he does suggest a distinct role for a physical and not merely visual or intellectual encounter.

Although they do not mention *understanders* as often as their later counterparts, Elizabethan dramas frequently represent a corporeal knowing that underlies and precipitates cognition.[68] Launce's understanding staff is one example, but *understanding* is only the period's most notable shorthand for signaling the physical resources of drama. Other terms with double sense, for instance *sense* and *feeling,* also mark the combination of physical sensation and cognition that distinguishes the understander and the fullness of an embodied drama that grounds and overreaches any narrowing (or defining) interpretation that can be applied to it. At its most material and least figural, such bodily plenitude registers only its own impact, as when in *The Comedy of Errors* Dromio of Syracuse asks Antipholus of Syracuse why Antipholus is beating him:

ANTIPH.S: Dost thou not know?
DROMIO.S: Nothing, sir, but that I am beaten.
(2.2.40f.)

The material fact of being beaten registers both on and in Dromio's head, but bears no further meaning for him.[69] Later, when Antipholus of Ephesus calls Dromio of Ephesus "sensible in nothing but blows" (4.4.27f.), the double meaning of *sensible* opens the space between body and thought that the understander also occupies. While physical sensibility, physical impact, beyond doubt is *something,* its force does nothing aside from registering itself. In this, though, it is unmistakable—and thus like the corporeal drama recognized by Baker and Prynne and sketched by Jonson and others. In *Comedy of Errors,* though, this double *sense* is practiced and experienced rather than analyzed from the outside. As pure physicality, Antipholus's and Dromio's horseplay is linked primarily not to the sense-making structures of thought but those of corporeal sense, the "nothing" that grounds thought. This is performance as noncognitive work of the kind that its understanders can also take part in.

In two pivotal scenes the drama demonstrates its kind of corporeal understanding through representations of the intellectual cognition to which it is opposed by Jonson and his followers. *King Lear* (c. 1605) figures in the person of Gloucester the world's inaccessibility to purely intellectual understanding, which the play metaphorically represents as sight and sanity. In his own words, the blinded Gloucester was "the superfluous and lust-dieted man / . . . that will not see / because he does not feel" (4.2.65–67); he "stumbled when he saw" (4.1.17).[70] The conversation when Gloucester encounters the mad Lear expresses his realization about the reality he overlooked:

LEAR: . . . Yet you see how this world goes.
GLOUCESTER: I see it feelingly.
LEAR: What, art mad? A man may see how the world goes with no eyes; look with thy ears.
(4.5.142–46)

The diction of *seeing feelingly* suggests that for this wrenching moment of recognition Shakespeare is recalling a similar scene in which knowledge is seen to amount to much more than thought or vision. This one is from Thomas Kyd's *The Spanish Tragedy* (c. 1587), in which Hieronimo at last discovers who is responsible for the murder of his son:

HIERONIMO: I ne'er could find
Till now, and now I *feelingly perceive,*
They did what heaven unpunished would not leave.[71]

Both scenes stage moments in which some crucial knowledge of the world, first revealed in an earlier scene but not then apparent to ordinary modes of thinking, is belatedly articulated; the ability to state it *now* indicates the impossibility of both experiencing *and* naming it *then*. For Gloucester, that existentially defining moment was earlier in the scene when, led by Edgar as Poor Tom, he tried to throw himself off what he believed were the Dover cliffs; for Hieronimo, it was the discovery of his son's corpse hanging in the darkness of an arbor (2.5). Both earlier scenes emphasize the inadequacy of thought and clear sight to grasp the felt experience of the world—in his blindness Gloucester believes Edgar's description that he is on a cliff's edge, while Hieronimo struggles to identify the body in the darkness and does not recognize his son until he cuts him down and feels what he is wearing. Recollecting these moments of true perception, Hieronimo and Gloucester identify in retrospect what they knew inarticulately before, obtained in the absence of clear sight through uncertainty, bodily touch, mistaking, as paradoxical synesthesias—as seeing or perceiving feelingly. In so doing, they identify themselves as having been understanders in the sense of the word that later writers mark to deride. They offer us a sense of the understander as a subject, albeit one who can name himself only retroactively, after having undergone the experience that makes him who he has become. Understanding as naming, articulating, in other words, follows understanding as experiencing.

   To be an understanding man in this sense is not to take the side of feeling against thought, as the distinction of *perceiving* and *feeling* might sentimentally suggest. When Hieronimo "feelingly perceives," he does not recognize through emotion or empathize; in fact, he is reading a letter that confirms his suspicions as much by its physical existence as by its contents. What the phrase means, rather, is to process information in a different way—corporeally, sensibly, tactilely, as experience not sundered from the whole experience of life.[72] When Hieronimo feelingly perceives, he surrenders the cognitive imperative of seeing and takes up the tactile one of feeling. To see feelingly is not to divide intellection and emotion, even in their most literal senses of cognition and corporeality, spirit and matter. It is not to divide at all, which is why it is so literally inarticulate; it is to take the whole sense of a lived world, and to make sense of it outside of speech. This understanding is out of joint—it cannot tell what it knows as it understands it.

To see feelingly, as Gloucester and Hieronimo do at their moments of greatest intensity and insight, is what the understanders in the theater do all along. To *understand* is to inhabit the theater's world as one who participates and experiences, as one who stands below and within it rather than viewing and judging it from a distance.[73] In this period the theater was not felt as an alienated spectacle that one viewed as if from outside it but as (literally) a circumstantial environment that one entered and in which one participated by attending, along with actors, book holders, onlookers, bystanders, understanders, captains, cutpurses, and vendors of oranges and bottle ale, each with particular tasks or expectations, but all engaged in the cooperative enterprise of the theater, of which the acted drama was only a small—if necessary—part. While the Elizabethan theater had no "fourth wall" in the sense that the phrase came to have in the nineteenth century—the imaginary, impermeable barrier at the edge of the stage separating audience from actors—it would be more accurate to say that the Elizabethan stage also lacked second and third walls (because it was on a thrust) and that the first wall was really a wall—not an imaginary barrier only, the surface of some represented space, but also the practical screen behind which characters changed costumes and grabbed props. Or perhaps it would be better to say that the Elizabethan theater *did* have a fourth wall, but one that encircled and included its audience.

Unlike modern theater, which with the edge of the stage divides passive audience from active player (a tendency that film exacerbates), early modern plays show the theater's whole circle, embracing both stage and pit, as set apart from the world outside it. Audience and actors have distinct parts, but they are mutually permeable. When the actors look out from the stage, they saw, and acknowledged that they saw, the people who were looking back at them from the theater. In moments of particular intensity or difficulty—beginning the play or reaching its climax, for instance—actors might reach across for the return acknowledgment of their audience. Thus in *Sir Thomas More* (c. 1592), as More advances to the scaffold for his execution and his friends drop away from him ("I perceive by your looks, you like my bargain so ill, that there's not one of you dare venture with me," 5.4.61–63), he discovers in the understanders a new set of allies within the theater: "Truly, here's a most sweet gallery, . . . By your patience, good people that have pressed thus into my bedchamber."[74] Asper in *Every Man out of His Humor* similarly notices the crowd during the Induction: "I not observ'd this thronged round till now" (51). Marston's *The Malcontent* opens with an Induction in which the actors Sly and Cundale (the Condell who, with Heminge, organized Shakespeare's 1623 Folio) place themselves within the theater's "company":

SLY: What do you thinke might come into a mans head now, seeing all this company?
CUNDALE: I know not sir.
SLY: I have an excellent thought: if some fiftie of the Grecians that were cramd in the horse belly had eaten garlike, do you not thinke the Trojans might have smelt out their knavery?

The onlookers are palpably present, crammed together into the wooden theater with the actors, creating shared atmosphere (as the garlic reminds us) in a very real sense.

Each of these moments comes at a transition, in which the audience is reminded that the represented world of the performance extends to encompass them, so that their experiences and responses become part of the play. But these Elizabethan plays balance the illusion of the scene and the presence of the audience to that illusion as illusion. The theater of physical understanding does not set author against player or player against spectator or auditor, and least of all representation from reality; all work together in a shared project of drama, which demands actors and understanders, real bodies and representations. Plays often call attention to the work of the performers in very physical terms: stalking, strutting, fretting, jigging. But the actors' work is represented as requiring the onlookers' understanding, whether this need is modeled by characters onstage or demanded more directly of the audience, which makes the theatrical production a mutual one. Actors and audiences share in the necessary work of the play, although they perform different tasks. Like Launce's staff or Herbert's prayer, they understand each other actively, comprehending and supporting. In "The Character of an Excellent Actor" (1615), attributed to John Webster, the actor is a corporeal counterpart to the orator, "for by a full and significant action of body, he charmes our attention; sit in a full Theater, and you will thinke so many lines drawne from the circumference of so many ears, whiles the *Actor* is the *Center*."[75] The actor does not stand apart from the audience; the actor creates the audience around him by his speaking and moving presence among them, just as, more explicitly, the actors who waded into the crowd calling "Make room!" physically formed their audiences. The circle of the theater building marks the outer limit of the acts of representation and presentation that define it—or that instantiate it, from the center outward. The importance of the understanders was their placement around the center of this ecosystem, embodying it.

Outside the circle of the theater stood the real world; within it was the special environment of the theater, a new community that was neither *oikos* nor *polis,* but which was voluntary, feeling, understanding, encompassing. Within the dramatic performance itself, the rapid and intricate shifting of emotions, dramaturgies, and events produces the same effect of ironization that inheres in the word "understanding"—that is, even when it looked like one was beholding a representation, there was always the undercurrent—the understand, perhaps?—of the concentricity of the actors and the audience, and the possibility that this might unexpectedly come forward in an encounter.

What are we to conclude from this last description, through Gloucester or Hieronimo, of what the understander experienced in perceiving feelingly? As performance studies have so often suggested, the experience of theater is a communal one, and performances of many sorts can be attempts to return, to rediscover the community that seems to be missing. But this sense of community, at least for the understanders in the Elizabethan theaters, is not most crucially a community of shared experience, of seeing or experiencing one thing or another. It is the community merely of being together in a place that continually calls attention to that togetherness, which is to say that what is sought is not metaphysical *presence* but a physical, ecological *present.* Stanley Cavell has argued that what drama calls upon us to do is to recognize that we cannot help those we behold onstage, that they are in our presence but we are not in theirs.[76] Cavell's argument is about drama generally rather than at any particular moment of its history, and the theater he describes is a mid-twentieth-century one, with seats and a darkened auditorium. But his description is even more apt for the understanders, who felt themselves present to what they saw, who were part of its representation and presentation, even if their part was to perceive it feelingly rather than to act on or in it. To be present to something is to understand it. To understand something in this sense is to be present to it.

In this present, understanding is more stimulus than meaning—or stimulus is the meaning, without other community, history, or other forces defining that meaning. Performances in the Elizabethan theaters were provocations toward meaning rather than representations of a meaning, or as a representation can be a provocation, a question demanding an answer. The response they demand is attention. Being there, understanding, no onlooker possesses a complete view of the action from a masterful distance—absence is what promises mastery, and Elizabethan theaters are arranged to resist that imaginary distance and control. What they could not control, though, the understanders could respond to. Raymond Williams describes what he calls "structures of feeling," as "the inalienably physical" present experience, undiscriminating but accurate (128). Such experience as present also challenges its own articulation, since such articulation renders experience in a fixed, and therefore altered, form. We can see this in the understanders, who do not express themselves to us, but rather leave shadows in the texts of others, and so only appear after their fact.

A final figure for the understander is Launce's dog Crab, that representation of recalcitrance and still more recalcitrant onstage presence.[77] Just after the dispute about how a staff understands, Speed asks Launce about the courtship of his master.

SPEED: But tell me true, will't be a match?
LAUNCE: Ask my dog. If he say ay, it will; if he say no, it will; if he shake his tail and say nothing, it will.
SPEED: The conclusion is then, that it will.
(2.5.33-38)

The content of Crab's response does not matter—what matters is *that* Crab respond. But he will respond, because his physical presence onstage is already cast as responsiveness, understanding, and thus Launce (and his other understanders) will have something to interpret. Insofar as they are there as critics of acting, knowing, or meaning, "the dog makes fools of the audience" (Boehrer, 165)—the audience, that is, as critic. But as an understander, and to an understanding auditory, Crab—attentive, responsive to his world, engaged, infinitely interpretable and so uninterpretable finally—fools nobody and makes a fool of nobody. In Launce's attempt to speak for him, we hear finally an understanding voice, the clown speaking the possibility of an Elizabethan theater of present understanding.

Notes

I am grateful to Mary Floyd-Wilson, Garrett Sullivan, and the anonymous readers for *Renaissance Drama* for their help in refining this essay, as well as to the questions of an attentive audience at the English department of Northwestern University, in particular those of Jeff Masten, whose understanding of what I wanted to say helped me to better articulate it here.

1. Gustav Binz, "Londoner Theater und Schauspiele in Jahre 1599," *Anglia* 22 (1899): 456-64, 458, records Platter's account in German. It is also widely reproduced in English, for example, Appendix 2:32 in Andrew Gurr, *Playgoing in Shakespeare's London* (Cambridge: Cambridge University Press, 1987), 213f. I have revised the translation found in Gurr. Interestingly, while Platter refers to the locations of a cockfight and a bearbaiting that he attends as "playhouses," he does not use this word for the theaters. See also Gabriel Egan's "Thomas Platter's Account of an Unknown Play at the Curtain or the Boar's Head," *Notes and Queries* 245 (2000): 53-56.

2. Andrew Gurr, *The Shakespearean Stage, 1574-1642,* 3rd ed. (Cambridge: Cambridge University Press, 1992), 122, citing E. K. Chambers, *The Elizabethan Stage* (Oxford, U.K.: Clarendon Press, 1923), 2:358. For a reproduction of the deWitt drawing, see R. A. Foakes, *Illustrations of the English Stage, 1580-1642* (Stanford: Stanford University Press, 1985), 52-55. That the extant drawing is recopied from deWitt's notes also suggests that the layout of the theaters was of enduring interest. English commentators also mention the tiered seating and the progressive system of charging admission, for example, William Lambarde, also in Gurr, *Stage,* 122, citing *ES* 2.359.

3. This division of audiences, and the hierarchy it implies, is older than the theaters; even *Mankind* (c. 1465-70), which certainly was not performed in a playhouse, distinguishes, "ye sovrens that sitt, and ye brothern that stonde right uppe," 904, in *Medieval Drama,* ed. David Bevington (Boston: Houghton Mifflin, 1975).

4. Gurr, *Playgoing,* uses "understander" almost as a technical term, including it, for instance, in the index. Interestingly, it is not indexed in his later *Shakespearean Stage.*

5. Francis Beaumont, *The Knight of the Burning Pestle,* ed. Michael Hattaway (New York: W. W. Norton, 1969); Ben Jonson, *Ben Jonson,* ed. C. H. Herford Percy and Evelyn Simpson, 11 vols. (Oxford, U.K.: Clarendon Press, 1925-52), 6:14. All references to Jonson's works are to this edition.

6. Jean Howard observes that, for antitheatricalist John Northbrooke, "In a strong sense, place . . . determines identity," *The Stage and Social Struggle in Early Modern England* (London: Routledge, 1994), 27. Recent works by Gail Kern Paster and Michael Schoenfeldt, among others, have similarly shown how fully and physically the early modern person was felt to be part, even an extension, of his or her environment, although their differing conclusions show how many-sided a problem the relations of mind, body, and world presented; among many works on this topic, see Paster, *The Body Embarrassed: Drama and the Disciplines of Shame in Early Modern England* (Ithaca, N.Y.: Cornell University Press, 1993) and *Humoring the*

Body: Emotions and the Shakespearean Stage (Chicago: University of Chicago Press, 2004); Schoenfeldt, *Bodies and Selves in Early Modern England: Physiology and Inwardness in Spenser, Shakespeare, Herbert, and Milton* (Cambridge: Cambridge University Press, 1999); and the introduction to *Reading the Early Modern Passions: Essays in the Cultural History of Emotion*, ed. Paster, Katherine Rowe, and Mary Floyd-Wilson (Philadelphia: University of Pennsylvania Press, 2004), 1–20. Given this sense of physicality and permeability, the position of the understander may be stranger to us than to one of the understanders' contemporaries; certainly the sense that an intellectual independence from physical placement or that thought might happen in detachment from physicality is a notion that is emergent rather than dominant in the period I discuss, and figures like Ben Jonson, whom I discuss below, are more innovative than reactionary in insisting on a distinction between cognitive and physical understanding. Nevertheless, as I argue, in a theatrical context at least, around 1600 it was not only possible but usual to distinguish between those whose reactions were seen as physically conditioned and those whose responses were imagined as more independent. See also note 17 below.

7. Except for those to *King Lear*, all citations from Shakespeare's plays are to *The Riverside Shakespeare*, 2nd ed., ed. G. Blakemore Evans (Boston: Houghton Mifflin, 1997).

8. James Shirley, *Six New Playes* (London : Humphrey Robinson and Humphrey Moseley, 1653). The play was first performed in the private Dublin playhouse and later moved to the Globe, "this meridian," although an earlier single play edition presents it "as it was acted at the private house in Black-Friers" (*The Doubtful Heir: A Tragi-Comedie* [London: Humphrey Robinson and Humphrey Moseley, 1652]). See also *Dramatic Works and Poems,* ed. William Gifford and Alexander Dyce, 6 vols. (New York: Russell and Russell, 1966 [repr. of 1833]), 4:279. The word "meridian" recalls the Induction to *Bartholomew Fair* (1614): "the *Author* hath writ it iust to his *Meridian* and the *Scale* of the grounded Iudgments here" (Ind. 55–57; 6:14), as well as the linking of personal temperament to geographic environment.

9. For a range of references to uncouth audiences cracking nuts, see W. J. Lawrence, "Those Nut-Cracking Elizabethans," in *Those Nut-Cracking Elizabethans: Studies of the Early Theatre and Drama* (London: Argonaut Press, 1935), 1–9; on bottle-ale, cf. John Stephens, *Essayes and Characters Ironical and Instructive* (London: Nicholas Okes, 1615), 191; qtd. in Gurr, *Playgoing*, App. 2: 107, as Stephens's *Satyrical Essayes Characters and Others* (1615), of which it is a much expanded edition.

10. Beaumont and Fletcher, ed. Cyrus Hoy, *Dramatic Works in the Beaumont and Fletcher Canon*, gen. ed. Fredson Bowers, 10 vols. (Cambridge: Cambridge University Press, 1976), 3:491. All citations of Beaumont and Fletcher's works are to this edition. Cf. the Induction to *Bartholomew Fair*, where Jonson endeavors to contract the individual members of the audience to judge no more than they pay for and to isolate the judgments of the members of the audience from one another. I am grateful to my student Maren Donley for suggesting this reading of that scene.

11. Pauline Kiernan, *Staging Shakespeare at the New Globe* (New York: St. Martin's Press, 1999), 13–17, in a discussion of the responsiveness of twentieth-century crowds in the new Globe Theater, cites several early modern texts to argue for the freedom of an audience to interrupt or even commandeer a performance. One source of Tarlton's popularity was that he incorporated this backtalk by taking "themes" from it for his impromptu verses in the jig;

see Richard Levin, "Tarlton in *The Famous History of Friar Bacon* and *Friar Bacon and Friar Bungay,*" *Medieval and Renaissance Drama in England* 12 (1999): 85f.

12. This also is older than the theaters: conflating sinful nature and bodily odor, Humanum Genus in *The Castle of Perseverance* (c. 1405-25) declares, "We have etyn garlek everychone," l.1369, in Bevington, *Medieval Drama.*

13. Act 5, no scene or line numbers, John Marston, *The Plays,* ed. H. Harvey Wood, 3 vols. (Edinburgh: Oliver and Boyd, 1934), 3:234; Gurr, *Playgoing,* App. 2:40. In the Prologue to *The Fawn* (1606), Marston condemns another crowd for their "ranke baudrie, that smels / Even thorow your maskes, *usque ad nauseam,*" like the composer of *The Castle of Perseverance* linking carnal sin and corporal scent (2:145). On the aural atmosphere of the playhouses, Bruce R. Smith, *The Acoustic World of Early Modern England: Attending to the O-Factor* (Chicago: University of Chicago Press, 1999). In light of Marston's remarks, we should perhaps attend to the olfactor as well.

14. Thomas Dekker, *The Guls Horne-Booke* (London: [Nicholas Okes], 1609), 2, 27, 28. The tobacco smell of the audience was as marked as the garlic; Gurr, *Playgoing,* Appendix 2 records a number on instances (2:31, 59). For "stinkards," see Gurr, *Playgoing,* App. 2:59 and 70 (both Dekker); Middleton, *Father Hubburds Tales* (1604), refers to "a dull Audience of Stinkards sitting in the Penny Galleries of a Theater," Gurr *Playgoing,* App. 2:52.

15. "To the Reader," *Complete Works,* ed. F. L. Lucas, 4 vols. (London: Chatto and Windus, 1966 [repr. of 1927]), 1:107.

16. See David Hillman, "*Homo Clausus* at the Theatre: Closing Bodies and Opening Theatres in Early Modern England," in *Rematerializing Shakespeare: Authority and Representation on the Early Modern English Stage,* ed. Bryan Reynolds and William N. West (New York: Palgrave, 2006), for a much fuller discussion of the ideology of embodiment as it relates to drama in this period.

17. Like the humoral physiology prevalent until well into the seventeenth century, modern cognitive science suggests that in fact corporeality is inextricably part of thinking; see, for example, George Lakoff and Mark Johnson, *Philosophy in the Flesh: The Embodied Mind and Its Challenge to Western Thought* (New York: Basic Books, 1999), and Mary Thomas Crane, *Shakespeare's Brain: Reading with Cognitive Theory* (Princeton: Princeton University Press, 2001). I argue ultimately that the implication of *understanding* in this period is much the same. But the joke on understanding presupposes an assumption that body and mind are distinct and even opposed, a belief also taking shape at this time. In the received psychology of the period, "understanding" often translates *intellectus,* the reasoning faculty of the intellective soul, although I suspect that this technical term forms a background to the theatrical usage rather than a direct engagement with it; see, for example, Pierre Charron, *Of Wisdome,* trans. Samson Lennard (London: Edward Blount, 1608), 46-54, and, more generally, Katherine Parks, "The Organic Soul," *The Cambridge History of Renaissance Philosophy,* ed. Charles B. Schmitt, Quentin Skinner, Eckhard Kessler, and Jill Kraye (Cambridge: Cambridge University Press, 1988), 464-84.

18. Brian Melbancke, *Philotimus: The War Betwixt Nature and Fortune* (London: Roger Warde, 1583), 152. Erasmus condemns those people who do not accept that they are human, try to live like gods, and thus become like monstrous giants, but I am not sure this is the passage Melbancke has in mind.

19. 4.4.1–39 and 2.3.1–32.

20. S.v. "understand" (n.), *OED*. Stewart's equivocation appears in a poetic diversion entitled "Ane New sort of rymand rym / Rymand alyk in rym and rym / Rymd efter sort of guid Rob steine; / Tein is to purchas Robs teine," in which the sound ending each line begins and ends the next line (*The Poems of John Stewart of Baldynneis,* ed. Thomas Crockett, STS n.s. [Edinburgh and London: Blackwood, 1913], 149–51, ll. 16f).

21. I.6.5; *Of the Laws of Ecclesiastical Polity: Preface—Book I—Book VIII,* ed. Arthur Stephen McGrade (Cambridge: Cambridge University Press, 1989), 70.

22. Janette Dillon, *Language and Stage in Medieval and Renaissance England* (Cambridge: Cambridge University Press, 1998), 77, observes that for the religious reformers of the sixteenth century "the other kind of 'understanding,' the kind that emerges *out of* shared practice, as opposed to producing it, could not be available." This conclusion, as well as the conventional association of Protestantism with interiority and individuality and Catholicism with form and community, is contested by Ramie Targoff, *Common Prayer: The Language of Public Devotion in Early Modern England* (Chicago: University of Chicago Press, 2001), 18–35. See also Mary Thomas Crane, "What Was Performance?" *Criticism* 43 (2001): 169–87, esp. 169–74.

23. *The Byble in Englyshe* ([London]: Edward Whitchurch, 1540), +iir.

24. *The Boke of Common Praier* (London: Richard Grafton, 1552).

25. Charles Hardwick, *A History of the Articles of Religion* (Philadelphia: Herman Hooker, 1852), 283.

26. Hardwick, *A History,* p. 282, article 24 and p. 281, article 24. In the 1552 articles, this is in article twenty-five. Individuals may pray privately in any language they understand.

27. *The Lay Folks Mass Book,* ed. T. F. Simmons (EETS orig. ser. 71, 1879), 158. The conversation supposedly dates from 1527, when Mary was thirteen. I was led to this by Dillon, *Language and Stage,* citing Susan Brigden, *London and the Reformation* (Oxford, U.K.: Clarendon Press, 1989), 14. On the challenges to understanding prayer, which were as much about hearing it in a noisy church as comprehending it, see Targoff, *Common Prayer,* 14–18, 22–28.

28. Crowley, *The Way to Wealth,* in *The Selected Works of Robert Crowley,* 129–50 (EETS orig. ser. 15, 1872), 141f.

29. Hobbes, *Leviathan* 1.2, "Of Imagination" (1651), ed. C. B. Macpherson (Harmondsworth: Penguin, 1968), 93f.

30. See Bruce Holsinger, *Music, Body, and Desire in Medieval Culture* (Stanford: Stanford University Press, 2001), on the interpenetration of body and soul through the medium of music in medieval thought.

31. Percy and Simpson, 3:435.

32. "An Expostulation with Inigo Jones," Percy and Simpson, 8:403, l. 39.

33. Percy and Simpson, 7:488.

34. Percy and Simpson, 3:421, l. 6ff.

35. Stanley Fish, "Authors-Readers: Jonson's Community of the Same." *Representations* 7 (1984): 26–58, makes a similar argument regarding Jonson's lyric.

36. Percy and Simpson, 5:291.

37. Percy and Simpson, 6:397.

38. Percy and Simpson, 6:15, 16.

39. This nostalgia for the staid error of the understander may surface as well in Jonson's late attempts to revisit older dramatic modes like the morality, the humors play, or the Robin Hood play in *The Devil is an Ass, The Tale of a Tub,* and *The Sad Shepherd,* his fragment of *Robin Hood.*

40. Philip Massinger, *Plays and Poems,* ed. Philip Edwards and Colin Gibson, 4 vols. (Oxford, U.K.: Clarendon Press, 1976), 3:[19].

41. E.g., Anthony Munday, *A Second and Third Blast of Retrait from Plaies and Theaters* ([London: Henry Denham], 1580), 3: "For while [the 'beholders'] saie nought, but gladlie looke on, they al by sight and assent be actors. . . ." Alexandra Halasz, " 'So beloved that men use his picture for their signs': Richard Tarlton and the Uses of Sixteenth-Century Celebrity," *Shakespeare Studies* 23 (1995): 19–38, 19, notes that after his death Tarlton serves as "a figure of affection and trust who functions to signify a site of pleasure and entertainment indisputably popular, non-exclusive—the ale-house, a place of community gathering, storytelling, merriment. . . ." The understander claims a similar communality. Note also Jim Bywater, the actor who played Launce in the new Globe's first season, quoted in Kiernan, *Staging,* 23: "The audience shares the actor's consciousness" of the play as an ongoing, changeable process. A more anxious version of this sharing of consciousness is expressed in the antitheatricalists' fear that "the spectator could be made compulsively to replicate the actor" (15), Laura Levine, *Men in Women's Clothing: Anti-theatricality and Effeminization, 1579–1642* (Cambridge: Cambridge University Press, 1994), 11–17.

42. This shift in the relative status of author and performer, and thus of reader and audience, is discussed in Robert Weimann, *Author's Pen and Actor's Voice* (Cambridge: Cambridge University Press, 2000), and Julie Stone Peters, *Theatre of the Book, 1480–1880: Print, Text, and Performance in Europe* (Oxford: Oxford University Press, 2000).

43. Beaumont and Fletcher, 3:491.

44. Beaumont and Fletcher, ed. Fredson Bowers, 10:559.

45. *Comedies, Histories, and Tragedies* (London: Isaac Jaggard and Ed. Blount, 1623), facsimile in *The Riverside Shakespeare,* 95.

46. *Riverside Shakespeare,* 95.

47. Jerzy Limon, *Gentlemen of a Company: English Players in Central and Eastern Europe, 1590–1660* (Cambridge: Cambridge University Press, 1985).

48. Moryson, *Shakespeare's Europe,* ed. Charles Hughes (London: Sherrat and Hughes, 1903), 304, qtd. in Peters, *Theatre of the Book,* 103.

49. Quoted in Limon, *Gentleman of a Company,* 1.

50. Kiernan, *Staging,* 26, also suggests that Webster's "understanding Auditory" may imply the understanders.

51. The *Epigrams* are first collected and published in the folio *Works.* Jonson finds the trope of the epigram as theater in Martial; for a further discussion of the *Epigrams* as a theater, see my *Theaters and Encyclopedias in Early Modern Europe* (Cambridge: Cambridge University Press, 2002), 163–65.

52. Donne, *Poems . . . with Elegies on the Authors Death* (London: John Marriot, 1633); Taylor, *A Juniper Lecture* (London: William Ley, 1639), A4r, excerpted in *Half Humankind: Contexts and Texts of the Controversy About Women in England, 1540–1640,* ed. Katherine

Usher Henderson and Barbara F. McManus (Urbana: University of Illinois Press, 1985), 290–304, 291.

53. *The Purple Island, or The Isle of Man* ([Cambridge]: Printers to the University of Cambridge, 1633), n.p.

54. *Complete English Poems,* ed. John Tobin (London: Penguin, 1991), 45f.

55. Halasz, "Richard Tarlton," 22, notes similarly that Tarlton's death—and thus his removal from circulation—allows for his image to be given a fixed signification and appropriated. See also the general theoretical point made by Raymond Williams, *Marxism and Literature* (Oxford: Oxford University Press, 1977), 129, that the dead can be reduced to fixed forms that do not capture the forward-looking temper of lived experience. It is worth noting that the understander is more mentioned as the dualism most often associated with Descartes, but not confined to his followers, gains ground as an explanation of human nature.

56. Of the plays I have mentioned, only *Every Man out of His Humor* and *Henry VIII* were definitely performed outdoors (*The Doubtful Heir* is doubtful but likely; see note 8) and only *Every Man Out* is Elizabethan. Shakespeare's *Two Gentlemen of Verona* (c.1590) and *Twelfth Night* (1601) were probably performed in outdoor theaters, but do not mention theatrical understanders.

57. Peters, *Theater of the Book,* 106–12, on the way that print and drama are mutually defining in this period.

58. For a remarkable attempt to formulate such a counterdiscourse, see Bruce Smith, "Hearing Green," in *Reading the Early Modern Passions,* 147–68.

59. See, for instance, my discussion of this in *Theaters and Encyclopedias,* 165–70.

60. Marston, *Plays,* 1:139, "To the Reader."

61. Marston, *Plays,* 2:144, "To My Equal Reader"; Webster, "To the Juditious Reader," *The Devil's Law-Case,* 2:236.

62. On the differences between semiology and phenomenology for performance studies, see Bert States, *Great Reckonings in Little Rooms: On the Phenomenology of Theater* (Berkeley: University of California Press, 1985), 6–14, 19–29.

63. Richard Jones, "To the Gentlemen Readers," *Tamburlaine 1,* ed. David Fuller, in Marlowe, *Complete Works,* 5 vols. (Oxford, U.K.: Clarendon Press, 1998), 5:2.

64. Smith, "Hearing Green," 161f.

65. While these arguments for the force of physicality on an audience could be called upon by supporters of the theater as readily as by its opponents, they are used less often than one might expect. Most Elizabethan and Stuart protheatrical writers seem to rely instead on traditional arguments of an edifying theater that teaches by example or by holding the mirror up to nature; see chap. 4 of my *Theatres and Encyclopedias,* "Holding the Mirror Up to Nature?" 111–42. The later seventeenth century offers more examples of trying to harness the physicality of performance and feeling for knowledge; see Katherine Rowe, "Humoral Knowledge and Liberal Cognition in Davenant's *Macbeth,*" *Reading the Early Modern Passions,* 169–91; for early eighteenth-century theories, see, for example, William Worthen, *The Idea of the Actor: Drama and the Ethics of Performance* (Princeton: Princeton University Press, 1984), 72–97. For the continental interrogation of the possibility of an educational, physical theater, see Jane Tylus, " 'Par Accident': The Public Work of Early Modern Theater," *Reading the Early Modern Passions,* 253–71.

66. My emphasis; *Histrio-mastix: The Players Scourge, or, Actors Tragedie* (London: E[dward] A[llde] et al., 1633), 714.

67. Sir Richard Baker, *Theatrum Redivivum, Or the Theatre Vindicated,* ed. Arthur Freeman, (London: 1662; facs. New York: Garland Publishing, 1973), 133. Baker cites the earlier passage from Prynne to deride the idea that there is any way to be acquainted with plays *except* experimentally, 62.

68. As I have suggested, perhaps one reason they do not note it is that, in a culture that generally accepted a humoral physiology, where cognition was constituted in a transaction with an environment, it was not important (or even possible?) to distinguish the experience of physical understanding from a more exclusively intellectual one.

69. On the meaning of beating, see Douglas Lanier, " 'Stigmaticall in Making': The Material Character of *The Comedy of Errors,*" in *The Comedy of Errors: Critical Essays,* ed. Robert S. Miola (New York: Garland Press, 1997): 319–26.

70. I quote throughout from the earlier quarto *History of King Lear* (1608), *The Complete Works,* ed. Stanley Wells and Gary Taylor (Oxford, U.K.: Clarendon Press, 1988), but in the passages I look at the folio *Tragedy* (1623) is identical. I have, however, used the traditional act and scene numbers, given in the Oxford edition along with its preferred scene numbers.

71. 3.7.54–56, my emphasis; *The Spanish Tragedy,* ed. J. R. Mulryne (New York: W. W. Norton, 1989). In my discussion I ignore the 1602 additions.

72. Williams, *Marxism and Literature,* 132, argues that what he calls structures of feeling are not feeling against thought, but felt thinking, so that what is thought is not reduced to pastness, distance, or objecthood, but incorporated into the world of the present moment. Antonio Gramsci sees understanding as a transformative activity rather an articulate description, like Williams privileging the actuality of experiences over words or thoughts (*Selections from the Prison Notebooks,* trans. Quentin Hoare and Geoffrey Nowell Smith [New York: International Publishers, 1971], 333).

73. Kiernan, *Staging,* 32–35, discusses the intensity of the interaction between audience and action in the new Globe.

74. 5.4.63–66; Anthony Munday, et al., ed. Vittorio Gabrieli and Giorgio Melchiori (Manchester: Manchester University Press, 1990).

75. Thomas Overbury, *New and Choise Characters,* (London: Thomas Creede, 1615), n.p.; Gurr, *Playgoing,* App. 2:109. On the shape taken by an audience around a performance, see Richard Schechner, "Towards a Poetics of Performance," *Essays on Performance Theory, 1970-1976* (New York: Drama Book Specialists, 1977), 108–39.

76. See the remarkable discussion of the acknowledgment of presence as the core of drama in Stanley Cavell, "The Avoidance of Love," in *Must We Mean What We Say? A Book of Essays* (New York: Charles Scribner's Sons, 1969), 331–49, 332. For Williams as well the function of art is to render the present—the world as open-ended process rather than the world as fixed form, *Marxism and Literature,* 128–35. I am also indebted here to Sarah Beckwith, *Signifying God: Social Relation and Symbolic Act in the York Corpus Christi Plays* (Chicago: University of Chicago Press, 2001).

77. See States, *Great Reckonings,* 33–35, and Bruce Boehrer, *Shakespeare Among the Animals: Nature and Society in the Drama of Early Modern England* (New York: Palgrave, 2002), 159–68, for Crab as a symbol of the actor's power and limitations in this drama.

Eating Air, Feeling Smells:
Hamlet's *Theory of Performance*

CAROLYN SALE

I N ACT III of *Hamlet,* just before he sits down with Claudius, Gertrude, and Ophelia to watch *The Mousetrap,* that play for which he has written sixteen lines, Hamlet says what may very well be the oddest of the many odd things that he says throughout the play: "I eat the air, promise-crammed" (3.2.92–93).[1] He later claims that he could eat a crocodile to express the depth of his feelings for the dead Ophelia, so his culinary tastes are clearly varied, but "I eat the air, promise-crammed," part retort, part self-definition, takes us to the heart of the play's interaction or transaction with its audience. In his talk of eating air, Hamlet suggests that the corporate body whose members appear to be but "mutes" in relation to the staged action may be as busy as the actor playing him. They may be feeding, as he does, "of the chameleon's dish" (3.2.92); that is, sitting down to the same table as those creatures who can change color upon command, actors, and taking in, across the course of the performance, the invisible matter that circulates between them, breath. Hamlet's odd statement would thus function as a metonym for the play's theory of performance, one that takes it beyond both mimesis and catharsis.

That this play offers its own theory of performance cannot be doubted. As Annabel Patterson noted some fifteen years ago, "this play contains more *information,* simply speaking, on the business of play-production than any other in Shakespeare's canon, and . . . this material is already *theoretical* when it reaches us, already, if incompletely, transformed by Hamlet's critical perspective."[2] A powerful and enthusiastic consumer of theatrical fictions, Hamlet does indeed have plenty to say about the theater's functions and workings, and is confident enough in his understanding of how the theater works to dole out advice to professional players. This may constitute some cheek, but elsewhere Hamlet displays his critical powers with a little more humility, and as he does so offers an all-important context for his odd remark about eating the air. When he leaps to the defense of an "excellent play" denounced by critics as "caviar to the general" or too fine a theatrical delicacy to "please . . . the million" (2.2.377–80), he defends the play's "honest method" by employing an extended metaphor of play-as-food: "excellent plays" well prepared and properly savored or spiced are palatable to and digestible by all, for their method, "as wholesome as sweet" (2.2.384–85), results in matter "well digested in the scenes" (2.2.380). Pursuing the methods by which the play aims to offer up fare that will "please the million," I seek to offer a specific sense of how, as Steven Mullaney has suggested, the Shakespearean theater operates as an "affective rather than a didactic forum" that "produce[s] new powers of identification, projection and apprehension in audiences."[3] I will do so by focusing on the promise of Hamlet's claim, or the ways in which the character's utterance speaks to idealistic conceptions of how the theater might work—or rather work upon, and perhaps ask work of, those who take a place within it as auditors and spectators.

"Promise-crammed," Hamlet may be speaking to an ideal transaction between play and playgoer, one in which something "as wholesome as sweet" may be offered up for consumption within the theatrical space. We could argue that in this play so concerned with addressing its culture's concerns about the theater, the promise is tied to the reform of theatrical practices that Hamlet urges, or rather to one aspect or another of the concerns that antitheatrical pamphleteers raised in their texts. From Stephen Gosson's 1579 *The Schoole of Abuse* onward, Elizabethan antitheatrical pamphleteers inveighed against the theater as a site of contagion, both physical and moral. In the first volley in a campaign to make potential playgoers run from the theater before they received any kind of "hurt" therein, Gosson conceived of their particular vulnerability in terms of the "winds" that might be in circulation in the theatrical space. Every other creature had been supplied, by God, with the capacity to "peyse their bodies" against these "winds":

But wee which are so brittle, that we breake with euery fillop, so weake, that we are drawne with euery threade; so light, that wee are blowen away with euery blast; so vnsteady, that we slip in euery ground; neither peyse our bodyes against the winde, nor stand vppon one legge, for sleeping too muche: nor close vppe our lippes for betraying our selues, nor vse any witte, to garde our owne persons, nor shewe our selues willing too shunne our owne harmes, running most greedely to those places, where we are soonest ouerthrowne.[4]

Although in this context, the winds appear to be merely figurative, the suggestion is that in the theater playgoers open themselves up to infiltration of one kind or another and a subsequent tempest that will leave them in one way or another debilitated. More moderate than his fellow pamphleteers, Gosson nevertheless held out the possibility that the theater's dangers might be mitigated, and set the players (and those who wrote for them) a challenge:

If Players can promise in wordes, and performe it in deedes, proclaime it in their Billes, and make it good in Theaters: that there is nothing there noysome too the body, nor hurtefull to the soule: and that euerye one which comes to buye their Iestes, shall haue an honest neighbour, tagge and ragge, cutte and longe tayle, goe thether and spare not, otherwise I aduise you to keepe you thence, my selfe wil begine to leade the daunce.[5]

It is an assurance of this kind that *Hamlet* offers, as it employs its own culinary metaphors to respond to Gosson's rhetoric of the noxious "dyet" that playgoers purportedly dine upon in the theatrical space.[6] The play reassures them that the things offered for their consumption in the theater will not only do them no hurt, but may very well do them some good. The "participation" that takes place as a result of this may be understood, as Anthony Dawson and P. A. Skantze have argued, as a kind of "secular transubstantiation,"[7] and there can be no doubt that for some playgoers in the Globe Shakespeare's theater operated as a venue for the transmission of a spirit that was very much religiously inflected.[8] I am not, however, interested in the religious aspects of the transmission here. I wish to pursue the play's theory and practice of the transfer of breath between actor and playgoer in purely material terms. The *success* or pragmatics of the play's theory of performance is not what is at issue here, but rather its character, in its full-blown idealism or "promise."[9]

Pursuing a sense of the play's transaction with its audience in material rather than spiritual terms, I mimic the play's own modus operandi, which is consistently to render the divine (and other complex discourses such as that of the law) into terms that are "plaine," "honest," "wholesome," and "sweet" for consumption and comprehension by "the general." To put this another way, the play consistently presents the high-flown, the philosophical, the abstract in what Hamlet calls "examples gross as earth" (4.4.46). In fact, the play engages in a relentless materializing of everything it discusses. Turn to almost any line of this text and you will find the immaterial or the abstract given material form. The text bestows upon the abstraction time either anatomical or architectural form (it is "out of joint" [1.5.191]), and those other abstractions, the false and the true, find themselves figured as fish: "Your bait of falsehood takes this carp of truth" (2.1.62). There is a decided tendency in this text not only to render things material, or give them forms and figures, but to turn one form after another into what we might call, echoing the text, "baser matter" (1.5.104); and in an environment in which everything is being rendered material in one way or another, reason becomes the ability to distinguish thing from thing, or one form, from another: "when the wind is southerly," Hamlet informs Rosencrantz and Guildenstern, "I know a hawk from a handsaw" (2.2.321–22). The line also suggests that certain winds, or forms of air, make possible a rationality or perspective that Hamlet would otherwise lack, a matter to which I shall return. In fact, in this play so insistently about the material, even thinking exerts a material force: it is a "cudgel[ing] of [the] brains" which produces effects elsewhere in the body: thinking, Hamlet tells us as he considers what can happen to a lawyer's skull after his death, makes the bones ache (5.1.87).

One important result of the text's tendency to construe everything as the product of material exchanges or friction between material bodies is that the Hamlet who unfolds before us insistently pursues questions of identity in what we might regard as the simplest, or the earthiest, of terms. Not only does Hamlet regularly consider how everything ultimately returns to dust, he himself continually performs a linguistic equivalent of this material turn, posing high-flown questions about being and action in language that a ten-year-old could understand. With a mere ten words, for example—"And yet to me what is this quintessence of dust?" (2.2.277–78)—Hamlet presents one of the most pressing questions about identity in terms that foreground his own materiality along with his alienation from it, an alienation that makes possible the crucial disjuncture between self-as-object and self-as-reflexive-thinker from which Hamlet wrings so much linguistic payoff. The insistent materialization of everything taking place under the "majestical roof fretted with golden fire" (2.2.270-71), that is, both the earthly and the theatrical space, means that even those aspects of identity that we would deem the most abstract and intangible (soul, conscience, memory) are "limed" for us (3.3.68), made material through metaphor, that trick of language through which word is made flesh in familiar terms. This concern with ways in which to give complex thought material form extends beyond the language of the page to the semiotics of the stage, so that what the spectator experiences in the Globe is the by-product of a material aesthetic—that is, an aesthetic that everywhere turns one form into a "baser" or simpler one not only to ensure the widest possible communicability of the text, but also to draw its audience into an experience—one sensual and physiological—through which it participates in material processes of transformation.

The play's language catches its spectators or auditors up in this materializing tendency in its talk of various forms of feeding or consumption. This talk insistently reminds playgoers of their own embodiment, and perhaps the fact that they are making their bodies available for some kind of transaction simply by taking their place in the theater. In its plainest terms, playgoers are induced to imagine that they will ultimately be, like Alexander the Great, nothing more than "dust" in a "bunghole" (5.1.193-94). Elsewhere, this rhetoric reminds playgoers not only of their own physicality and mortality but also of the ways in which their embodiment is caught up in political forms of consumption: "We fat all creatures else to fat us, and we fat ourselves for maggots. Your fat king and your lean beggar is but variable service—two dishes, but to one table" (4.3.21-23). The play's critique of sociopolitical dynamics in terms of the ingestion of one form of matter by another casts Hamlet's claim that he eats air as political: eating air, he removes himself from the material circuit that makes some men fat while leaving others lean, and places only men like Osric, who are "spacious in the possession of dirt," at the king's table (5.2.75).[10] Hamlet fashions a political discourse in which the king is made an object and stripped of the mystery whereby he exerts his power over others and claims certain feeding privileges denied to others: "The king is a thing," he informs Rosencrantz and Guildenstern—"of nothing," he adds, when Guildenstern presses him for elaboration (4.2.25-27). This thing he desires to turn into the "offal" with which he may fat "kites" (2.2.518-19). The "fine revolution" threatened in all of this—Hamlet attributes substance and meaning to beggars along with their bodies, while depriving the king of the same—is one of the things that makes Hamlet the "hectic" in Claudius's blood (4.3.65); figuratively crammed with Hamlet, Claudius is in desperate need of a cure. But I am interested in the obverse of all this: not how Hamlet conceives of Claudius's unjust "fatting" of himself at others' expense, but the play's compensation for the operations of the polis in terms of the fare it serves up to its audience. The action of the play will culminate in Hamlet finally taking revenge upon Claudius but in the course of these representations of action, what does the audience consume? Joining Hamlet in his eating of air, the audience will take in a substance that nourishes them more than any fare they could have if they too had a "crib . . . at the king's mess" (5.2.73–74). Eating the air they will take in a substance, moreover, that renders them active rather than passive, allowing them to imagine a more positive transaction with other bodies or materials than that which Hamlet imagines in his talk of the king's progress "through the guts of a beggar" (4.3.30).

I am certainly not the first scholar to suggest that playgoers in the Globe were ingesting various forms of matter as they took in a play. Scholarly discussion has so far, however, focused on what Sir Francis Bacon called "visibles" and "audibles." On the impact of these two "species" of matter, Bacon wrote:

The *Species* of *Visibles* seeme to be *Emissions* of *Beames* from the *Obiect seene;* Almost like Odours; saue that they are more Incorporeall: But the *Species* of *Audibles* seeme to Participate more with *Locall Motion,* like *Percussions* or *Impressions* made vpon the *Aire.* So that whereas all Bodies doe seeme to worke in two manners; Either by the *Communication* of their *Natures;* Or by the *Impressions* and *Signatures* of their *Motions;* The *Diffusion* of *Species Visible* seemeth to participate more of the former *Operation;* and the *Species Audible* of the latter.[11]

Bacon's statement is vague, especially in regard to "visibles," which somehow communicate their natures by a form of "emission" he can describe at best by way of simile: they pass into the spectator "like Odours," or as if they were scents or smells. The species of "audibles" has proved more tractable material for both sixteenth-century and contemporary theorists, precisely because of the "percussions" that Bacon attributes to them here. The idea of direct material transfer from actor to playgoer of sound is captured most famously, perhaps, in John Webster's description of the "excellent actor" as a figure whose riveting of playgoers' attention lets

Webster imagine he sees lines of transmission between the actor's body and playgoers' ears: "he charms our attention: sit in a full theatre, and you will think you see so many lines drawn from the circumference of so many ears, while the actor is at the center."[12] The "percussions" that move along those lines between actor's body and playgoers' ears have been pursued by both Joseph Roach and Bruce Smith. Joseph Roach has famously read the transaction between actor's body and playgoers' ears in terms of kinetic energy—the actor's voice and gestures both create waves of sound and motion that infiltrate playgoers through their ears to exert a physical force inside them, stirring up their passions.[13] More recently, Bruce Smith has argued that the Globe serves as a physical instrument for the transmission of sound, in which every playgoer's body becomes a smaller instrument through which sounds play and resonate.[14]

Smith's argument is important for moving us away from an idea of the theater as predominantly discursive arena. He suggests that with sound the playgoers communicate materials that are prediscursive: playing with a phrase from Wright's *Passions,* he argues that by "hearing green" the playgoer in the Globe may enjoy the viscerality of the theatrical experience simply by thrumming with "audibles" and without processing them into phonemes.[15] I wish to go beyond the idea of the theater as a place where a material transfer of theatrical representations takes place through the conduits of eyes and ears, and beyond the idea of the Globe as an organ for the transmission of sound, in pursuit of a material and a theatrical experience that is more ephemeral and more elusive. I start by not resting content with Bacon's simile, "like Odours." Let us use *Hamlet's* relentless materializing to cut through that simile. *Hamlet* makes literal what is figurative in Bacon and Roach to provide a theory of performance that reads the exchange between actor and playgoer in terms of the actual infusion of one body with the materials of another, through breath.

The terms in which *Hamlet* discusses the species of "visibles" and "audibles" are, as we might expect from my earlier discussion of the materializing tendencies of the play, elemental. It presents "visibles" in gritty terms, or should I say, terms of grit: the spectacle that the Ghost presents, for example, is a "mote . . . to trouble the mind's eye" (1.1.112). Horatio's metaphor imagines "visibles" as things that can get inside one, causing in their transit into another form of matter some friction or rub. The body of the "visible" may be microscopic, a "mote," but it produces physical effects: seeing makes the eyes ache. Given that this is a play in which a character digs a grave, we may imagine many actual motes going into circulation, depending on whether the playing company makes a property out of that substance of which Hamlet keeps speaking and the vigor with which the actor digs. But the play is also concerned with that other species of matter that Bacon designates, "audibles." In the course of objecting to Rosencrantz and Guildenstern's attempts to make him a tool for their own advancement, Hamlet focuses on that other species by imagining his own body as a "little organ" or "pipe" upon which they attempt to play (3.2.362-64). The act of blowing that would be required for them to play upon him as a pipe would result in sound, but the sound would be a by-product of their breath passing through him: "Give it breath with your mouth," Hamlet says (3.2.352-53). Neither words nor sounds are the primary material here. The material of which both sounds and words are composed is, as Ophelia tells us, "sweet breath" (3.1.98).

When we focus on the transaction between actor and playgoer in the Globe as the transmission of breath, we find another answer to the question that Thomas Wright raises in *Passions of the Minde in Generall* as he considers the immense power of the passion that can be communicated in performance: "what qualities carie simple single sounds and voices, to enable them to worke such wonders?"[16] Working toward an answer, Wright claims that passion in an orator, actor, or any other "perswader" seems to him to "resemble the wind a trumpeter bloweth in at one end of the trumpet."[17] As his description continues, the simile shifts into metaphor ("the passion proceedeth from the heart, & is blowne about the bodie, face, eies, hands, voice . . .")[18] but it is only elsewhere that he approaches the issue in material rather than figurative terms, writing that "sound it selfe . . . is nothing else but a certaine artificiall shaking, crispling or tickling of the ayre (like as we see in the water crispled, when it is calme, & a sweet gale of wind ruffleth it a little . . .)."[19] This last statement provides support for theories (both sixteenth century and of our own moment) that posit that sound through its "crisplings" stirs the passions of the hearer. But I would like us to think of the air not, as Wright does, as the thing that is stirred or blown about by something else, but rather as the thing that stirs. Air, wind, or breath is not simply the medium, carrier, or agent of sound and words; in its issuance, in the theatrical arena, from actors' mouths, it is a propulsive force. The matter that emanates from actors is not "like odours" and does not simply "resemble the wind"; it *is* the "sweet breath" of which all of their enunciations, whether they are verbal or prelinguistic, are composed.

In a text where characters regularly make use of ejaculations such as "hum," "pooh," and "ha," the play suggests that nonverbal forms of communication have matter in them, or rather carry matter that is neither sound nor words. Not only can the "windy suspiration of forced breath" (1.2.79) express passion (grief, in the context of Hamlet's assertion that he does not simply *seem* woeful), it may emit, exude, or simply comprise matter: "There's matter in these sighs" (4.1.1) Claudius informs Gertrude when he finds her heaving after her confrontation with Hamlet. The sighs carry some sense that he wishes her to unfold in words, but the sighs are also the vehicle for matter of another kind, the passion with which Hamlet's words have filled her, a passion so great that it is crowding out her own breath. Hamlet, himself suffering from the effects of another's passionate communication (the effects, that is, of "incorporeal air" as mysteriously embodied in his father's ghost), also experiences the impact of sighs, at least according to Ophelia's report: he breathes a sigh of such force in a visit to her that it seemed to "shatter all his bulk / And end his being" (2.1.94-95).

Gail Kern Paster's extensive work on the humoral body and the "ecology of the passions" helps us understand the physiological force that the actor playing Gertrude is feigning when confronted by Hamlet. As "passion's slave," Hamlet is the victim of his own physiology, stirred into a state of great excitation, disturbance, and distraction by his encounter with that thing of air, his father's ghost. "The narrative of physiology is," Paster writes, "one of assimilation of nature's raw matter—its food and water and air—into the stuff in which consciousness must lodge, the bodily stuff of self."[20] This assimilation requires an intermixing of "nature's raw matter" with the body's humors (black bile, yellow bile, blood, and phlegm) in the "containing vessels" of the body's arteries, and "the compression of incorporated air and fire moving along the liquid streams of [these] containing vessels" makes possible action.[21] It also causes "explosions of air and fire within the body's dense liquidity" that may manifest itself in overly forceful outward action, as Paster's quotation of Bacon suggests: "wee knowe that simple *Aire,* being preternaturally attenuated by *Heate,* will make it self Roome, and breake and blowe vp that which resisteth it."[22] Dealing with the effects of the "winds of passion" inside him that have been stirred up the Ghost, Hamlet speaks of himself as having been plunged into "Vulcan's stithy" (3.2.83). In more recent work Paster provides a detailed reading of the First Player's speech about Pyrrhus which shows how Pyrrhus, as a thing "roasted in wrath and fire," becomes a figure for Hamlet's physiological state after his encounter with his father's spirit.[23] The air is the agent here, stirring or "exagitating" one person's spirits so that he in turn stirs or "exagitates" another's.[24] But the communication of passion in the form of breath between actor and playgoer need not work such deleterious effects. In fact, we could argue that when Hamlet advises the players not to "saw the air" (3.2.4) around them with their hands, he is seeking to ensure a gentle, noncoercive transfer of breath from actor to playgoer. When the actor "saws" the air, he risks subjecting the playgoer to an onslaught of kinetic energy, perhaps even risks altering the nature of the thing being transferred: with the sawing, the "sweet breath" may become something else entirely, a barrage of motion waves that disperse it before it ever reaches the playgoer. It may also do a kind of violence upon the person who receives it: "Ayre so carued," Wright writes, "punisheth and fretteth the heart."[25] In the language of Shakespeare's text, it serves up to the playgoer a "whirlwind of . . . passion" (3.2.6) that he or she may not have the power to ingest. The play represents the effects of such airs or such a "whirlwind" in a decidedly negative inflection en route to ensuring that its own "chameleon's dish" (3.2.92) will be "wholesome" and "sweet" (2.2.385), the product of its own players "us[ing] all gently" (3.2.5).

The play cultivates the sense that the matter in sighs and the matter of breath may be communicated to playgoers or infused through them gently, as something already "well digested," by appealing to another of their senses, the sense of smell. "Affection [or passion] poureth forth it self by all meanes possible," Wright notes;[26] and while Wright believes that the most powerful of the senses for the transmission of passion is sight ("no sense hath such varietie of objects to feed and delight it . . . no sense sooner moueth"),[27] and though he devotes a great deal of attention, as Smith has noted in his reading of *Passions,* to sound, he also suggests the importance of smell to what he calls the "discoverie" of passions. "Passion smelleth," he writes.[28] The remark suggests that as passion percolates through the body (a "machine," according to Hamlet [2.2.124]), it gives off an odiferous by-product or a chemical stink. Shakespeare knows this: he has Claudius attribute a rankness to his "offence" of killing his brother, which "smells to heaven" (3.3.36). Writing of the difficulties that insincere men or those who dissimulate pose to those who would discern their true natures or motives, Wright claims that his readers can smell their way to the truth: "in all suiters presents," he suggests, by way of example, "a man of a bad sent may easily feele a smell of profit, which perfumeth those gifts."[29] Attributing to objects a scent or perfume, Wright gives passions a body, matter or substance in the form of odors that makes them discernible even to a man of "bad sent." This matter will allow him to apprehend or *feel* the smell of profit in the gifts. The wonderful catachresis of "feele a smell" not only underscores the physicality of smelling one's way toward apprehension or understanding, it also marks for us the invisible transit of material in the act of breathing, material that we can *feel* even if our sense of smell fails us.

In addition to indicating that smells can offend (Hamlet recoils from the stink of Yorick's skull, for example, at 5.1.190 ["And smelt so? Pah!"]), all three of *Hamlet*'s texts present scent, as Wright's text does, in relation to gifts or presents. In 3.1, Ophelia informs Hamlet that he is to take back his letters and the tokens of love that he has given her for their "perfume" is "lost" (3.1.99). In other words, for the benefit of her father and Claudius, Ophelia pretends that she can no longer feel the smell of Hamlet's gifts; this act, in which she dissociates herself from her own passions, will lead eventually to her madness and drowning; but the reference invites playgoers to think of objects as exuding some invisible matter that may be apprehended by smell, and perhaps *only* by smell. The most important reference to scents comes from the Ghost, about a third of the way through the long speech to Hamlet in which he explains how he was murdered. Brought up short in his tale-telling by his recognition that morning is approaching, the Ghosts says, "But soft, methinks I scent the morning air" (1.5.58). Scenting the morning air, the Ghost may not only be breathing it in, but in a now obsolete meaning also exhaling it.[30] A thing of air himself, he is therefore a medium or organ for air's transmission, and the actor who stalks onstage to personate him gives body to that which he himself exudes in motes (on first encounter, Hamlet suggests that the Ghost either trails "airs from heaven or blasts from hell" [1.4.41]). Scenting the air, the Ghost also feels smells, as the typographical appearance of "scent" as "sent" in both Q2 and the Folio underscores, for "sent" draws our attention to the word's etymological roots in French (in the verb "sentir") and Latin (in the verb "sentire"): to scent is to feel or perceive.[31] Performing for playgoers the act of scenting or feeling smells, the actor playing the Ghost on the Globe's stage (Shakespeare, as legend would have it) draws the audience's attention to the importance of the act of breathing, especially in the space of the wooden O, which becomes, with the single word of "scent," a vehicle for feeling and apprehension through smell, but also the medium for the transmission of scent and breath to others. Drawing breath, the actor takes in not only a scent or perfume but also the air that carries it; exhaling it, he perfumes it in turn, as he returns to the environment around him what he took from it. The performance of the act of "scenting" stimulates the audience's sense of smell and its ability to scent, priming its members to understand the air of the theater as perfumed—filled, that is, with the breath of the actors, which they may "scent," ingest or, as Hamlet's suggests, "eat." The "miraculous organ" in which they find themselves and of which they are a part functions, then, not only as a globe or head filled with words that may stir them to intellection, as Hamlet suggests the Ghost does, but also as another body part: a pair of lungs that scatters throughout its environment a "baser matter" in the form of perfume.

What work does this air or breath do? Let me first consider the ways in which it does *not* work. In its suggestion that playgoers may, like Hamlet, "eat the air" or feed on what is transmitted by it, the play goes well beyond any idea of the theater tied to mimesis. It also goes beyond the transmission of breath for or as language. The play, I suggest, although it exploits what mimetic representation can offer, is also suspicious of the kinds of effect to which mimesis lends itself; and Hamlet is of course famously dismissive of words. The fact that Hamlet is himself the instrument of mimetic principles at their most coercive should not deter us from accepting some of his other ideas about the function of the theater. As Robert Weimann has noted, this is a strange play in which both Hamlet and Shakespeare articulate an "equivocal position": "the demand for 'reform' and the refusal to comply with it in one and the same play is," for example, "largely unparalleled."[32] In Hamlet's hands, the mimetic character of the theater becomes a weapon that he uses both to provoke some show of Claudius's guilt and to threaten him (the *Mousetrap* shows a nephew poisoning his uncle). He uses mimetic principles even more aggressively with Gertrude as he holds up a glass wherein she may see the inmost part of her. Hamlet is in fact so forceful with Gertrude that he renders her breathless: when he asks her to swear not to tell Claudius about his confrontation of her, she assures him that she could not if she wanted to: "Be thou assured, if words be made of breath, / And breath of life, I have no life to breathe / What thou hast said to me" (3.4.197–99). Hamlet has gone too far. To borrow a word that Wright uses when writing of passion's forcible effects upon an auditor, Hamlet's confrontation of Gertrude, an exhibition of mimetic principles wrested to coercive ends, threatens to "exanimate" her (175). Using mimetic principles to such ends, Hamlet veers from the project that the Ghost has assigned him, a project that involves a purgation of the state through a bringing-to-account of Claudius. What the audience experiences here, palpably, even if they are too far away to see what might easily appear here, the actor's breath upon the mirror, is the forcefulness of one practice of mimesis. Given that Hamlet also fails to achieve the effects that Thomas Heywood will later claim for mimesis in his *Apology for Actors* (1612) as he aims to demonstrate the moral utility of the theater (Gertrude is not prompted to any show of guilt in relation to the murder), the scene thus seems, as Jane Tylus has suggested, to "militate *against* the very 'work' theater is ideally supposed to perform as a discoverer of hidden passions."[33] But that is not the work that this play, I am arguing, sets out to do. Hamlet's roughness with Gertrude constitutes a practice of mimesis that the play's theory of performance as an exchange of breath counters. Articulating a theory of its exchange with the audience in terms of the eating of air, the feeling of smells, the drawing of breath, the play offers an idea of the theater as an organ for an exchange that works to fill playgoers with breath in its most positive character rather than expose them to any kind of force that would compel it from them. The breath that the actors transmit works to the very opposite effect that Hamlet pursues with Gertrude: it does not exanimate, but inspires. It motivates and mobilizes. The organ of the theater operates as a pair of lungs that takes through that "canopy" that is no proper roof at all a material that, harnessed by the actors in their acts of breathing and speaking, passes outward to the audience, who may receive the breath as "mutes," but who do not remain mute; they receive the breath as "patients," as materials that are acted upon, but what they receive renders them active, or rather creates in them the capacity or the potential to become that which they observe: the breath makes them "capable" by turning them all into potential actors.

Wright helps us further this line of thinking. Advocating that his readers turn to the theater, and to players in particular, for models for their own passions, he suggests that they go to the theater to learn how to act—not on the stage, but in the world. His language posits a circuit of exchange in

which the players, basing their personation of action on their observation
of the passions around them, make themselves into superlative models of
passionate action for others:

The first is, that we looke vpon other men appassionate, how they demeane
themselues in passions, and obserue what and how they speake in mirth, sadnesse,
ire, feare, hope, &c, what motions are stirring in the eyes, hands, bodie, &c. And
then leaue the excesse and exorbitant leuitie or other defects, and keepe the
manner corrected with prudent mediocritie: and this the best may be marked in
stage plaiers, who act excellently; for as the perfection of their exercise consisteth
in imitation of others, so they that imitate best, act best. And in the substance of
externall action for most part oratours and stage plaiers agree: and only they differ
in this, that these act fainedly, those really; these onely to delight, those to stirre
vp all sorts of passions according to the exigencie of the matter.[34]

What begins with the actions of men and women in the world (those
who act "really," in Wright's wording) finds itself perfected by players on
the stage (those who "act fainedly") and the "fained" becomes the model
for the "externall action" of those who act "really." What the playgoer
receives, then, in Wright's view, when they go to the theater, are lessons
in acting for which they were the source material. The refinement of
the "externall action" in which they are always engaged comes back to
them from the players. The exchange is thus two-way, and in its double
character offers a challenge to subjectivity, for what the actor personates,
whether he is confined within the bounds of the O or walking London's
streets, performing his actions "really," is always already someone else, or
the many bits of sundry other persons which he cobbles together in an
inheritance from others that has no proper point of origin, no proper
author, no one person. What passes between actors and playgoers, then,
in the exchange of breath, that material that allows for the expression of
passion, is no particular idea of subjectivity, and no discursive end. "We
move," Wright writes, comprehending himself as a player too, if only in
terms of his grammar: " . . . we moue, because by the passion thus wee
are moued, and as it hath wrought in vs so it ought to worke in you."[35]
In its intransitivity (the players move others, but to no particular object
or end), Wright's formulation suggests that what the players transmit as
they perform passion is the principle of action: they are moved, in turn
move, and make possible further moving in those moved. *Hamlet*'s famous
formulation for action spoken by the first Clown—action is "to act, to do,
to perform" (5.1.12-13)—goes a step beyond Wright's formulation, both

in terms of its grammar and what it is actors do, liberating action from both subject and object, stripping it naked, leaving it all verb. It untethers action from any particular source and any particular end, rendering it a pure, enlivening force that can be accessed, through the act of breathing, by all. The material through which all of this is accomplished is unconfined and unconfinable. It may move through bodies with a certain power or energy, as the actor's breath does when the Ghost's voice booms through the wooden O in the opening act, but, like the Ghost's voice, it is simultaneously everywhere and nowhere, all around them and yet in no one place. It may gather force as it moves through the enclosed spaces of the actors' bodies and the shell of the theater itself, and take on or carry other material as it does so (including sound, as Smith has argued so persuasively), but, in its ideal formulation, it is always free and unrestrictive: available to all, coercive with none.

Indeed, within the physiological terms that Gail Kern Paster has so extensively elaborated, within the theatrical space, each and every playgoer becomes a "containing vessel," in which this breath stirs up the animal and vital spirits to make possible action. The breath—or the air of the chameleon's dish of which they all eat—excites the physiological processes in which they are all "stithies." The work that they engage in is both individual and collective. Each playgoer must deal with the effects of the passionate transmission—that is, take in the passion received from the actors in the exchange of breath, and bear any potential negative consequences, en route to permitting the purgative effects of the stirring up or enlivening of their own passions. If we note, along with Stephen Orgel, that the Greek word that signifies the thing from which playgoers are released or relieved in the experience of catharsis is "pathemata," and that this word, usually translated as "sufferings," "implies, literally, passive action," or as Orgel paraphrases it, "what happens to you, as opposed to what you do," the theory of performance to which the play thus speaks might be understood as an elaboration of Aristotle's theory of catharsis: where they join the actor playing Hamlet in his eating of the air, and when they weep at the character's death, playgoers make themselves available for a physiological alteration that frees them from the inaction or passivity that "pathemata" connotes to "make them capable."[36]

If we take all of this literally, as Gail Kern Paster urges us to do, we might imagine playgoers engaged in a larger process of collective purification. The play repeatedly draws our attention to one distillate of the physiological processes that playgoers may experience as the play unfolds, the salt that gets left behind on playgoers' cheeks when they weep. This weeping is a result of the tragic action. Within the fiction, Hamlet's action of killing the king figuratively clears or purifies the "pestilent congregation of vapors" (2.2.272–73) in Denmark; and the represented purgation, by provoking real-world physiological effects that include but are by no means limited to crying, may refine or purify the air that playgoers "scent." Within the "ecology of the passions," Paster notes, breath "moves into and out of the body," and in its ambiguity makes our constitution ambiguous; we are the product of both internal and external forces, and the product of parts that are always our "own" (bones, flesh, organs) and something that we share with others (the air that we draw in with our breath).[37] This suggests that both our capacity to act and our physical being are always tied both to the ecological system within us (that tempestuous interaction of air, fire, and water that makes meteorological metaphors so apt for their description) and the ecology without, that environment that one finds without, as one crawls, as Hamlet puts, it between heaven and earth. In the Renaissance, the circulation of materials between these two environments—that of the individual's body and that of the larger physical environment in which he or she is situated—was understood, as Paster has argued, literally: "That which is bodily or emotional figuration for us, preserved metaphors of somatic consciousness, was the literal stuff of physiological theory for early modern scriptors of the body," she writes as she urges us to resist the tendency to let "semantic differences between past and present discourses of the body . . . occlude early modern habits of bodily sensation and self-experience . . . and lead us to substitute figurative where literal meanings ought to remain."[38] As I noted at the outset, the play's own relentless materializing also encourages us to resist a metaphorical turn. If we are as obstinately literal in our conception of the exchange as the First Clown is, within the fiction, about other things ("How absolute the knave is!" [5.1.129]), we might argue that within the space of the theater, both actors and playgoers are joint contributors to a process of ingestion, digestion, and refinement of the air that circulates between them that results ultimately in its purification. The notion that what Hamlet calls "more rawer breath" (5.2.108) might be refined, in the collective "stithy" of the theater, into something more delectable is clearly idealistic, and certainly no virulent antitheatrical writer or preacher would have acknowledged it as a genuine possibility. But the invitation that the play extends to playgoers is that each of them might become a pipe through which a sweeter air might flow.

The connection between the exchange of breath in the theater to which the play speaks and Hamlet as the instrument of purgation was beautifully suggested in Trevor Nunn's 2004 production of the play for the Old Vic. Nunn used the material of breath in a pointed way in relation to Hamlet's act of killing the king. This act has important legal aspects that I pursue at greater length elsewhere.[39] Let me here offer simply the upshot, which is that Hamlet, as he strikes at Claudius, is in the terms of the case that the Clown nonsensically redacts in his presentation of the "three branches" of action, *Hales v. Petit,* a dead man walking: he is already killed, but still capable of taking action against Claudius. At the moment that Hamlet discovers that he is killed, and just before he seizes the opportunity to act, Hamlet inhabits a strange liminal space and moment between life and death. He is about to die, but is in some sense at this moment at his most alive, for he is free to take action against Claudius not only in "perfect conscience" but also without anyone, including any representative of the law and his own accusatory self, being able to "charge" him with anything at all. In that moment, the young actor playing Hamlet in Nunn's production, Ben Whishaw, took a sturdy, deep, deliberate breath, the performance of which was inescapable. The audience watched the actor/character breathe, and then the breath result in an action: Whishaw rose, stepped forward, and touched Tom Mannion, the actor playing Claudius, with his foil so gently, so lightly, that the foil barely connected with Mannion's body. By preceding these actions with such a deliberate performance of the act of breathing, Whishaw and Nunn turned the moment and the play into an exhibition of contemporary Shakespearean performance as a vehicle not for Shakespeare's "voice" (as Bill Worthen has shown us so many contemporary acting manuals advocate)[40] but for the replaying of the circulation of the material in which Shakespeare and his fellow actors dealt, the material of breath.

The text of *Hamlet* offers its most explicit and its final expression of the idea of the theater as a place for the exchange of breath in Hamlet's final speech. As the play draws to a close, Hamlet requires that Horatio continue to "draw breath" in this harsh world awhile so that he may tell Hamlet's story (5.2.331). Horatio conceives his role as storyteller, as executor of the legacy Hamlet has left him, as a passing on of Hamlet's voice and breath: he will speak "from his mouth whose voice will draw on more"

(5.2.375). Speaking from Hamlet's "mouth," Horatio becomes a vessel for, or pipe whereon, that voice may play, but more important the figure for the transfer of Hamlet's breath to others. He functions as the audience's proxy, eating once of the air that exudes from Hamlet with his final utterance, in that string of O's that Bruce Smith has called Hamlet's "omega."[41] This omega is not, however, only an expression of Hamlet in sound or as sound, as Smith suggests. The string of O's signifies the moment in which the actor looses Hamlet's breath, setting it free for uptake and safe-keeping by Horatio. With that string of O's, the actor playing Hamlet performs the loss of the character's life, but as he does so, or to do so, must let loose his own breath. Hold up your hand before your mouth while breathing Hamlet's string of O's and you will feel a gentle variant of the exhalation of breath that the actor is called upon to perform. The character's breath and the actor's exhalation are in fact enfolded, and that which is "fained" and that which is "real" here collapse into one another; in the fiction, the character dies and in the space of the Globe the actor playing him passes on something material to the constituency around him—not something "like Odours," not something that "resembles the Wind"—but breath itself. As a result, two things occur: the character who imagined that he would be happy "bounded in a nutshell" becomes, within the larger shell of the theater, a kind of food, a figurative nut meat, for playgoers; at the same time, along with that "fained" food, or the imaginary consumption, the playgoers in the Globe who scent the air for the perfume or exhalation of the actor take in something that is not "fained" at all, the breath that is set loose to disperse among them in motes.[42]

With this loosing of the actor's breath in the play's closing moments, the play simply makes explicit what has been occurring during the entire passage of the actors' two hours' traffic upon the stage (or four hours, as the case may be). The play in performance has been offering up to its constituency from its start a fare that not only takes the character of its interaction with the audience well beyond the bounds of mimesis, but also takes it beyond Wright's goal for all those who deal in passionate presentations, which is to find the most effective way of communicating passion to "the common people."[43] By appealing to their sense of smell and encouraging them to believe that they are partaking of a particular delicacy, the play not only reminded playgoers that they were processing machines, but invited them to feel what would otherwise be so usual with them, so common, that it would go unnoted, unmarked, the progress of air through the matter of the body. The act of breathing would thus become one means of experiencing the subtle way in which we are continuously infiltrated by materials from outside us and would thus unsettle or make more tenuous the apparent or provisional integrity of human identity as it is defined in or around the vessel or machine of the body. The invitation of the play, then, to eat the air or scent it is an invitation to experience a heightened sense of one's own embodiment along with a paradoxical liberation from it: the process of "feeling smells" or of experiencing the felt progress of air through the machine of one's own body induces a sense of participation in a larger body, a body united and constituted by the breath that passes in a continual state of flux through one and through others in an endless scattering and dispersal, and reconstitution and remembering, that challenges the integrity of individuals even as it animates and revitalizes them.[44]

If, then, the play is, in performance, the occasion for a form of "breathing time" (5.2.156), a form of recreation in which playgoers may experience the propulsive, animating and generative force of breath, and find themselves, through the act of breathing, or their eating of the "chameleon's dish," made part of a larger "miraculous organ," the sensual experience afforded by smell or the physicality of using the diaphragm to take the breath of actors into the machine of the body is unique to the moment of performance: words in printed form may conjure up images in the mind's eye and sounds in the mind's ear, but there is no substitute for the materiality of the breath exchanged within the Wooden O. On the page, Hamlet's final string of O's may hint at the passage of breath onstage, but it cannot act, do, or perform it. The participation in the theater's "breathing time," is in short utterly and completely ephemeral: it is the "perfume and suppliance of a minute" (1.3.9). But by capturing some idea of this ephemeral aspect of the Shakespearean theater for us, the play as printed suggests why it pleased all in performance: all playgoers needed to do to have the core of its theatrical experience, and partake of its finest fare, was "scent the air" for the actor's loosed breath. Then they too might become, in Shakespeare's "stithy," things of "quick sail" (5.2.101).

When we recall that the voice and breath that the actor playing Hamlet passes on or disperses to the audience has its origin within the fiction in the Ghost, and its origins as theatrical representation in the person of Shakespeare, the loosing of the breath that playgoers capture when they "scent the air" has implications for our understanding of the character of

Shakespearean authorship. This play makes play-going about the giving away of words and breath—for a price, it is true, the price of the penny given at the gate, but for a price not commensurate with what is yielded in return. In the sense that the price paid cannot equal what is bestowed in return, the play in performance is a gift, and the gift is in large part a sharing out of the writer and his conceptions.[45] The aesthetic of the play thus counters materialist arguments that would construe the Shakespearean theater as thoroughly embroiled in, and unable to extricate itself from, market forces. I suggest that Hamlet's disavowal of a proprietary relationship with words—to Claudius's claim "These words are not mine," Hamlet retorts "No, nor mine now" (3.2.94–96)—stands, at least in relation to this play, as a gesture of disavowal on Shakespeare's part: the organ of the O takes his words and disperses them to all gathered there, and as they part from him, whether or not they issue from his own mouth, in the part that he takes on actor, or from other actors' mouths, the words are no longer his own. With this play, Shakespeare uses the "aire" to "set passions aloft,"[46] and that air or wind, in the form of each of the actors' breaths, disperses both words and breath for eating by all of the playgoers gathered there. With that dispersal, the perfume of the gift infuses through the Globe and scatters.[47] We cannot "scent the air" as playgoers in the Globe did to "recover the wind" that was set free there (3.2.340): the perfume is lost. It was always lost, for at the end of each performance the "wind" moved out the Globe's large mouth, back to the air beyond its shell again; and the playgoers moved out the other points of egress in that body, that shell, in which they had been all temporarily bound together in a sharing of space and breath, to scatter too.[48] We can, however, use the artifact of the text to articulate the remains of the theatrical experience, and reconstruct our sense of the gift, the thing shared, by recapturing an idea of what *Hamlet* offered up to playgoers, for their "breathing time."

Notes

I would like to thank Will West and Stephen Deng for their comments on an earlier version of this paper at the 2004 meeting of the Shakespeare Association of America. Their comments were instrumental in turning me in the direction that I pursue here.

1. This and all other references to the play are, unless otherwise noted, to *The Tragical History of Hamlet Prince of Denmark*, ed. A. R. Braunmuller (Penguin, 2001).

2. Annabel Patterson, *Shakespeare and the Popular Voice* (Oxford: Basil Blackwell, 1989), 13-14. Patterson seeks to mediate between opposing views of the Shakespearean

theater as represented by the work of Ann Jennalie Cook and Walter Cohen, Cook arguing that Shakespeare wrote for a "privileged" educated audience and Cohen that the Shakespearean theater catered to a "social heterocosm" that included "artisans and shopkeepers" and was in turn shaped by their desire for a populist and nationalist theater (15-17). She also resists Stephen Greenblatt's theory of containment ("We need to return to a less impersonal, less totalitarian account of how Shakespeare's theater probably functioned"[25]). To do this, she argues that Hamlet, a transgressive and radical character, speaks in a "mocking, dynamic, subversive, popular, and 'general' voice" (98), and that the play opposes "academicism," then and now (29-31), and that with this voice, and its critique of certain ways of thinking, the play speaks simultaneously to "the judicious few" and the "underprivileged many" (100). She posits that the play displaces philosophical speculation to restore to playgoers "the ground, the trust in material reality, that philosophical speculation had excavated way" (118). Here I pursue *the means* by which it does so.

3. See Steven Mullaney, "Mourning and Misogyny: *Hamlet, The Revenger's Tragedy* and the Final Progress of Elizabeth I, 1600-1607," *Shakespeare Quarterly* 45:2 (1994): 139-62, esp. p. 144.

4. Stephen Gosson, *The Schoole of Abuse* (London, 1587), STC 12098, 50.

5. Ibid., 52.

6. For one discussion of culinary metaphors in antitheatrical rhetoric, see Jeremy Lopez *Theatrical Convention and Audience Response in Early Modern Drama* (Cambridge: Cambridge University Press, 2003), 27-31.

7. For Anthony Dawson's discussion of the ways in which Shakespeare's theater offered Shakespeare's first audiences an experience related to and perhaps a substitution for their experience of Christ's real presence in the Mass, see chapter 1, "Performance and Participation," 11-37, in Anthony Dawson and Paul Yachnin, *The Culture of Playgoing in Shakespeare's England: A Collaborative Debate* (Cambridge University Press, 2001). P. A. Skantze recapitulates Dawson's arguments in terms of a "secular transubstantiation" in *Stillness in Motion in the Seventeenth-Century Theatre* (New York: Routledge, 2003), 15.

8. Those who wish to argue that Hamlet offers its audience an experience of breath or air that is spiritually or religiously inflected could argue that it extends a Catholic theatrical tradition of creating an experience of the divine in the form of the Holy Ghost through appeals to the senses that is best epitomized in the medieval drama in the *Digby Play of Mary Magdalene.*

9. In " 'A History of the Air': Shakespeare and the Evaporating Self," a paper delivered to the Shakespeare Association of America in March 2002, Carla Mazzio discussed the toxicity or noxiousness of the air that playgoers had to breathe in Elizabethan and Jacobean London in relation to texts by Shakespeare, Bacon, and Donne. In that paper, she raises the possibility that the Shakespearean drama may have offered a "restorative poetics"; through weeping, she suggests, audience members may have brought about an "elemental alteration, self-evaporation, a 'clearing of the air' of the self, soul and environment."

10. Robert Weimann's suggestion that "air" puns on "heir" puts another political aspect of the statement into play. Hamlet is left eating air as the heir, that is, as someone whose own claim to the throne has been preempted, at least temporarily, by Claudius's. Weimann discusses the kinetic energies that are embodied and released in Hamlet, but not the impli-

cations of this statement for the play's theory of performance. See *Author's Pen and Actor's Voice: Playing and Writing in Shakespeare's Theatre,* ed. Helen Higbee and William West (Cambridge: Cambridge University Press, 2000), 176–77.

11. Francis Bacon, *Sylva Silvarum,* qtd. in Bruce R. Smith, "Hearing Green: Logomarginality in *Hamlet,*" Conclusion, *Early Modern Literary Studies* 7.1 (May, 2001): 5.1–7 <URL: http://purl.oclc.org/emls/07-1/logomarg/conclus.htm>, 4.

12. John Webster, qtd. in Joseph Roach, *The Player's Passion: Studies in the Science of Acting* (Newark: University of Delaware Press, 1985), 32.

13. See chapter 1 of *The Player's Passion,* especially 44–45.

14. See Bruce Smith, "Hearing Green: Logomarginality in *Hamlet,*" Physical Frame. *Early Modern Literary Studies* 7.1 (May 2001): 2.1–4 <URL: http://purl.oclc.org/emls/07-1/logo marg/physic.htm>, 2. See also Smith's more recent essay, "Hearing Green," in *Reading the Early Modern Passions: Essays in the Cultural History of Emotion,* ed. Gail Kern Paster, Katherine Rowe, and Mary Floyd-Wilson (Philadephia: University of Pennsylvania Press, 2004).

15. See Smith, "Hearing Green: Logomarginality in *Hamlet,*" Physiological Frame. *Early Modern Literary Studies* 7.1 (May 2001): 3.1–3 <URL: http://purl.oclc.org/emls/07-1/logo marg/physiol.htm>, 2.

16. Thomas Wright, *The Passions of the Minde in Generall,* ed. Thomas O. Sloan (Urbana: University of Illinois Press, 1971), 168.

17. Ibid., 174.

18. Ibid.

19. Ibid., 170.

20. See Gail Kern Paster, "Nervous Tension: Networks of Blood and Spirit in the Early Modern Body," 106–25, in *The Body in Parts: Fantasies of Corporeality in Early Modern Europe,* ed. Carla Mazzio and David Hillman (New York and London: Routledge, 1997), 116.

21. Ibid., 110.

22. Ibid., 108–9.

23. Gail Kern Paster, "Roasted in Wrath and Fire: The Ecology of the Passions in *Hamlet* and *Othello,*" 25–76, in *Humoring the Body: Emotions and the Shakespearean Stage* (Chicago and London: University of Chicago Press, 2004), esp. 34–40.

24. The word is Robert Burton's translation of a passage on air in the work of Levinus Lemnius, as quoted in Paster, "Roasted," 41.

25. Wright, *Passions,* 170.

26. Ibid., 176.

27. Ibid., 151.

28. Ibid., 177.

29. Ibid., 255.

30. *OED,* entry for "scent" v. <http://80-dictionary.oed.com.webvoy.uwindsor.ca:2048/ cgi/entry/00215171>. The obsolete meaning is the third definition that the OED offers: "3. To exhale an odour, to smell. [So F. *sentir.*] Now *rare* or *Obs.*"(October 27, 2004).

31. *OED,* entry for "scent" v., <http://80-dictionary.oed.com.webvoy.uwindsor.ca:2048/ cgi/entry/00215171> (October 27, 2004).

32. See Weimann, *Author's Pen,* 123.

33. Jane Tylus, " 'Par Accident': The Public Work of Early Modern Theater," 253–71, in *Reading the Early Modern Passions,* 269.

34. Wright, *Passions,* 179.

35. Ibid., 176.

36. Stephen Orgel, "The Play of Conscience," 129–42, in *The Authentic Shakespeare and Other Problems of the Early Modern Stage* (New York and London: Routledge, 2002), especially 133–34.

37. Paster, "Roasted," 41.

38. Paster, "Nervous Tension," 110.

39. "Hamlet's Cause," in *Shakespeare and the Law,* ed. Karen Cunningham and Constance Jordan (New York: Palgrave, forthcoming).

40. See chapter 3 of W. B. Worthen, *Shakespeare and the Authority of Performance* (Cambridge: Cambridge University Press, 1997). Worthen quotes the actor Simon Callow on the experience of acting as the "incomparable feeling" of having "another person . . . breath[e] through your lungs" (144).

41. See Smith, "Hearing Green: Logomarginality in *Hamlet,*" Dramaturgical Frame. *Early Modern Literary Studies* 7.1 (May 2001): 4.1–4 <URL: http://purl.oclc.org/emls/07-1/logo marg/dramat.htm>, 3.

42. The line "O God, I could be bounded in a nutshell, and count myself a king of infinite space—were it not that I have bad dreams" occurs only in the Folio. See the *Riverside Shakespeare,* 2.2.254.

43. Wright, *Passions,* 175.

44. The process of "feeling smells" therefore works to a very different end from civilizing processes that work to establish various kinds of propriety, inculcate certain forms of behavior, and uphold the integrity of the individual. In "Acting with Tact," Mazzio discusses how civilizing processes give rise to the mode of behavior we call "tact," which encourages sensitivity to "a kind of vulnerable air in the space between persons." Tact, we could argue, treats the "vulnerable air" between bodies as a body in its own right to discourage contact or make any move toward contact through touch tentative; the process of "feeling smells" breaks "tact" down, as it involves intimate contact between bodies at a remove. See Mazzio, "Acting with Tact: Touch and Theater in the Renaissance," 159–86, in *Sensible Flesh: On Touch in Early Modern Culture,* ed. Elizabeth D. Harvey (Philadelphia: University of Pennsylvania Press, 2003), esp. 186.

45. Robert Weimann also writes of the economic exchange that takes place in terms of some kind of return to the audience: "that audience, which had not come empty-handed, did not leave empty-minded. Their contribution, a profitable commodity, was rewarded with a volatile sense of 'imaginary puissance.' " His emphasis falls, however, on what Shakespeare's company gets rather than what it gives: "What remained in the theatre was the sum total of all the pennies paid, together with the desire and the need to have more of them from returning audiences." See *Author's Pen,* 216–17.

46. Wright, *Passions,* 168.

47. Here I extend Bruce Smith's notion of the dispersals that take place in the Globe. In "Hearing Green," Smith offers a descriptive formula by which sound leads to "spiritus," which is in turn dispersed through the entire space. He may write of sound, and I, of breath, but

clearly the phenomena of which we write, though they differ crucially, are very intimately related. See Smith, "Hearing Green," Physical frame, 1. Weimann's discussion of digestion in relation to the prologue to *Henry V* and the Globe's space is also a useful point of reference here. I extend his discussion of the ways in which the Globe's space digests things by applying it specifically to the dispersal of breath. See Weimann, *Author's Pen*, 75.

48. Both Smith and Weimann write of the Globe's "canopy," Smith focusing on the actual canopy above the stage and Weimann the canopy of the air to which Hamlet refers. Smith focuses on the actual canopy to explain how the shell of the Wooden O contributes to the acoustical properties and experience of plays in performance: "the presence of a canopy, however, meant that sounds originating under that canopy were reflected from top to bottom as well as from side to side, producing a more diffuse, harder to locate sound," he writes. See "Hearing Green," Physical frame, 2. Weimann suggests that Hamlet's reference to the canopy of the air "conjoins the global circumference of this 'goodly frame the earth' with the protruding place of the stage as a 'promontory' jutting out into the pit . . . ." (*Author's Pen*, 215). Imagining the canopy as a mouth through which the air outside the theater is ingested and then released again gives us another way of talking about Hamlet's claim that "excellent plays" offer up matter that is "well digested."

All Swell That End Swell:
Dropsy, Phantom Pregnancy, and
the Sound of Deconception in
All's Well That Ends Well

JONATHAN GIL HARRIS

I BEGIN WITH A sound premise—or rather, a premise about sound: the title of Shakespeare's *All's Well That Ends Well* conceals a punning phantom. This is, after all, a play of whose characters one might say less that All's Well than All Swell. Pregnancy, tumescence, puffing, and as Patricia Parker has noted, dilation are arguably the play's signature movements.[1] While Helen's putative pregnancy at play's end might suggest to some readers that All Who Swell End Swell, in the hokey American sense, other references to swelling in the play don't lend themselves to such blithe interpretation. Paroles's quips on the fruits of sex in the first scene serve to align what he calls bodily "increase" with an "undermin[ing]" that will "blow you up" (1.1.113).[2] The King's fistula, which in the play's source is described as a "swelling upon his breast," threatens rather than produces life.[3] And just as strikingly, the King's advice to Bertram after the latter has protested Helen's choice of him for a husband—"Where great additions swell's, and virtue none, / It is a dropsied honour" (2.3.123-24)—underlines the play's insistently pathological coding of swelling.

The King's invocation of "dropsy" suggests how the reservedly optimistic thrust of the play's title is potentially shadowed by another, sicker trajectory. This might be a play in which All's Well That Ends Well, as is suggested by the providential movement from crisis to resolution embodied in Helen's seemingly successful conception and the promise of a next generation. But it is also a play in which All Swell That End Swell, with

169

its intimation of a movement that is recursive or pleonastic, embodied in a sick swelling that bears no fruit other than itself. For if the trajectory of All's Well That Ends Well is exocentric, directed toward a future that transcends and redeems current dilemmas, the movement of All Swell That End Swell is relentlessly endocentric, where the "end" is both syntactically and chronologically impossible to differentiate from the "beginning." This movement of swelling without clear issue or resolution is the condition that I term deconception.

In this essay, I tease out the macrocosmic implications of deconception in *All's Well That Ends Well*—that is, what the play's instances of swelling without clear issue might reveal about the larger environments its bodies inhabit. Recent studies of the premodern body, most notably by Gail Kern Paster and Mary Floyd-Wilson, have reacquainted us with the fundamentally ecological understandings of corporeality that characterized cultures from ancient Greece to Renaissance England. In the Hippocratic and Galenic medical traditions, the embodied self was in and of the world, linked to the latter not only as its microcosmic template but also as a symbiotic organism with which it shared elemental properties such as wind and water. And indeed, one could make the case that swelling links the bodies of *All's Well*'s characters to larger environmental forces. But I am interested in how the play stages a somewhat different macrocosm. The early modern cosmology that rendered the human body both a component and a map of the larger universe did more than imagine the body of man and the body of the world. As numerous Tudor and Stuart writers insisted, these two bodies were the extreme instances of a mediated continuum that also included the body politic. In *The Boke of the Governor,* for example, Thomas Elyot figured the "publike weale" as a "body lyuyng, compact," a system whose organization corresponds to "the order, that god hath put generally in all his creatures."[4] For Elyot, this was no mere analogy. The body was instead embedded in a divinely authorized network of correspondence and symbolic substitution that was political as much as physical.

Rather than locate the ecology of swelling exclusively in the relation of the body to the physical world, I follow Elyot in reemphasizing the political ecosystem within which it also participates. *All's Well*'s swelling bodies are interarticulated with conceptions of the body politic in two ways. First, the swollen body—whether pregnant or pathologically bloated— provides a homological template for the body of the nation, fruitfully swollen with the promise of a future generation or distended with the barren disorders of the present. But the swollen body is not just a map of the *corpus politicum*. It is also the gateway into a social macrocosm of sound, whose elements are joined to each other not through meaningful *homology* between the body of man and the body politic but through far more random *homophonic* relations. As will become apparent, early modern writers identified a certain type of swollen body by its production of seemingly significant sounds—sounds that do not have transparent meanings, however, but instead signify only by sounding *like* other sounds. This sonorous swelling that promises yet defers the delivery of meaning is the paradox I am terming deconception; it is, I will argue, the condition of Shakespeare's play. Deconception assumes, even as it destabilizes, a theory of signification embodied in the tension between visible conception and homophonic emptiness that characterizes early modern accounts of pregnancy and dropsy. This tension, I will also argue, literally resonates with the white noise of its historical moment, and in ways that underscore how swollen bodies, pregnant or dropsied, were thoroughly implicated in discourses of the English body politic. Swelling in *All's Well That Ends Well* is a condition inseparable from political problems endemic in late Tudor England, particularly in the declining years of its childless monarchs' reigns.

From Conception to Concept

The King's reference to "dropsy" highlights the play's linking of problems of swelling and problems of naming. It is worth examining his remark in full:

> Where great additions swell's, and virtue none,
> It is a dropsied honour. Good alone
> Is good without a name, vileness is so:
> The property by what it is should go,
> Not by the title.
> (2.3.123–27)

In his warning to Bertram, the King draws an implicit distinction between a dropsied swelling derived from the accumulation of mere titles or names, and a virtuous swelling that "is good without a name." The accumulation of unpropertied titles puffs up the accumulator illegitimately, bloating him with phantom signifieds—phantom inasmuch as they are simultaneously invoked yet invalidated, present yet absent.[5]

By contrast, the virtuous sweller needs no title—she contains within her the "property" or thing itself. This distinction glances ahead to Helen, swollen at play's end if not by virtue, than at least by Bertram's and her baby. Her pregnancy entails a privileging of both referent and concept over name. This much is made clear by how Helen's unborn child is presented as the solution to not simply a matrimonial but also a linguistic riddle, posed by Diana:

> Dead though she be she feels her young one kick.
> So there's my riddle; one that's dead is quick.
> And now behold the meaning.
> (5.3.299-301)

The relentless riddling of *All's Well That Ends Well,* which works to defer any clear signified, is seemingly resolved by Diana's speech in favor of a singular concept or conception. This literally embodies the play's transcendence of equivocal titles, including its own, through teleological movement toward a pregnant "meaning" that can be "beheld." To the extent that it models successful signification, and the transcendence of visible concept over mere title, Helen's pregnancy echoes Augustine's repeated figuration of the Virgin Mary as the vessel for the living word of God, whereby the mother is venerated for the logos she bears: "Mary, too, is blessed, because she heard the word of God and kept it. . . . Christ as truth was in Mary's mind, Christ as flesh in Mary's womb; that which is in the mind is greater than what is carried in the womb."[6] Like the pregnant Mary, Helen seemingly embodies an ideal of transparent signification, carrying within her a plenitude of meaning derived from mental as much as from sexual conception. Admittedly the mere "titles" that the King belittles *are* at stake in Helen's pregnancy: by conceiving, she acquires for herself—at least in Bertram's eyes—the legitimate title of "wife." But the latter is a name that derives from the fact of Helen's conception, unlike those dropsied titles where name precedes, and is never quite delivered of, concept.

Yet to embrace this logocentric reading of the play, according to which All's Well That Ends Well, is to arbitrarily refuse the power of All Swell That End Swell, in which the accumulation of uncertain titles cannot help but obstruct the movement to conception. What I want to show is how Shakespeare's play, in its invocation of dropsy, obliquely mines a premodern discourse of phantom pregnancy that potentially contaminates and throws into question the play's issue. As we will see, the King's reference to dropsied swelling acquires considerable power when read in conjunction with the canon of midwife manuals from the Middle Ages to the late seventeenth century, in which dropsy figures prominently. Indeed, one might say that the premodern discourse of pregnancy is equally a discourse of dropsy; as the King's implied differentiation of "dropsied honour" from "virtuous" pregnancy suggests, the one species of swelling could not be imagined without the other.

Dropsical Ultrasound

Dropsy is a term that has more or less fallen out of the English language. Deriving from the Greek *hydrops,* or water, it was widely understood in the humoral schema as a swelling of the belly caused by an excess of a waterish humor or phlegm. As a result, many early modern physicians understood dropsy to be a pathological condition induced by heavy drinking, whether of alcoholic or nonalcoholic liquids. Thomas Sydenham, in his treatise on the disease, wrote that "great drinkers are most subject to the *dropsy.*"[7] But the affliction was not attributed simply to waterish superfluity. Galenic practitioners customarily distinguished between three types of dropsical swelling, each of which had a different cause. Whereas Ascites and Anasarca were both believed to be swellings arising from an excess of water, a third, Timpanites, was seen as the product of excess wind or *"Ventosa."*[8]

The centrality of wind to Timpanites would seem to link dropsy with the "pneumatic character" of premodern corporeality discussed by Gail Kern Paster in *Humoring the Body.*[9] As Shigehisa Kuriyama notes,[10] the Greek word for both breath and wind—*pneuma*—is illustrative of the symbiotic relationship that ancient Greek practitioners of medicine, such as Hippocrates, believed to obtain between microcosm and macrocosm. In Paster's insightful analysis, this pneumatic symbiosis equally characterizes early modern culture, and foregrounds how the relationship between body and world in Shakespeare's drama is less analogical than ecological. Citing Katharine Eisaman Maus on the difficulty of knowing when "a bodily analogy is really an analogy" and "when we are dealing with metaphor and when with a bare statement of fact," Paster tends to resolve this difficulty in favor of the factual or physical.[11] But I shall argue that an ecological reading of dropsy in *All's Well* need not interpret any given reference to swelling as implying simply a relation between the early modern body and its physical environment. The play's understanding of dropsy equally presumes an ecosystem of sound and (elusive) signification, a macrocosm closer to what Bruce R. Smith, in his brilliant study of the acoustic world of early modern England, has termed "an ecology based on listening."[12] Dropsy's winds blow inside and outside the body, but in a fashion that diverges somewhat from the physical circulations of Paster's and Kuriyama's ecosystems. Instead, dropsy's winds constitute an airy yet sonorous nothing within both the swollen body (the realm of the physiological) and the swollen words that pass between it and other bodies (the realm of the social). My aim here, then, is to recover a pneumatics less of the physical ecosystem than of a swollen body politic that literally re-sounds in deconception.

The symptoms of dropsy in all its incarnations were repeatedly—even obsessively—associated with sound. As its percussive name might suggest, Timpanites in particular prompted such comparisons. In his 1398 translation of Bartholomaeus Anglicus, John of Trevisa asserted that when the "wombe" of a Timpanites victim is struck, "it sowneth as a taboure";[13] the medieval English translation of Lanfranc noted that "it wole sowne as it were a tought lether ful of wynd" and "a tympan";[14] and the Scottish physician Andrew Boorde claimed in the 1540s that Timpanites "doth make ones bely to swell lyke a taber or drounslet."[15] Boorde did not confine sound effects to Timpanites; he noted also that in cases of Ascites, "the bely wyll boll & swell, and wyl make a noyse as a botel halfe full of water."[16] These assessments were still current well into the seventeenth century. In 1612, James Guillemeau wrote that the dropsical belly "soundeth like a Tabour";[17] half a century later, Richard Turner observed that in Ascites, "the Belly swelleth like a Blader, and soundeth like a drum-head."[18] This emphasis on sound is notable, and all the more so in the midwife manuals in which these percussive similes repeatedly appear. In the manner of Derrida's tympan, the drumlike belly of dropsy fails to deliver, offering mere sound in place of meaningful concept or conception.[19] For premodern physicians, the term "ultrasound"—had it existed—would have conjured up not proofs of pregnancy, but its absence. As Nicholas Culpeper observes in 1676, pregnancy "differs from a Dropsie in the Womb"; in the case of the latter, "if you strike vpon the Belly, there is a noise, but not in Conception."[20]

Culpeper's ultrasound test is of especial relevance to the phantom pregnancy of Mary Frith, better known as Moll Cutpurse, the Roaring Girl (the historical figure on whom Middleton and Dekker's play of the same name is based). Frith's alleged diary of 1662 chronicles how, late in life, her

"Belly, from a withered, dryed and wrinckled piece of Skin . . . was grown the titest, roundest *Globe* of flesh, that ever any beautuous young Lady strutted with, to the Ostentation of her Fertility."[21] Notably, the Augustinian language of concept and conception figures in her narrative of swelling: "I could not but proud my self in it; and thought nature had reserved that kindnesse for me at the last, insomuch that I could have almost been impregnated . . . with my own Fancy and Imagination, my *conceit* proving the same with *conception.*"[22] As Moll explains, her swelling was not too much of a miracle by the standards of the day. She observes that "a Woman of my Age then living in *London,* was brought a bed of a Son, which was very certainly true; and an old Parson in the *North,* one Mr. *Vivan,* of neer a Hundred years old, was juvenilized again, and his age renewed, as to all his senses he enjoyed before at Fifty."[23] Moll reads these, and her own, swellings macrocosmically—but in such a way as to connect them not to the physical environment, but to the fortunes of the body politic: "these were signal Miracles and presages of a *Revolution* in the state,"[24] that is, the forthcoming restoration of the monarchy.

This optimistic gynecological and political reading of her swelling, however, is undermined by her discovery that her putative pregnancy is a phantom. Employing Culpeper's ultrasound test, Moll rediagnoses her bloated belly as "a *Dropsie*": "there was no blood that was *generative* in my belly, but only that *destructive* of the *grape,* which by my excesses was now turned into water, so that the Tympanied skin thereof sounded like a Conduit door."[25] Moll's "tympanied" belly underscores the sonorous quality of phantom pregnancy. It also foregrounds how, as in the medical literature, the key trope of dropsy is simile: the struck belly of the Timpanites patient always sounds *like* something else—a tabor, a bottle, a tympan, a drumhead, or in this case, a conduit door.[26] And that door is itself instructive. It is a barred entrance, behind which lies nothing certain other than watery darkness, an endless network of pipes, and the empty reverberation of sound. Moll's dropsy figures a very different body politic from that implied by her pregnancy. Rather than a teleological movement forward to a *visible* signified, as instanced by the "Ostentation of Fertility" or the "signal . . . *Revolution* in the state" promised by what had previously seemed to be her successful conception, Moll's Timpanites entails a recursive slippage through simile to other empty *noises.* What lies behind the conduit door is a social macrocosm of sound, characterized by a potentially infinite chain of homophonic substitutions.

The premodern midwife manuals—like Moll Cutpurse—rhetorically distinguish between the meaningful conception of pregnancy and the sonorous deception of dropsy. But they also—again like Moll, who initially believes herself pregnant—acknowledge and in some cases even insist on the difficulty of telling the difference. "Ther ben many diverse tokens to know oone from another," says the author of the first English gynecological textbook, the so-called *Medieval Woman's Guide to Health*. Yet when a woman suffers from an excess of "wynde & of fleumatyke humours," she "swellith with this ydropseie as though sche were with childe."[27] Jakob Ruff, the sixteenth-century German physician, observed that women suffering from "hydropsie . . . swell, as if they were conceived of child" and that the symptoms of the disease "are also common to a true conception."[28] Louise Bourgeois Boursier, the seventeenth-century French midwife, similarly notes that "False conception hath many signs, common with the true conception," including "suppression of the flowers, depraved appetite, vomitings, swelling of the belly, and of the breasts."[29] Culpeper observes in his *Directory for Midwives* that "many are the wayes Authors have left for women to know whether they be with Child or not";[30] but he also concedes that in cases of dropsy, women exhibit the principal symptoms of pregnancy, with the consequence that "Doctors and Midwives are often deceived"[31]—a term frequently used in gynecological and midwife manuals as an antithesis to "conceived."

There are numerous instances of such deception. James Guillemeau, the French king's physician, writes of a woman who was believed to be with child, but was then "deliuered of certaine gallons of water."[32] The confusion could work the other way. William Sermon claimed that "many have undertook to Cure women, telling them that they had the Dropsie, &c. (when they were with child)."[33] Indeed, such was the difficulty of telling the difference that Timpanites and its colloquial synonyms also became derogatory synonyms for pregnancy. Dick Tarlton speaks of a maid who "fell sicke, and her disease was thought to be a timpany with two heeles."[34] And Richard Carew notes that "our ladies . . . haue so many *prophylactica* to keepe their bellies from tympanizing."[35] The difficulty of telling the difference is particularly apparent in medical accounts of dropsy that effectively transform Timpanites into an aberrant subset of pregnancy. In his treatise on dropsy, Sydenham observes that several kinds of the disease exhibit "the signs of pregnancy," either through "false conception" of a "preternatural fleshy excrescence" called a *"mola,"* or by an excess of wind:

"And such," Sydenham writes, "feel the child move from the customary time, to the usual time of delivery, and withal are sick between times, as pregnant women commonly are, and their breasts swell and have milk in them."[36] Here dropsy is no longer a straightforward deception; assuming all the signs of pregnancy, including a "false conception" of a "fleshy excrescence"—a process notably different from the *failure* to conceive— the disease deconstructs its fruitful opposite or, rather, deconceives it.

Deconceived Successions

The difficulty of telling the difference between pregnancy and dropsy was more than just a medical or semiological problem. It also became a problem of pressing political significance in the mid-sixteenth century. The childlessness of Queen Mary was a matter of considerable concern to those who hoped for a Catholic succession. Hence there was widespread relief in the spring of 1555, when rumors spread that Mary was, at last, expecting. In May, the merchants of Antwerp received news that the queen had been delivered of a baby boy on April 30, and the church bells of London pealed in celebration. But the joy proved premature; no child had arrived. On June 1, Mary claimed to feel labor pains; her doctors predicted a delivery date of June 6, which they subsequently revised to June 24 and then July 1. The French ambassador privately speculated that she might be suffering from a tumor or a *mola,* but the queen and her lady courtiers continued to insist that she was indeed pregnant. Though some were still hopeful of an imminent royal birth as late as December (long after her husband Philip had given up any hope and left the country on August 26), it became increasingly clear that Mary's pregnancy was a phantom.[37]

For Protestant commentators, Mary's failure to come to term acquired an unmistakable, if complicated, pathological dimension. Resorting to the characteristic deception/conception binary of the midwife manuals, John Foxe claimed that Queen Mary was "deceived by a Timpany,"[38] an assessment echoed by Holinshed: "she was deceiued by a timpanie or some other like disease, to thinke hirselfe with child, and was not."[39] Indeed, Foxe goes so far as to suggest that the cause of Mary's death was her "false conception . . . that turned into a dropsy."[40] Equally prominent in Foxe's narrative of Mary's terminal illness is the problem of the succession. In an ironic invocation of the biblical Mary, Foxe talks of the crib prepared for her English namesake's unborn child, which (he claims) bore the inscription

"Quam Mariae sobolem, Deus optime, summe, dedisti / Anglis incolumem redde, tuere, rege [The child which Thou to Mary, O Lord of might! Hast sent, / To England's joy, in health preserve,—keep, and defend!]." Foxe immediately appends his own "Carminis Inversio" [inverted prayer]: "Quam Mariae sobolem, Deus optime, summe, negasti, / Hanc ferat auspiciis Elisabetha tuis [The child which Thou to Mary, O Lord of might! hast denied, / May Elizabeth bear by Thy auspices!]." Foxe, in other words, reads the Tudor succession as an instance of All's Well That Ends Well, inasmuch as Mary's sterile Catholic line gives way to Elizabeth's bountiful Protestant one. With an astute pun on "deliver," Foxe wryly notes "what cause we Englishmen have to render most earnest thanks unto Almighty God, who so mercifully . . . hath delivered us in this case; which otherwise might have opened such a window to the Spaniards."[41]

Yet inescapably lurking in Foxe's narrative is also the pathological tale of All Swell That End Swell, fueled by his conviction that Mary's failed pregnancy allegorizes a larger, national failure to move forward. Here he draws on a customary figuration of dropsy as a false conception whose fraudulence also figures an illegitimate social power. We see precisely this figure in the King's reference to "dropsied honour" in *All's Well;* it appears also in John Donne's invective against "this Timpany, or false conception, by which spiritual power is blowne vp, and swelled with temporall,"[42] and in Robert Burton's complaint about the Pharisee "puffed up with this Timpany of self-conceit."[43] Protestant diagnoses of Mary's affliction likewise reassert the difference between dropsy and pregnancy at not a physiological, but a moral level; they do so by employing a rhetorical figure of diabolical inversion, in which Catholicism perverts the true church, dropsy perverts pregnancy, and deception perverts conception. Hence William Camden, noting like Foxe that Mary ultimately died of "a tympany,"[44] asserts in his history of Elizabeth's reign that "the Reader may be pleased to looke a little backe into the Reigne of [Elizabeth's] immediate predecessor Queene *Mary,* and consider with himselfe, how unfortunate, how unprosperous, how disasterous it was to her selfe and the whole Realme, how all things went backward, and nothing succeeded well."[45] Mary's reign is collapsed into her pregnancy, or rather its failure: both are unprosperous, incapable of succession, tugging antiteleologically "backward." Protestant historians thus fashioned Mary's regime as the structural antithesis to the reign of Elizabeth, which was styled as the embodiment of a swelling progress.

There is a second way in which Foxe's narrative of Mary performs All Swell That End Swell. If the first is homological, whereby Mary's swollen yet barren body stands in for the sterile English body politic, the second is homophonic. Foxe's discussion of the inscription on Mary's crib—"Quam Mariae sobolem"—depends on a pun that bloats the signifier "Maria" and robs it of any clear meaning that can be beheld: Mary the fruitful Virgin blurs homophonically into Mary the barren queen. The inscription suffers at one and the same time from an overabundance and a deficiency of meaning; it generates an acoustic *mola* that converts Mother Mary into a deconceptive Moll, within whom concept and conception are equally deferred. The sonorous specter of deconception, however, is exorcised in Foxe's "Carminis Inversio" by its syntagmatic and paradigmatic movement from "Maria" to "Elizabeth," whose conceptual singularity promises semiotic as much as corporeal and political issue.

The only problem, of course, is that the virtuous Protestant opponent of dropsical Catholic swelling herself never conceived. The succession under Elizabeth was therefore a fraught issue—and all the more so in 1603, the approximate date when Shakespeare wrote *All's Well That Ends Well*. Elizabeth's childlessness prompted writers to embrace other, nonreproductive metaphors of royal succession. Chief among these was the image of the phoenix. In Thomas Dekker's *Magnificent Entertainment,* which recounts the various spectacles produced for King James's coronation pageant in 1603, an actor eulogizes Elizabeth by mourning her as "A *Phoenix* [that] liu'd and died in the Sunnes breast." The actor then addresses James as "that sacred *Phoenix,* that doest rise / From th'ashes of the first."[46] The image is reproduced by Shakespeare in *All Is True (King Henry VIII)* when Cranmer predicts that Elizabeth will be a "pattern to all princes living with her, / And all that shall succeed"; on her death, "the maiden phoenix, / Her ashes new create another heir / As great in admiration as herself" (5.4.22-23, 40-42). As Madhavi Menon has noted, however, this nonreproductive vision of succession is rhetorically vexed. With its "endogamous endgame" that repeats the past rather than moving forward from it, Cranmer's remark constitutes "a rhetorical inflection of history that seriously compromises the ends to which history is deployed."[47] Indeed, Hegel believed the sterility of the Orient to be exemplified by the myth of the self-resurrecting phoenix. This myth, Hegel claimed, "is only Asiatic; oriental, not occidental." By contrast, occidental "spirit—consuming the envelope of its existence—does not merely pass into another envelope, nor rise rejuvenescent from the ashes of its previous form; it comes forth exalted, glorified, a purer spirit."[48] The Asiatic phoenix, then, was Hegel's version of Foxe's Catholic dropsy: both are the hallmarks of deconception, of reproduction without progression.

As I shall show, *All's Well That Ends Well* is suffused with the rhetoric of Elizabethan accounts of Mary's dropsy, particularly the language of "things going backward," not succeeding, and swelling. Like Protestant histories of Mary's phantom pregnancy and the transition to Elizabeth's supposedly productive reign, the play also expresses nervousness about the efficacy of the pregnant ideal it supposedly embodies. Like Foxe's pun on the queen's name, the play generates acoustic *molas* out of its titles. And like Hegel's reading of the phoenix, the play is haunted by the fear that seeming succession may amount to little more than dropsical deconception, and that the end may be merely a sterile repetition of the beginning rather than an advance on it. In the process, we can glimpse something of the widespread anxiety that accompanied the problem of the soon-to-be Jacobean succession.

'S Well

All's Well seems to reproduce the structural opposition of dropsy and pregnancy that pervades midwife manuals and Protestant accounts of Queen Mary's "tympany." Helen's pregnancy, as we have seen, contrasts the barren dropsical swelling that the King warns Bertram against. Her pregnancy also seems to promise succession, the antidote to the specter of retrograde movement that is raised repeatedly throughout *All's Well.* Helen's wit, which the play associates with her ability to conceive mentally and physiologically ("Our remedies oft in ourselves do lie" [1.1.199]), is presented as the teleological antithesis of a widespread idiocy that "doth backward pull / Our slow designs" (1.1.201–2). The failure of French society to produce a new generation as noble as Bertram's father—a failure supposedly voided later by Helen's wit and Bertram's reformation— threatens to produce a culture of "goers-backward" (1.2.48), whether in imagination like the sick King, nostalgically dwelling on memories of Bertram's and Helen's dead fathers, or physically like Paroles, to whom Helen remarks that "you go so much backward when you fight" (1.1.186). The backwardness of the French body politic was a readily available slur in Shakespeare's England, of course, in light of France's recent slide "back" into Catholicism. But it is also subliminally stressed by the King's particular affliction. Though Shakespeare's source-text calls it a "swelling on the breast," the play refashions it as a fistula, an ailment that could be located anywhere on the body but that was most frequently associated with the anus.[49] Like the physical and temporal "goers-backward" of the French court, then, Helen—not to mention *All's Well*'s audience—is forced to peer in the rear.

Helen's manifold powers, then, provide the seeming remedy to the French court's regressive movements. As Alexander Leggatt has noted, "she alone has forgotten the past and is launching with romantic aspirations into the future."[50] Her future-oriented disposition is of a piece with her medicinal skills in healing, which are initially rejected by the backward-looking King.[51] But I would argue that whatever healing powers Helen may possess reside less within her physical potions than within her language. "If thou proceed / As high as word," the King tells her, "my deed shall match thy deed" (2.1.208-9)—in other words, Helen is as good as her word; her language delivers on its promise, and seemingly most literally in the last act, where her pregnancy seems to convert her professed purpose into swelling flesh.[52] Yet I shall suggest that the play also works to destabilize Helen's redemptive swelling and the forward movement it represents. As we will see (or hear), the purposeful succession promised by Helen's pregnancy is deconstructed—deconceived—by *All's Well That Ends Well*'s obsessive rehearsal of the noisy symptoms of dropsy.

One character in particular embodies the dropsical swelling to which Helen's pregnancy is opposed: Paroles. His character and very name, neither of which is in Shakespeare's source-text, draw attention to the play's repeated disparagement of mere "titles" as dropsied *words* that fail to deliver their conceptions. Indeed, Paroles is repeatedly compared to swollen yet empty vessels that recall the sonorous hollowness of Timpanites: a "bubble" (3.6.6), a "pasty" (4.3.120), a "good drum" (5.3.254). When Lafeu first "exposes" him, he refers to Paroles as a "vessel" (2.3.198) and a "casement" that he "need not open, for I look through thee" (2.3.205-6); later he tells Bertram, "there can be no kernel in this light nut" (2.5.39-40). And in language that pointedly recalls the deception/conception opposition underwriting the early modern discourse of dropsy and pregnancy, Bertram pronounces himself "deceived" by "this counterfeit module" (4.3.95). All form and no content, all swelling and no conception, Paroles is phantom pregnancy made flesh or, more accurately, made sound: "these balls bound," he says, praising Bertram's puffed-up language, "there's noise in't" (2.3.281).

The figurative vocabulary of dropsy haunts one episode in particular: the sequence in which Paroles proposes, for the sake of his honor, to recover his battalion's lost drum. Indeed, the tympanous object of his spectacularly failed quest becomes his soubriquet in the play's last acts, during which he is repeatedly referred to as "Jack Drum." Even before Paroles's renaming, his drum is presented as less a missing stage property than an integral if pathological part of his corporeality:

BERTRAM: How now, monsieur? This drum sticks sorely in your disposition.
SECOND LORD: A pox on't, let it go. 'Tis but a drum.
(3.6.39–41)

The drum "sticks sorely" in Paroles's "disposition" yet it is "but a drum"—a pathological affliction, in other words, that is both full and empty of significance. The Paroles subplot, which is not in Shakespeare's sources, has been the subject of much critical speculation.[53] I would argue that the subplot, particularly the tale of Paroles's drum, draws much of its force from the discourse of dropsy invoked by the King. The drum's loud noise and emptiness—not to mention its failure to materialize in Paroles's supposed quest for it—finds a counterpart in his, as he terms it, dropsically "dilated" language (2.1.56), which is all sound and fury that fails to produce any issue other than more sound.

Like the witches of *Macbeth,* who prophesy the "swelling act / Of the imperial theme" (1.3.135–36) that will produce political success yet sterile nonreproductivity for that play's title character, Paroles—both character and concept—is associated with an equivocation that simultaneously involves an excess and deficiency of meaning. He is lambasted as a "double-meaning prophesier" (4.3.96), a "damnable both-sides rogue" (4.3.210), a "manifold linguist" (4.3.224), and an "equivocal companion" (5.3.250). Yet I would argue that Paroles is the play's scapegoat, by means of which dropsical swelling can be punished and its universality disavowed.[54] As much as his failure to signify with clarity is ridiculed in him, it is clear that signs fail to signify clearly throughout *All's Well That Ends Well.* Even the play's stage properties—in a manner that also recalls the easily confused signs of pregnancy and dropsy—can involve a confusion of opposites: the patch of velvet Bertram wears after the war, for example, ambivalently suggests both a heroic war wound and a shameful mark of syphilis. But we never get to see what, exactly, lies beneath it. Bertram's velvet patch is thus an objective correlative to the play's language, which likewise inhibits the delivery of visible signifieds. It does so by repeatedly drawing attention to its sound, either by being explicitly nonsensical—for example, the incoherent "gabble" spoken by the French Lords upon capturing Paroles (4.1.18)—or because it oversignifies at the level of sound. Like the belly of the Timpanites patient, words in this play always sound like something else. The most flagrant instance occurs in Bertram's letter to his mother, where he repudiates any sexual investment in Helen through a nasty pun on the nuptial "knot": "I have wedded her, not bedded her, and sworn to make the 'not' eternal" (3.2.20–21).[55] In its inversion of a religious formula, Bertram's letter echoes Foxe's "Carminis Inversio"; it draws, moreover, on the same deconceptive logic of homophonic slippage as Foxe's "Quam Mariae sobolem," whereby a seemingly fruitful signifier acoustically blurs into its barren opposite. But this is a tendency audible throughout the play.

If *All's Well that Ends Well* is all about the sonorous dropsy of titles, it is perhaps only to be expected that even the word "title" should be used as a pun, on "tittle," meaning a tiny amount. As Lavatch tells Paroles, "To say nothing, to do nothing, to know nothing, and to have nothing, is to be a great part of your title, which is within a very little of nothing" (2.4.21–23). Yet it is not just Paroles's name that sounds the slide of lofty title to denigrated tittle. The name of Helen slips homophonically into Shakespeare's other, earlier Helen, as Lavatch's song "was this the fair face?" suggests (1.3.62).[56] Along the same lines, when Helen affirms her intent "to go to Paris" to cure the King and secure her future (1.3.203), we can hear in her remark not only a move forward, but also a recursive loop back at the homophonic level of the signifier to her Greek predecessor's Trojan lover. Helen is just as much noisy "parole," then, as she is bearer of a concept-oriented "logos."

This recursiveness afflicts not only the play's names and titles, but also its very plot. For a work called *All's Well That Ends Well*, it is surely extraordinary that the play's end is not the end. As critics have noted, the last scene offers neither progress nor closure; in granting to Diana the power that he has previously granted to Helen—to choose her husband and therefore ennoble herself—the King simply recreates the conditions that led to the play's initial crisis.[57] But closure is thwarted also at the level of the riddle-solving "meaning" we are meant to "behold." Unlike Shakespeare's source, where Helen's counterpart Giletta produces twins for all to see, we are denied in Helen the "ostentation of fertility" conventionally associated with conception. Instead we have only her and Diana's *words* for it that she is pregnant. And like *All's Well*'s other "paroles," these terms fail to come to term. This is not to argue that Helen's pregnancy is really phantom or a case of dropsy. But the deferral of the fruits of her mental and sexual labors is typical of the play's logic of deconception, which strands theatergoers indeterminately between pregnancy and dropsy, visible conception and audible deception, spectatorship and audienceship.[58]

To schematize the play's visual and acoustic registers in this fashion might seem to privilege the former over the latter, to valorize the eye rather than the ear as the reliable sensory organ. But deconception undermines the primacy of the visible by disclosing sight's occulted dependence on hearing. Indeed, the auditory economy of the Shakespearean theater necessitated that sound help shape its field of vision. Early modern playgoers saw female characters onstage in part because various verbal cues—proper names, spoken references to unseen body parts—prompted them to translate boy-actors into "women" (even when those boy-actors were not wearing women's clothes, as the cross-dressed heroines of the comedies make clear). Similarly, modern and early modern playgoers alike believe Helen to be carrying Bertram's child—and hence to be in possession of a "meaning" that can be "beheld"—not because they see physical evidence of her swelling, but because they hear words that conjure up the ghost of her pregnancy. This is, of course, the familiar logocentric trick of speech, whose seeming purpose is transparent access, if only in the mind's eye, to visible concepts. But deconception has a habit of reversing the teleological trajectory from sound to sight. As the homophonic slippages of *All's Well* repeatedly suggest, sound not only enables but also obstructs what playgoers believe themselves to see. As a result, *All's Well*'s audiences are diverted into a sensory netherworld that falls short of pristine sight, whereby—like Bottom—they are more likely to "see a voice" or "hear [a] face" (*A Midsummer Night's Dream*, 5.1.190-91); in both plays, the auditory register simultaneously conceives and deceives the visible, or rather, deconceives it.

The play's logic of deconception is thus in some ways a transhistorical product of the acoustic properties of both speech and the theater. But as I have suggested earlier, deconception in *All's Well* also resonates with the white noise of its historical moment. Even as the play foregrounds the social ecosystem of homophonic resemblances and slippages that are persistent features of human communication, it does so partly by invoking a historically specific discourse of dropsy and pregnancy that engages, even at a symbolic remove, the anxieties attendant upon royal succession. This is not to claim that either Helen or her unborn child is an allegorical stand-in for King James, a promise of youthful futurity and progress after the aged court of Elizabeth or the barren one of Mary. We cannot see history so transparently in *All's Well*. But we can *hear* it in the play's sounds. In his account of Mary's tympany, John Foxe not only delineated the contours of Tudor fears—both Marian and Elizabethan—of pregnancy turning into dropsy and progress sliding into sterility; he also *enacted* this fear in his homophonic collapse of the fruitful Virgin Mary into the barren Queen Mary. Shakespeare's play, like Foxe's "Carminis Inversio," ties together the deconceptive discourse of pregnancy/dropsy and the deconceptive strategy of homophonic slippage, and in the process generates a social text of sound without singular conceptual issue that is literally embodied in the swellings of its words and characters.

All Swell That End Swell, with its suggestion of recursive rather than forward movement, thus bloats *All's Well That Ends Well* like a sonorous *mola*. The play's name promises an arrival at conceptual clarity; but in a drama that constantly reminds us of the hollow reverberation of titles, it only makes sense that the play's very title makes not sense so much as other sounds. This is especially the case with its keyword "well," which appears countless times in the play. What interests me is that, in the last act, the word invariably appears after the letter "s": Lafew says of Bertram "He looks well on't" (5.3.31); the King says "all yet seems well" (5.3.327) and, a few lines later in the epilogue, notes that "all is well ended" (2). Subliminally, then, the play insists that "all swell" even as it reassures us that "all's well." That punning swerve, that dropsical swelling audible in the deconceptive conversion of titles into tittles, guarantees that, in the end, there is no end to the play of sound that is All Swell That End Swell.

Notes

1. See Patricia Parker, *"All's Well That Ends Well:* Increase and Multiply," *Creative Imitation: New Essays on Renaissance Literature in Honor of Thomas Greene,* ed. David Quint, et al. (Binghamton, N.Y.: Medieval and Renaissance Texts and Studies, 1992), 355–90. All references to *All's Well That Ends Well* are to *The Norton Shakespeare,* ed. Stephen Greenblatt, Walter Cohen, Jean E. Howard, and Katharine Eisaman Maus (New York: W. W.

Norton, 1997 [based on the Oxford edition of Stanley Wells and Gary Taylor]). Although certain of Wells and Taylor's editorial choices are cause for debate, I prefer their restoration of the Folio edition's "Helen" at the expense of the now more customary "Helena"; see n. 51.

2. The play's opening line likewise associates pregnancy with death, the Countess lamenting that "in delivering my son from me, I bury a second husband" (1.1.1–2).

3. William Paynter, "Giletta of Narbona,"reprinted in *All's Well That Ends Well,* ed. G. K. Hunter, 3rd ed. (London: Methuen, 1967), 145–49, esp. 146.

4. Thomas Elyot, *The Boke of the Governor* (London, 1537), sigs. A1, A3. For two very different discussions of the body politic metaphor and its embeddedness within a larger cosmology of correspondence, see Leonard Barkan, *Nature's Work of Art: The Human Body as Image of the World* (New Haven: Yale University Press, 1975), and David George Hale, *The Body Politic: A Political Metaphor in Renaissance English Literature* (The Hague: Mouton, 1971). See also Jonathan Gil Harris, *Foreign Bodies and the Body Politic: Discourses of Social Pathology in Early Modern England* (Cambridge: Cambridge University Press, 1998) and *Sick Economies: Drama, Mercantilism and Disease in Shakespeare's England* (Philadelphia: University of Pennsylvania Press, 2004).

5. For a more thorough discussion of the problem of naming in the play, see François Laroque, "Words and Things in *All's Well That Ends Well,"* in *French Essays on Shakespeare and His Contemporaries: "What Would France with Us?"* ed. Jean-Marie Maguin and Michèle Willems (Newark: University of Delaware Press, 1995), 213–32.

6. St. Augustine, *Works of Saint Augustine: Sermons* (Hyde Park, N.Y.: New City Press, 1994), 72/a, 7.

7. Thomas Sydenham, *The Entire Works of Dr. Thomas Sydenham, Newly Made English from the Originals: Wherein the History of the Acute and Chronic Diseases and the Safest and Most Effectual Methods of Treating Them, are Faithfully, Clearly, and Accurately Delivered,* trans. John Swan (London, 1742), 464–65.

8. R. Turner, *De Morbis Feomineis, The Womans Counsellour: Or, The Feminine Physician, Enlarged* (London, 1686), 174. For a clear summation of the taxonomies of dropsy, see Andrew Boorde, *The Breuiary of Helthe* (London, 1547), sig. T3.

9. Gail Kern Paster, *Humoring the Body: Emotions and the Shakespearean Stage* (Chicago: University of Chicago Press, 2004), 9.

10. Shigehisa Kuriyama, *The Expressiveness of the Body and the Divergence of Greek and Chinese Medicine* (New York: Zone, 1999), 236.

11. Katharine Eisaman Maus, *Inwardness and Theater in the English Renaissance* (Chicago: University of Chicago Press, 1995), 196; Paster, *Humoring the Body,* 24.

12. Bruce R. Smith, *The Acoustic World of Early Modern England: Attending to the O-Factor* (Chicago: University of Chicago Press, 1999), 29. My argument diverges in one respect, however, from Smith's extraordinarily suggestive "historical phenomenological" analysis of the early modern acoustic world. Even as Smith claims that "if it is Presence that this book is after, it is not the Presence of the Word, but of *sound*" (29), he nonetheless tethers his analysis of sound to communication systems theory and its logocentric investment in the conveyance of meaningful information. I am interested in how sound inhibits as much as it enables communication; hence my essay might be dubbed an exercise in the "ecology of *hearing"* rather than the "ecology of *listening,"* which tends to presume the translation

of sound into meaning. In this respect, my argument is closer to that of Kenneth Gross in *Shakespeare's Noise* (Chicago: University of Chicago Press, 2001). For another thoughtful approach to the Shakespeare's use of sound, see Wes Folkerth, *The Sound of Shakespeare* (New York: Routledge, 2002).

13. John of Trevisa, *On the Properties of Things: John Trevisa's Translation of Bartholomaeus Anglicus' De Proprietatibus Rerum* (Oxford, U.K.: Clarendon Press, 1975), 7.iii.

14. *Lanfrank's "Science of Cirurgie,"* ed. Robert von Fleischhacker (Millwood, N.Y.: Kraus Reprint Co., 1975), 283.

15. Boorde, sig. L1v.

16. Ibid., sig. F3.

17. James Guillemeau, *Child-birth or, The Happy Deliuerie of Women* (London, 1612), sig. C1.

18. Turner, 167.

19. Jacques Derrida, *The Margins of Philosophy,* trans. Alan Bass (Chicago: University of Chicago Press, 1982), ix—xxix.

20. Nicholas Culpeper, *Directory for Midwives, or, A Guide for Women in Their Conception, Bearing, and Suckling Their Children* (London, 1675), sig. F2v.

21. *The Life and Death of Mrs. Mary Frith,* ed. Randall S. Nakayama (New York: Garland, 1993), 165 (277).

22. Ibid., 166 (278).

23. Ibid., 166 (278).

24. Ibid., 166 (278).

25. Ibid., 167 (279).

26. Compare Paster, *Humoring the Body,* 137–45, who likewise insists on the importance of simile in early modern discourses of the body. The difference between the types of simile that Paster illuminates and the ones I consider here, however, is that whereas the former operate in the field of *homology,* assuming a "doctrine of natural correspondences" (142) between micro- and macrocosmic domains, the latter function within a purely *homophonic* field.

27. *Medieval Woman's Guide to Health: The First English Gynecological Handbook,* trans. Beryl Rowland (Kent, Ohio: Kent State University Press, 1981), 108.

28. Jakob Ruff, *The Expert Midwife, or An Excellent and Most Necessary Treatise of the Generation and Birth of Man* (London, 1637), 140–41.

29. John Pechey, *The Compleat Midwife's Practice Enlarged, in the Most Weighty and High Concernments of the Birth of Man* (London, 1698), 60.

30. Culpeper, *Directory,* sig. H3.

31. Ibid., sig. F4.

32. Guillemeau, *Child-birth,* sig. A1v.

33. William Sermon, *The Ladies Companion* (London, 1671), sig. C1.

34. Richard Tarlton, *Tarlton's Jests and News out of Purgatory (1844),* ed. James Orchard Halliwell (Whitefish, Mont.: Kessinger Publishing, 2003), 78.

35. Richard Carew, *The World of Wonders* (London, 1607), 157.

36. Sydenham, *Entire Works,* 465. For a useful discussion of *molas,* "false conception," and the diseases of the womb, see Gail Kern Paster, *The Body Embarrassed: Drama and*

the Disciplines of Shame in Early Modern England (Ithaca, N.Y.: Cornell University Press, 1993), 169–74.

37. In early 1558, Mary again believed herself to be pregnant; making her will, she declared that she believed herself "to be with child in lawfull marriage." By November that year, of course, she was dead. See Rosalind K. Marshall, *Mary I* (London: HMSO, 1993), 143–47.

38. John Foxe, *Actes and Monuments* (London, 1563), VII.126.

39. Raphael Holinshed, *The Chronicles of England, Scotland, and Ireland* (London, 1587), 1131.

40. *The Christian Martyrology*, ed. J. Milner (London: Knight, 1839), 947.

41. *Actes and Monuments*, VI. 581.

42. John Donne, *Pseudo-Martyr* (London, 1610), 365.

43. Robert Burton, *The Anatomy of Melancholy: What It Is, with All the Kinds, Causes, Symptomes, Prognostickes, & Seuerall Cures of It* (London, 1621), 22.

44. William Camden, *Annals, or The Histories of the Most Renowned and Victorious Princesse Elizabeth, Late Queen of England . . . Translated in to English by R. N. Gent* (London, 1635), 21.

45. Ibid., 7.

46. Thomas Dekker, *The Magnificent Entertainment* (London, 1604), sigs. F1v—F2.

47. Madhavi Menon, *Wanton Words: Rhetoric and Sexuality in English Renaissance Drama* (Toronto: University of Toronto Press, 2004), 165.

48. G.W.F. Hegel, *The Philosophy of History*, trans. J. Sibree (Amherst, N.Y.: Prometheus Books, 1991), 73.

49. Melissa D. Smith helpfully distinguishes between fistulas *in ano* and other related afflictions in "A Tale of Two Helens: Syphilis, Healing, and Female Embodiment in *Troilus and Cressida* and *All's Well That Ends Well*," unpublished paper, delivered at the 38th Medieval Congress at Kalamazoo, May 8, 2003.

50. Alexander Leggatt, "*All's Well that Ends Well:* The Testing of Romance," *Modern Language Quarterly* 32 (1971): 21–41, esp. 24.

51. Much of the critical debate has centered on which school of medicine Helen professes. For a useful discussion, see Barbara Howard Traister, " 'Note her a little further': Doctors and Healers in the Drama of Shakespeare," *Disease, Diagnosis, and Cure on the Early Modern Stage*, ed. Stephanie Moss and Kaara L. Peterson (Burlington, Vt.: Ashgate, 2004), 43–52.

52. Of course, the teleological progress suggested by Helen's pregnancy redounds to Bertram and the patrilineal succession he represents. For a thoughtful discussion of how the play's fascination with conception is entangled with patriarchal politics, see Michael D. Friedman, " 'Service is no heritage': Bertram and the Ideology of Procreation," *Studies in Philology* 92 (1995): 80–101.

53. For discussions of Paroles's character and function in the play, see J. Dennis Huston, " 'Some Stain of Soldier': The Functions of Parolles in *All's Well That Ends Well*," *Shakespeare Quarterly* 21 (1970): 431–38; Jules Rothman, "A Vindication of Parolles," *Shakespeare Quarterly* 23 (1972): 183–96; Jeremy Richards, " 'The thing I am': Parolles, the Comic Victim, and Tragic Consciousness," *Shakespeare Studies* 18 (1986): 145–59; and R. J. Schork, "The Many Masks of Parolles," *Philological Quarterly* 76 (1997): 263–69.

54. One might also think, for example, of the instance of Lafeu. Although Lafeu mocks

Paroles for his empty dilations, we are told that his own speech "special nothing ever prologues" (2.1.90). Lafeu's never-ending "prologues" are deconception in action, where progress is promised yet never delivered.

55. For a particularly useful discussion of Bertram's letter, see David Thatcher, "Shakespeare's All's Well: The Case of Bertram's Letter," *Cahiers Elisabéthains* 53 (1998): 77–80.

56. In the Folio edition, the leading character's name usually appears as "Helen." Although modern editors have emended it to Helen, theirs is a loaded choice. It is an attempt to assert a distinction from the promiscuous, deceptive Helena of Shakespeare's *Troilus and Cressida,* and to confer on the play's heroine a clear signified unique to her (or shared with her more benign namesake in *Midsummer*).

57. See, for example, David Scott Kastan, *"All's Well That Ends Well* and the Limits of Comedy," *ELH* 52 (1985): 575–89; and Garrett A. Sullivan Jr., " 'Be this sweet Helen's knell, and now forget her': Forgetting, Memory and Identity in *All's Well that Ends Well,*" *Shakespeare Quarterly* 50 (1999): 51–69, 68–69.

58. For a discussion of the auditory as well as visual dimensions of the first scene, see J. L. Styan, *"All's Well That Ends Well:* On Seeing and Hearing the Opening Scene," *Connotations: A Journal for Critical Debate* 7 (1997–98): 215–18. On deferral generally in the play, see Susan Snyder, " 'The King's Not Here': Displacement and Deferral in *All's Well That Ends Well,*" *Shakespeare Quarterly* 43 (1992): 20–32.

The Devil's in the Archive:
Doctor Faustus *and Ovidian Physics*

KRISTEN POOLE

We may not staye here within the limites of our owne reason, which is not able to reach vnto, or to comprehend what way Deuils should be able to haue such operations. We may not I say measure their nimblenes, & power, & subtilties in working, by our owne vnderstanding or capacitie.

—George Gifford,
A Discourse of the Subtill Practises of Deuilles by Vvitches and Sorcerers (1587)

I

The problem is, how can we take the devil seriously?

That is to say, how can "we"—reasoning, skeptical, worldly individuals, skilled in analysis, prejudiced against superstition—approach Satan, reeking of brimstone, wreaking havoc with people's lives? How can we write a history of experiencing the devil without sterilizing or rationalizing the demonic? How can we look back through that period we have called the Enlightenment and study the devil's earlier dark participation in the world without bringing an innate mistrust of the tales we read and a latent condescension toward the people who tell them? How can we really study a devil we don't think is real?[1] At one time, of course, the devil was as real as God—in a way, even more real, since he could be perceived directly as even the omnipresent deity could not. In the seventeenth century, John Rogers (the future Fifth Monarchist) saw devils everywhere. "[F]ear of Hell and the devils" consumed him, he writes. "I thought I saw every foot in several ugly shapes and forms, according to my fancies, and sometimes with great rolling flaming eyes like saucers, having sparkling firebrands in one of their hands, and with the other reaching at me to tear me away to torments."[2] Rogers's environment was saturated with the demonic. Today, our response would be to diagnose him with a mental disorder; he would almost certainly be medicated and perhaps even institutionalized. But within his own period, Rogers's experience would not have been

191

that atypical. While his ongoing perception of demons might have been extreme, the presence of devils in the world was a given, and something that the ordinary Englishman or woman would have experienced on a regular basis. From thunderstorms to erotic dreams, from the workings of the cosmos to the musings of the soul, the devil was an immediate, active presence in people's lives. He was ubiquitous and unavoidable.

I have taken Rogers's quote from Keith Thomas, who includes it in his seminal study *Religion and the Decline of Magic*.[3] Not that we should read it too closely: at the end of the previous paragraph, Thomas observes that "[t]he Devil who provoked high winds and thunderstorms, or who appeared dramatically to snatch a poor sinner in his cups and fly off with him through the window, is difficult for us today to take seriously."[4] For all of the emotional intensity of Rogers's experience, Thomas primes us to take it lightly, or at least notes our propensity to do so.

Within the field of Renaissance studies, there are entrenched historical and cultural impediments to taking the devil seriously. In reading sixteenth- and seventeenth-century accounts of demonic activity it is, as Thomas suggests, sometimes hard to remain straight-faced. The devil provided a rational explanation for seemingly irrational events, such as medical conditions and weather systems. It is not so much that early modern people did not understand such things—they understood perfectly well that they were the work of the devil. But since our own understanding has shifted toward the invisible machinations of cells and atoms, their reason has become our irrationality.

Irrational beliefs are often associated with childhood, and there has long been a scholarly tradition of portraying the inhabitants of the six- teenth and early seventeenth centuries as immature versions of our more worldly selves. The models of history that we inhabit invite us, perhaps even compel us, to conceptualize time as moving in terms of human development. Metanarratives of the Renaissance are especially prone to this developmental scheme, given how fundamentally the work of Jacob Burckhardt defined the field. The Renaissance, in Burckhardt's view, is a glorious story of coming-of-age; the entry into modernity is marked by the abandonment of (childish) superstition in favor of a more rational (adult) skepticism. Crucial to this process is the expulsion of the supernatural, as the "faith, illusion, and childish prepossession" of the Middle Ages gives way in the Renaissance to an "*objective* treatment and consideration of the State."[5] Other metanarratives, perhaps in spite of themselves, follow a similar developmental pattern, at least when it comes to analyzing belief in the supernatural. In a discussion about the devil, Sigmund Freud likens "neurotic illnesses in earlier centuries" to the "neuroses of childhood."[6] Keith Thomas gives this familiar teleology a twist. Where Burckhardt maps the historical evolutionary process onto human maturation (the child of the Middle Ages gradually becoming the adult of the nineteenth century), Thomas maps it onto global development (with medieval demonic beliefs frequently likened to those of "primitive," African cultures).[7] In different shapes and forms, then, the cognitive mode of organizing time in developmental terms naturalizes the idea that we are more sophisticated than our predecessors.

As a profession, today we are more sensitive to the ideological implications of these metanarratives, and our job is to work through the complexities of medieval and early modern cultures, not to extol their simplicities. But the teleological, developmental paradigm is so ingrained in our critical tradition that it is hard to escape. Although this paradigm may have become more subtle as it moved its way through the influential work of authors ranging from Norbert Elias to Charles Taylor, it has nonetheless remained central for organizing discussions about early modernism.[8] Even more subtly, though more pervasively, the progressive teleology is implicit in our current label of choice, "early modern."[9] This historical orientation has led us to trace, rather single-mindedly, the etiology of modernity rather than the legacy of medievalism. An underlying obstacle to studying the devil of the sixteenth and seventeenth centuries is thus our predisposition, witting or not, to construe history as analogous to human growth and development and the inherent tendency to patronize the youth that attends this mode of thought.

One consequence of this historical orientation has been an undue focus on historical skeptics and disbelievers, those whom we perceive as emerging modern voices. In particular, we have appreciated those who exhibit a healthy skepticism toward the devil; we are more at home, for example, with Reginald Scot's *Discoverie of Witchcraft* than with King James's *Daemonology* (since, as Katharine Eisaman Maus observes, "to us the skeptics look obviously right and the witch-hunters are hard to take seriously").[10] Our propensity to gravitate toward the disbelieving Scot as a spokesman for sixteenth-century attitudes on witchcraft is symptomatic of our desire to find kindred spirits within the period. This desire has caused us to overlook the fact that in his own day Scot's views would have been considered more radical than rational; as Stuart Clark has discussed, the vast majority of sixteenth- and seventeenth-century writing on witchcraft eschewed extravagant positions of excessive belief or disbelief, espousing a middle ground between these positions.[11]

The predilection to view Scot as a voice of reason finds a counterpart in our tendency to locate fellow skeptics among early modern playwrights. One recent critic confidently proclaims (with no supporting evidence whatsoever) that, "We can surmise with almost complete certainty that Marlowe's attitude towards witchcraft would have been much the same as Scot's."[12] Like Marlowe, Shakespeare has also been perceived as reassuringly modern on account of his apparent disinterest in the devil. John Cox has recently considered the evolution of our understanding of Shakespeare as a skeptic, arguing that the historical narrative put forth by E. K. Chambers in *The Medieval Stage* (1903) continues to shape the critical approach to stage devils. In Cox's analysis, Chambers constructed a "scheme that interpreted stage devils in a narrative of teleological secularization."[13] According to this scheme, stage devils were a feature of "the religious superstructure that drama eventually outgrew" as it made its "gradual evolution toward its brilliant secular flowering in the work of Shakespeare."[14] Shakespeare's canon contains only two stage devils, both in the early *Henry VI* plays, but as Cox shows, devils appeared in no less than forty plays staged between *Faustus* and 1642. Shakespeare, in other words, was not the death of the devil.

Cox's account of Chambers's continuing influence might be overstated,[15] but in some ways Chambers's scholarly response to devils is not so different from ours a century later. In *The Elizabethan Stage,* Chambers sets out to create a comprehensive archive of the documents pertaining to the Elizabethan theater. His efforts mark a rejection of Romantic approaches to literary study, largely reliant upon subjective character analysis, in favor of a more historiographical approach. But inevitably, given the time in which the documents were produced, the archive contains traces of the supernatural that, for Chambers, sit uncomfortably with other forms of historical records. While Chambers dutifully includes these documents, he cordons them off, segregating them from texts that he considers to have more legitimacy. He notes, for example, how Marlowe's *Doctor Faustus* "became the centre of a curious *mythos,* which was used to point a moral against the stage."[16] This *mythos,* as students of the period well know, is that during the performance of *Doctor Faustus* actual devils were wont to appear onstage.[17]

Chambers cites as an example of this phenomenon:

N.D. "J.G.R." from manuscript note on "the last page of a book in my possession, printed by Vautrollier" (1850, *2 Gent. Mag.* xxxiv. 234), "Certaine Players at Exeter, acting upon the stage the tragical storie of Dr. Faustus the Conjurer; as a certaine nomber of Devels kept everie one his circle there, and as Faustus was busie in his magicall invocations, on a sudden they were all dasht, every one harkning other in the eare, for they were all perswaded, there was one devell too many amongst them; and so after a little pause desired the people to pardon them, they could go no further with this matter; the people also understanding the thing as it was, every man hastened to be first out of dores."[18]

Exeter was not the only place that experienced theatrical demons. Chambers also notes William Prynne's account in the antitheatrical compendium *Histriomastix* of

[t]he visible apparition of the Devill on the stage at the Belsavage Play-house, in Queen Elizabeths dayes (to the great amazement both of the actors and spectators) while they were there prophanely playing the History of Faustus (the truth of which I have heard from many now alive, who well remember it) there being some distracted with that feareful sight.[19]

Chambers's framing of these accounts as a "curious *mythos*" categorically relegates them to the world of fantasy, the quaint relics of an immature age. "Curious" not only gestures toward the bizarre, but toward the curioso, or the curiosity; *"mythos"* designates them as antiquated and untrue. Appearing after the serious, scholarly matter of dating all of the extant editions of the play, these accounts are presented as merely an amusing little something for the collector to put in his *Wunderkammer* of theatrical oddities. These are not, Chambers would have us believe, documents that have a practical function or that deserve serious analytical scrutiny.

In labeling the onstage appearance of *Faustus*'s demons as a myth "used to point a moral against the stage," Chambers offers his own pragmatic explanation for the accounts, suggesting that they were circulated as antitheatrical propaganda. No doubt William Prynne took a certain amount of glee in deploying a story that provided proof of the theater's status as the devil's playground. Maybe Prynne even made the story up: although he claims to be able to produce witnesses that remember the event from Elizabethan days, he has no supporting evidence. Or maybe the old people who claim to remember seeing the devils are themselves spinning old wives' tales or have memories fogged with time. But what Prynne's account does indicate is that the possibility of devils on the stage was a real one for him and a real one for his audience; even if the account is a form of propaganda, it would only work as such if it were believed to be true. This was a matter in which "the people . . . [understood] the thing as it was": the real incursion of demonic agents into the daily space and time of their lives. We could, of course, offer theories of mass hallucination to justify the tales of Faustus's devils, but such explanations would need to willfully, perhaps condescendingly, explain away contemporary claims of the "truth" of this experience. Prynne's account, whatever its motivation, is signaled as a real event, with witnesses still testifying to its veracity.

Literary scholars have followed Chambers's lead in relegating these stories to the realm of anecdote rather than archive, even though they appear in the same type of document that we trust for other types of theater history. While the "myth" of *Faustus's* onstage devils is widely known, it seems only to be deployed for the purposes of seasoning an undergraduate lecture or adding a little zest to a scholarly essay.[20] It has not, to the best of my knowledge, been the subject of any sustained, pointed inquiry. But the degree to which our own culture is dismissive of the possibility of devils onstage is countered by the degree to which early modern people took such events seriously. Although the accounts are brief, they indicate an acceptance of real demonic presence that spanned the divide between actor and audience, theatergoer and antitheatrical polemicist, Elizabethan and Carolinian.

If our own position of disbelief (at least vis-à-vis the devil) can be an intellectual asset, allowing for greater objectivity, it can thus also be a liability, leading us to dismiss that which we consider "illusion" (in Burckhardt's term) as a valid field of inquiry. Not that the devil has been entirely off limits, but we have tended to view him only anamorphically, most often through studies of witchcraft. As the subject of sociological investigation, witches are used as a means of analyzing complex communal structures and relationships.[21] As a locus of feminist analysis, the testimonies of early modern women claiming allegiance with the devil are read—however sympathetically—through a diagnostic lens that reveals responses to the strictures of patriarchy.[22] In the interest of cultural critique, the devil is generally explained away, rationalized, sanitized.

Even if we do want to confront the devil directly, to "understand the thing as it was," it is difficult to analyze the supernatural in a manner that adheres to familiar evidentiary protocols. The devil's archive slides between the mundane and the fantastic. Take, for instance, a type of document that appears regularly in witchcraft trials: the demonic contract. This paper, a signed agreement between an individual and Satan, was frequently used as legal evidence, its terms, both then and now, subject to scrutiny by legal scholars.[23] But analysis of the bond's content can lose sight of the extraordinary nature of the object itself, which could move freely between hell and earth, and which sometimes had to be retrieved from the beyond. These types of documents are the closest thing we have to a text written in the devil's hand, and their material properties are a constitutive element of their reception. This materiality offers us a mode of analyzing sixteenth- and seventeenth-century demonic belief that circumvents illusion and fantasy.

II

So, then, to refine my original question: How do we approach demonic contracts on their own terms, especially if we don't believe in hell? Oddly enough, I find direction for such an inquiry in the writings of Sigmund Freud. In his essay entitled "A Seventeenth-Century Demonological Neurosis," Freud immerses himself in the study of demonic contracts. The introduction to the essay provides a pithy synopsis of Freud's explanation for the devils seen in earlier centuries: "the demons are bad and reprehensible wishes, derivatives of instinctual impulses that have been repudiated and repressed."[24] The demons that today are internalized, so the reasoning goes, were once projected into the external world. Freud's assertion that the appearance of devils was a neurotic manifestation is predictable enough, but the essay takes an unexpected turn once he begins to scrutinize the archive itself.

The essay opens, as usual, with a case history. The subject is Christoph Haizmann, a seventeenth-century Bavarian painter. Haizmann, it appears, had the rather ill-advised habit of entering into pacts with the devil. This tendency first came to light in 1677, when Haizmann experienced convulsions while visiting a church. Suspicious local officials began to inquire if

Haizmann had by any chance held intercourse with Satan, and a repentant Haizmann soon confessed that he had, alas, signed a pact with the devil, a bond that was due in just a few short weeks. Through the benevolence of a village priest, Haizmann was taken to the shrine at Mariazell, where it was hoped that the Blessed Virgin would intervene and recover the bond, a document which happened to be written in blood. At Mariazell, Haizmann underwent an intense period of penance and soon encountered the devil himself, who, in the shape of a dragon, returned the bond. (The attending clerics themselves did not see the demon; Haizmann simply ran from the priests to a corner where he perceived the devil and then returned, miraculously, with the fateful document in hand.) After this encounter a happy and healthy Haizmann departed to live with his sister in Vienna, but he was soon beset by more demonic seizures. Haizmann suddenly recalled that there had in fact been a *second* devilish bond, this one written in ink; he returned to Mariazell where another undisclosed miracle retrieved this paper as well. Free at last, Haizmann entered the Order of the Brothers Hospitallers, resisted the devil's subsequent bargaining attempts (which took place only after Haizmann had indulged in too much wine), and died uneventfully in 1700.

This case was brought to light by the director of the former imperial Viennese record office, who discovered the manuscript account in his library's holdings and solicited Freud's medical opinion on the matter.[25] Freud is quickly impressed by the factual, even clinical nature of the documents. After Haizmann's first encounter with the dragon-devil, Freud interjects an editorial paragraph on the reliability of the evidence. He writes, "At this point a doubt as to the credibility of the clerical reporters may well arise in our minds and warn us not to waste our labours on a product of monastic superstition. . . . But the . . . testimony dispels this doubt."[26] Throughout, the priestly scribes and witnesses are praised for their candor and "veracity" in disclosing the facts of the case. The document, in Freud's hands, is neither a piece of clerical propaganda nor religious fantasy, but a credible account suitable for further analysis.[27]

Indeed, Freud spends a good part of the essay analyzing the features of the document itself, apparently reveling in the opportunity to play textual scholar. Unlike his other case notes, this report is full of bibliographic and paleographic detail. He detects chronological inconsistencies in the supposed relationship of the two bonds, the one written in blood (let's say the A-text) and the other in ink (the B-text), and he enters into an extended and intricate attempt to date them. Finally (after five full pages of such analysis in the Standard Edition), Freud comes to the conclusion that the bonds were fraudulent—that is, they were written by Haizmann in an effort to deceive the clerics. The conclusion is a startling one, not because we are shocked to discover that the documents were of mundane origin, but because it becomes apparent in retrospect that an alternative outcome to Freud's line of inquiry might have been to confirm an infernal origin (for why else would he spend so much time disproving a demonic occurrence?).

At this point, we might find ourselves taken aback by the bizarre fervor that Freud brings to his task of dating the documents, and even more so by the fact that he seems to be entertaining the logical possibility of human traffic with the devil. Freud anticipates our response; it seems fair to say he has even set us up for it. He acknowledges the secular sophistication of his audience, asserting, "Now I am writing for readers who, although they believe in psycho-analysis, do not believe in the Devil."[28] These readers find themselves, incredulously, arguing with Freud about the devil's existence. "For, they will say," Freud contends, ventriloquizing our own response, "the bond in blood was just as much a product of his phantasy as the allegedly earlier one in ink. In reality, no Devil appeared to him at all, and the whole business of pacts with the Devil only existed in his imagination."[29]

Freud responds, "I quite realize this." The statement serves as both an acknowledgment and a retort to the readers' concerns. Freud aims to redirect the readers' questions and line of reasoning; at issue here is not whether the devil is real or imaginary. And while elsewhere in the essay Freud is content to diagnose Haizmann's devil as a father figure, and while elsewhere in his writings Freud goes so far as to diagnose organized religion as a collective neurosis, here he seems relatively unconcerned with the operations of the psyche. Instead he insists upon the importance of the bonds' material existence. Back to Freud's own words: "I quite realize this. . . . But . . . the matter goes further. After all, the two bonds were not phantasies like the visions of the Devil. They were documents, preserved, according to the assurances of the copyist and the deposition of the later Abbot . . . , in the archives of Mariazell, for all to see and touch."[30] This materiality gives us a certain purchase on demonic belief— if not Haizmann's particular neurosis, then the beliefs of the clerics, a belief system that is not merely recorded but sustained by its habits of documentation. The documents at hand tell us not only *what* was believed, but *how* the belief was processed and negotiated.

This case complicates what Peter Gay has referred to as Freud's "stark vista of a historic confrontation in which educated atheists were pitted against unlettered believers."[31] Here the confrontation is presented in terms of two groups of educated believers: the honest clerical scribes and the savvy Viennese intelligentsia. Freud's willingness to defend the former before the almost scoffing dismissal of the latter does not, of course, indicate a latent belief in the devil. Rather, Freud is playing, as it were, devil's advocate. Freud's mode of archival analysis confronts these documents on their own material terms, and in the process accepts an episteme in which eschatological figures interact with worldly individuals.

By privileging the fact that the documents *exist,* that they are there in the archive "for all to see and touch," Freud seems to be feeling his way toward the precepts of historical phenomenology. In such a methodology, as Bruce Smith writes, "Texts not only represent bodily experience; they imply it in the ways they ask to be touched, seen, heard, even smelled and tasted."[32] The material artifacts of human experience are not only its record, but its constitutive elements. They provide a means of reconstructing subjective experience—of tracing the subject's movement through, perception of, and engagement with the world. The demonic contract is a particularly salient text for this purpose, since it not only serves to document an abstract agreement, but is in and of itself the mediator between Satan and the self, the material trace of the interaction between devil and human, the form through which this encounter takes place.

And yet the demonic contract also takes us to the edges of phenomenology. The demonic contract might reek, for example, of brimstone; it was a document that could be stored on earth or archived in hell. Our own experience of the everyday doesn't prepare us for analyzing a document that has an infernal provenance. Our experience with material texts hasn't led us to question the laws of physics. But the demonic contract, in its material form, raises the question: How do we historicize matter itself? Or, to ask it otherwise: how do we study the historical experience of phenomena when past ontological understandings differ so significantly from our own? How do we overcome our Newtonian sensibility, which favors the assumption that matter adheres to immutable laws, an understanding that is so innate we don't even recognize it as a prejudice?

III

Let's return to Faustus. Both as a play and as a character, Faustus revolves around the vicissitudes of material text. *Doctor Faustus,* or, more properly speaking, the *Doctor Fausti,* have bedeviled scholars for years, as the A- and B-texts have romped through the centuries, wrestling for supremacy, alternately finding themselves crowned with legitimacy and spurned as bastards. The debate over the authenticity of these play texts remains ongoing, as it is often more about changing scholarly attitudes toward the theater, authorship, and materiality than it is about the texts themselves. But these are not, per se, the two texts I have in mind. For within *Doctor Faustus* we find a sort of embedded demonic archive in the form of the two bonds Faustus writes up committing himself to the devil. (Shall we say the A^1-text and the B^1-text?)

The contracts (especially the first) are emphatically, even hyperbolically material. Faustus initially seems to think that an oral gentleman's agreement will suffice to sell his soul to the devil, but Mephistopheles is determined to procure a written bond for his master.

FAUSTUS: Now tell me what saith Lucifer thy lord?
MEPHISTOPHELES: That I shall wait on Faustus whilst he lives,
So he will buy my service with his soul.
FAUSTUS: Already Faustus hath hazarded that for thee.
MEPHISTOPHELES: But now thou must bequeath it solemnly
And write a deed of gift with thine own blood,
For that security craves Lucifer. . . .
Then, Faustus, stab thy arm courageously,
And bind thy soul that at some certain day
Great Lucifer may claim it as his own,
And then be thou as great as Lucifer.
FAUSTUS [*cutting his arm*]: Lo, Mephistopheles, for love of thee
Faustus hath cut his arm, and with his proper blood
Assures his soul to be great Lucifer's,
Chief lord and regent of perpetual night.
View here this blood that trickles from mine arm,
And let it be propitious for my wish.
MEPHISTOPHELES: But Faustus,
Write it in manner of a deed of gift.
FAUSTUS: Ay, so I do. [*He writes.*] But Mephistopheles,
My blood congeals, and I can write no more.
MEPHISTOPHELES: I'll fetch thee fire to dissolve it straight. . . .
See, Faustus, here is fire. Set it on.

FAUSTUS: So. Now the blood begins to clear again.
Now will I make an end immediately.
[*He writes.*] . . .
Consummatum est. The bill is ended,
And Faustus hath bequeathed his soul to Lucifer.
(2.1.30–75)[33]

I include this passage at length to demonstrate the overdetermined materiality of the demonic bond. From Faustus's perspective, the act of cutting
his arm, and the blood which trickles from his wound, is testament enough
of his oath, as if he is engaging in a ritual of blood brotherhood. But
for Mephistopheles, the blood is ink; he adamantly requires a written
document, claiming that the piece of paper is necessary for Lucifer to
have the "assurance" and "security" he needs to trust in the arrangement.

The mechanics of writing are highlighted throughout this scene, and
it becomes artificially protracted, emphasizing the production of the text
and its material form. Faustus's declaration of "*Consummatum est.* The
bill is ended, / And Faustus hath bequeathed his soul to Lucifer" would
seem to draw the moment to a close, and indeed we soon find ourselves
watching a dumb show of devils, giving clothes and crowns to Faustus and
then performing a little dance. After this interlude we might expect the
dramatic action to move on, but we discover that this was only a break in
the contract-signing scene, and we return to the issue of the bond.

FAUSTUS: Then Mephistopheles, receive this scroll,
A deed of gift of body and of soul—
But yet conditionally that thou perform
All covenants and articles between us both.
MEPHISTOPHELES: Faustus, I swear by hell and Lucifer
To effect all promises between us both.
FAUSTUS: Then hear me read it, Mephistopheles.
"On these conditions following:
First, that Faustus may be a spirit in form and substance.
Secondly, that Mephistopheles shall be his servant, and be by him commanded.
Thirdly, that Mephistopheles shall do for him and bring him whatsoever.
Fourthly, that he shall be in his chamber or house invisible.
Lastly, that he shall appear to the said John Faustus at all times what shape and form
soever he please.
I, John Faustus of Wittenberg, Doctor, by these presents, do give both body and soul
to Lucifer, Prince of the East, and his minister Mephistopheles; and furthermore

grant unto them that four-and-twenty years being expired, and these articles above written being involate, full power to fetch or carry the said John Faustus, body and soul, flesh, blood, into their habitation wheresoever.
By me, John Faustus."
MEPHISTOPHELES: Speak, Faustus. Do you deliver this as your deed?
FAUSTUS [*giving the deed*]: Ay. Take it, and the devil give thee good of it.
(2.1.88–111)

Once again we seem to arrive at a moment of closure when Faustus proclaims "receive this scroll," and yet he still goes on to read the document in its entirety. The bond contains little, if anything, that the audience doesn't already know; the purpose of reading the contract (probably with a large scroll as a stage prop) is to underscore its material presence. The document functions, of course, both as the inscription of an abstract contract and as the material record of a transaction between Faustus and the devil, but at this moment the bond's evidentiary qualities take precedence. Here, form trumps content, as the play insistently draws our attention to the document's materiality.

The scroll creates a disconcerting juxtaposition of the mundane and the supernatural, but perhaps even more powerfully it creates a paper trail— not as a record of past events, but as something that we can trace (or not) moving through different cosmic spheres. As a familiar object moving between earth and hell, the scroll invites all sorts of speculation: How will it get there? Will it have the same appearance in hell? Where will it go once it gets there? Does Satan have a secretary?

Some of these issues seem to be on Faustus's mind, too, for his first question after delivering up the contract is "Tell me, where is the place that men call hell?" (2.1.116). The subsequent discussion about infernal geographies is not incidental or a non sequitur to the lengthy bond writing, but an extension of the scene, describing the space into which the bond will be transported. Mephistopheles's answer for the location of hell at first seems evasive, as he responds that hell lies

> Within the bowels of these elements,
> Where we are tortured and remain for ever.
> Hell hath no limits, nor is circumscribed
> In one self place, but where we are is hell,
> And where hell is there must we ever be.
> And, to be short, when all the world dissolves,

> And every creature shall be purified,
> All places shall be hell that is not heaven.
> (2.1.119-26)

Mephistopheles's description wanders from identifying a specific location, to paradoxically proclaiming that hell is limitless, to asserting that it is more of a state of mind, to positioning it within a language of essential elements and alchemical purification. The answer presents not so much a list of options as an interconnected set of conditions, in which space and mind and physics are mutually constitutive and dependent. It vacillates between the multiplicitous logic of analogy and the rigors of binarism. It layers forms of belief.

Faustus himself embodies this layering. To Mephistopheles's account of hell, Faustus bluntly proclaims: "I think hell's a fable" (2.1.127). The comment, in a conversation with Mephistopheles, carries obvious ironies. Faustus's smirking denial of hell's existence continues even in a dialogue with hell's ambassador:

MEPHISTOPHELES: Ay, think so still, till experience change thy mind.
FAUSTUS: Why, dost thou think that Faustus shall be damned?
MEPHISTOPHELES: Ay, of necessity, for here's the scroll
In which thou hast given thy soul to Lucifer.
FAUSTUS: Ay, and body too. But what of that?
Think'st thou that Faustus is so fond to imagine
That after this life there is any pain?
No, these are trifles and mere old wives' tales.[34]
(2.1.128-35)

Taken off the stage, Faustus's skepticism may seem (to us) a familiar, comforting rationalism. But within the context of the play, his refutation of hell is clearly irrational. What is so strange about this moment is that Faustus becomes Freud and Haizmann at once. Faustus maintains a detached cynicism about the existence of hell even as he has personally signed a demonic contract and conversed with devils. Like many modern historians, he fictionalizes evidence of the demonic;[35] proof of hell, he contends, comes only from narrative, and the lowest kind at that—"fables," "trifles," "old wives' tales." But Mephistopheles counters this accusation by brandishing the bond that Faustus himself has just written (and which we, the audience, witnessed). Mephistopheles's argument might border on the tautological, except that it is not so much the content of the bond as its form that matters. Mephistopheles emphasizes the material text ("for here's the scroll") as its own form of evidence; it has already become archive.

When he declares hell a fiction, Faustus finds himself in company with the reformer William Tyndale, who, as Stephen Greenblatt has recently discussed, declared purgatory to be "a poet's fable."[36] In his study of purgatory, Greenblatt opens up avenues for exploring how an early modern poetic sensibility directed perceptions of eschatology. Greenblatt asks, "what if we take seriously the charge that Purgatory was a vast piece of poetry?"[37] In other words, what if we push on the metaphors that pervade sixteenth-century eschatological discourse until we arrive at the extreme position that the entire purgatorial ideology was itself a poetic construction? This is the path that Faustus seems to have taken in his own contemplation of hell (at least at this point in the play—he later has a desperate change of heart, prompting the composition of the second bond). Faustus's skepticism is part of what makes him familiar—part of what identifies him as a Renaissance man in a play so indebted to medieval dramatic forms. But if his disbelief locates him closer to us (Freud's idealized audience of those who "do not believe in the devil"), it estranges him from many, probably even most, of his contemporaries. As Bruce Smith notes, inhabitants of sixteenth- and seventeenth-century England would have been more likely "to see material reality where our own preconceptions prompt us to see only metaphor."[38]

We have been prompted to see only metaphor, for example, in studies of early modern appropriations of Ovid. Jonathan Bate contends that the Elizabethan understanding of Ovidian metamorphosis was "psychological and metaphorical instead of physical and literal"; it is a contention with which Lynn Enterline seems to agree.[39] At first glance, *Doctor Faustus* hardly seems to be an Ovidian play. But references to the classical poet are threaded through *Doctor Faustus:* in the performance of the Seven Deadly Sins, Pride is "like to Ovid's flea" (2.3.108-9);[40] the opening Chorus likens Faustus to Icarus (20-21), and Faustus woos Helen by comparing her to the nymph Arethusa (5.1.111), both characters in *The Metamorphoses;*[41] Faustus "plays Diana" and puts horns on Benvolio, who had just declared that "[he'll] be Actaeon and turn [himself] into a stag" (4.1.101; 109-100). The reference to Actaeon and Diana seems to bring us into the realm of Petrarchan poetics, where Ovid's tale does indeed establish a complex constellation of metaphoric relations. In *Faustus,* however, the emphasis is not on the fragmentation (literal and figurative) of the subject, but on the possibility of transformation, of metamorphosis.

The play transforms the metamorphic metaphor into a mode of physical reality. In his musings on the advantage of demonic servants, Valdes assures his friends that

> Like lions shall they guard us when we please,
> Like Almaine rutters with their horsemen's staves,
> Or Lapland giants, trotting by our sides;
> Sometimes like women, or unwedded maids.
> (1.1.118-21)

We might at first hear similes, but as the play progresses it becomes clear that this "like" is not performing a metaphoric operation but a literal one. The last and seemingly most important item in Faustus's demonic contract is the ability to dictate Mephistopheles's form: "Lastly, that he shall appear to the said John Faustus at all times what shape and form soever he please." (Lucifer, in turn, promises Faustus that "thou shalt turn thyself into what shape thou wilt" [2.3.160].) The "pliant" (1.3.29) Mephistopheles soon transforms himself from a dragon to a friar at Faustus's command ("I charge thee to return and change thy shape"), setting off a chain of transforma- tions. The play becomes one of shape-shifting: Mephistopheles says to Dick, "be thou turnèd to this ugly shape, / For apish deeds transformèd to an ape," and to Robin, "Be thou transformed to a dog" (3.3.41-42, 45); Robin later recounts that "one of [Faustus's] devils turned me into the likeness of an ape's face" (4.5.50); Faustus and Mephistopheles take on the shapes of the cardinals (3.1.116-17); Benvolio proclaims, "an I be not revenged for this, would I might be turned to a gaping oyster and drink nothing but salt water" (4.1.163-64); a "horse is turned to a bottle of hay" (4.4.33); Wagner threatens the unfortunate Robin "I'll turn all the lice about thee into familiars" (1.4.20) and promises "I'll teach thee to turn thyself to a god, or a cat, or a mouse, or a rat, or anything" (1.4.41-42).

Since the days of Eden, shape-changing has been one of the devil's greatest tricks, a central element of his modus operandi. But in *Faustus* this idea of metamorphosis, like the demonic contract, becomes overde- termined. (The heightened emphasis on bodily transformation is all the more striking given its performative limitations.) Indeed, Faustus's initial fantasies of power are about changing the world—literally. He wants the ability to modify the cosmos ("Be it to make the moon drop from her sphere . . ." [1.3.35]) and to reconfigure the planet ("I'll join the hills that bind the Afric shore / And make that country continent to Spain" [1.3.105–6]). The endless allusions to transformation in *Faustus* indicate a material world that is eminently plastic. The ability to move continents, to reshape the world, is but an extension of the logic that allows demonic agents to transform men into gods, cats, mice, and rats.

Thus while Ovid's poems certainly had a profound impact on the psychological and metaphoric life of many inhabitants of sixteenth- and seventeenth-century England, his writings may also have influenced an understanding of the physical and the literal. The fundamental trope of *The Metamorphoses* is one that reinforces—and arguably conditioned—cultural understandings about the acts of the devil and his minions. (It is important to note that early modern commentators often cite Ovid as a classical source on witchcraft.)[42] Far from being incongruous with the concerns of *Doctor Faustus,* Ovid and the notion of metamorphosis enhance the play's portrayal of the devil and his world. Just as the devil's contract is emphatically material, so too the notion of transformation is decidedly physical: in *Doctor Faustus,* metamorphosis is not working in the service of poetics, but of physics. Indeed, *Doctor Faustus* operates according to what I will call Ovidian physics, an understanding of the world in which matter and space are perceived as fluid and plastic.

Such a conception may seem to be the stuff of fantasy or antique "illusion." Stevie Simkin describes *Doctor Faustus* as "the most archaic of Marlowe's works, predicated as it seems to be on an understanding of the world that takes for granted the existence of the supernatural realm. Indeed, physical reality and the spiritual cohabit the stage in a way that roots the play in the medieval tradition of mystery and morality drama."[43] Such a reading, however, is based upon a fundamental misunderstanding of early modern notions about the supernatural. As Stuart Clark reminds us, our own use of the label "supernatural" for the demonic is itself anachronistic; within the period, debates about the devil emphatically claim him as part of the natural world.[44] In fact, studying the acts of the devil was seen as a key to understanding God's universe. Far from being a retrograde medieval holdover, demonology was a primary field of exploration for the natural philosophers. Clark writes that "we would do better to associate demonology with development and, indeed, 'advancement,' in natural knowledge than with stagnation or decay. If the devil was a part of early modern nature, then demonology was, of necessity, a part of early modern science."[45] Clark's own magisterial study demonstrates how inquiries into the demonic played a crucial role in natural philosophy, including speculation on physics.[46]

The actual physics of demonic metamorphosis were a topic of debate; at stake were the properties of matter and the devil's power over the material world. The case for the devil's ability to transform people into animals had some powerful advocates, including the influential Jean Bodin and Paracelsus, who believed that the devil could transform witches into dogs, cats, or werewolves.[47] On the whole, however, experts were inclined to disbelieve the phenomenon. Clark writes: "Witchcraft narratives and confessions often depended on the changing of witches or their victims into animals, and the case of lycanthropy was especially well discussed. Yet . . . [experts could not] accept the phenomenon itself as real. It was philosophically and morally distasteful to suppose that the human *anima* could function in an animal body (and vice versa), and impossible for the devil to either effect the transfer or transmute substantial forms."[48]

The conflicted beliefs surrounding demonic metamorphosis are illustrated in John Cotta's *The Triall of Witch-craft, Shewing the True and Right Methode of the Discouery* (London, 1616), a text that frames its discussion of witchcraft in terms of natural philosophy.[49] Cotta discusses metamorphosis at great length, first in the context of "the workes of the Diuell by himselfe, solely wrought without the association of man."[50] Working solo, "the Diuell doth shew himselfe by voices and sounds in trees, caues, statues, and the like: so doth he in diuers other outward shapes and formes of other creatures. Thus he appeared vnto *Eua,* and spake vnto her in the shape of a Serpent. . . . Of his appearance in diuers other formes likewise are many testimonies."[51] Thus the devil can—and regularly does— morph his own being. Assuring his audience that his sources on the subject are far from superstitious old wives' tales, Cotta contends that he will only discuss authors

[a]s by the common consent of times, and generall voice of all Writers, exact credit and esteeme. In this kinde what a multitude of Examples doth the whole current and streame of all Writers of all ages afford? Who almost that readeth any ancient classical Author, can auoide the common mention of fained gods . . . offering themselues vnto men and people, sometimes in one shape, sometimes in another. . . . All Christians, who know God, his word, and truth, and thereby beleeue one onely true God, must needs assure themselues that all these were, euill Spirits, and Diuels. That such were, all times, ages, histories, and records of times with one vniuersall consent confirme.[52]

To these classical authors, Cotta adds biblical authority, citing, among other examples, that "*Pharaoh* [did] see & view with his eyes those great and mighty Sorceries, water turned into blood, rods into Serpents, Frogges caused to issue out vpon the face of the earth."[53] But while Cotta's devil can transform himself and other matter, he is constrained by the laws of nature when it comes to putting human souls into animals.

It is written by some Authors, that the diuel hath perswaded some foolish Sorcerers and Witches, that hee hath changed their bodies and substances, into Catts, Asses, Birds, and other creatures, which really and indeed without illusion . . . is impossible vnto him to doe. For there can be no reall or true transmutation of one substance or nature into another, but either by creation or generation. . . . [H]ee cannot be able to command or compasse any generation aboue the power of Nature, whose power is more vniuersall and greater then his.[54]

The reader of Cotta's account thus emerges with a sense of both the possibilities and the limits of demonic metamorphosis; it is at once a fundamental part of the devil's existence and yet irreconcilable with the human constitution.

If the actual metamorphosis of humans into animals was deemed unlikely, scholars nonetheless acknowledged the reality of the *perception* of such change and attempted to account for it in ways that conformed to their understanding of the natural order. The devil had many tricks up his sleeve, many ways to play a sleight of hand with physics. He had speed on his side: he could replace a human being with a wolf so quickly that it would appear that the man had been transformed. He had the skill of deception: he could wrap men in the shape of a wolf and thus deceive the senses. He could manipulate the elements: he could condense the air between viewer and object to create an illusory "aerial effigy." And, in an explanation that lies a hair's breadth away from true metamorphosis, he "could achieve . . . 'transfigurations,' changing not the substance but the accidents of things to give them the appearance of more drastic alteration."[55]

These esoteric explanations for the appearance of metamorphosis did not trickle down into popular understandings of the demonic, however. Even if they had, demonologists admitted that the devil was so skilled at illusion that it would take an expert to distinguish between real and illusory physical effects.[56] And even if people did understand that metamorphosis was an illusion, this understanding would provide small consolation for the devil's victims. As Maus writes, " 'Imaginary' effects are no less threatening, to many witchcraft believers, than 'real' or material ones. . . . That a young girl may not 'actually' have become a filly, but only seemed to become a filly to herself and others, is almost a distinction without a difference in a system in which mental convictions play such a crucial role."[57] Thus for most people in early modern Europe metamorphosis remained firmly entrenched as one of the devil's talents. Witchcraft narratives and confessions—again, documents that fully qualified as legal evidence—frequently depended upon claims of metamorphosis, and witchcraft pamphlets of the period commonly assert that the devil changed people into animals. (The transformation of people into animals had a pragmatic function: "The popular belief was that witches often turned themselves into cats, wolves, and other animals, sometimes in order to enter houses undetected, sometimes to make aerial voyages to the Sabbats, and sometimes for the purpose of killing or injuring their enemies' livestock.")[58]

Metamorphosis, then, was commonly perceived as an integral part of the reality of Marlowe's world. Demonic transformations were part of an epistemology that accepted the belief that meat turns into maggots, the idea that devils take to the stage, the logic of alchemy, and the notion that documents are transported between earth and hell.[59] This was an epistemology that was not yet subject to the seventeenth-century mechanistic philosophy (most potently articulated by Descartes) that "declar[ed] matter to be totally inert, completely devoid of any interesting property."[60] At the end of the sixteenth century, the possibilities of natural magic, occult phenomena, and demonic intervention were all still very real. My interest here is not simply in tracing how *Doctor Faustus* maps onto contemporary debates in natural philosophy, but in contemplating how the play presents a model of inhabiting a metamorphic environment—how it creates a sense of the lived experience of Ovidian physics. This is the shift, in other words, from new historicism to historical phenomenology.

IV

Metamorphosis is the space between binaries; it is the moment of both/and rather than either/or. It is about process and movement rather than static ontological conditions. The distinction between the psychological and the physical, or between the physical and the spiritual, or between the metaphorical and the literal ceases to hold. Ovidian physics is at once poetic, a product of the imagination, and material, a way of experiencing the world. It is, in the dual meanings of the word, literal—that which is written and that which resists metaphor, that which is produced by text and that which pertains to the physical world.

We find an analogy for this relationship in another Ovidian trope, that of dismemberment (a phenomenon also present in *Faustus,* as the play ends with a discussion of the doctor's severed limbs). This notion of fragmentation affected both the abstract construction of self (a shattered one, according to Cynthia Marshall) and the material practices of early modern Europe (the "culture of dissection" described by Jonathan Sawday).[61] The idea of bodily fragmentation spanned the poetic and the physical, rendering them not only interconnected but intertwined and mutually constitutive. So too the metamorphic sensibility I am describing weaves together, or between, the intangible and the tangible. Smith writes that historical phenomenology "accepts the ontological premises of deconstruction but directs attention to the sentient body caught up in that situation, positioned among the cultural variables set in place by new historicism and cultural materialism."[62] Ovidian physics is just such a deconstructive ontology taken into the material world; the same sliding, morphing properties we now recognize in text were once, and for many, properties of the very space in which they lived. Such was the world of the devil.

To take the devil seriously, then, is to accept the reality of Ovidian physics, to acknowledge an environmental, material consciousness and comprehension that differed radically from our own. This might seem like a tall order, but we can draw lessons from the wealth of recent research on the humoral body. Such work has not simply examined the theory of the humors as a quirky, arcane medical belief system, but explored how the belief of inhabiting a humoral body shaped lived experience. Indeed, the analogue between humoral theory and Ovidian physics is an integral one. Both notions are governed by a logic of fungibility and mutability. That the world could be malleable is a logical conclusion if the environment plays macrocosm to the microcosm of the humoral body. (And vice versa—the humoral body reflects the plasticity of the environment.)[63] Ovidian physics might be perceived as humoral logic writ large in the universe—"cosmologic," as Gail Kern Paster puts it.[64] Just as fluids in the humoral body morph into one another, so too, in the world of Ovid, matter is eminently transformable. Men can be transformed into stags, girls into birds, nymphs into water.

In early modern England, this environmental perception is reflected in the understanding of the devil. For those in the sixteenth and early seventeenth centuries, belief in a devil that could transform himself into a bush, or in fluid eschatological spaces with their inherent distortion of matter— belief in a universe that was molten—was a given. John Rogers, whom I quoted at the beginning of this essay, further articulates his experience of the demonic: "I thought trees sometimes good Angels, sometimes bad, and looked upon bushes as the Dens of Devils."[65] Rogers perceived a world of shape-shifting and unstable matter. We should note that Rogers's comments appear in the context of a spiritual autobiography, and that these experiences of the devil took place between 1639 and 1642, when Rogers was twelve to fifteen years old. The commentary carries its own degree of irony, as the mature author (the narrative ends in 1665, when Rogers was thirty-eight) reflects on the imaginative excess of his youth, when the world was perceived "according to [his] fancies." Rogers's mapping of his own development vis-à-vis the devil corresponds with that of his time: a metamorphic understanding of the universe was becoming archaic by the end of the seventeenth century. As Lorraine Daston has discussed, Robert Boyle attacked natural philosophers who endowed nature "with plastic powers and capricious deviations."[66] A developmental paradigm was emerging that would cast the beliefs of even someone like Prynne as the follies of youth. The narrative arc of Rogers's autobiography is thus the story that would be told of modernism outgrowing superstition. Rogers anticipates, scripts, and self-consciously embraces the trajectory that Burckhardt and his followers would impose upon an epoch.

Central to the creation of this paradigm was the divorce of empirical science and the fictional imagination. Thomas Sprat writes in *The History of the Royal-Society of London* (1667) that the aim of the society was "to make faithful *Records,* of all the Works of *Nature,*" and that "to accomplish this, they have indeavor'd, to separate the knowledge of *Nature,* from . . . the devices of *Fancy,* or the delightful deceit of *Fables.*"[67] (It was "the *Poets* [who] began of old to impose the deceit.")[68] Ovidian physics, as the duality of the term suggests, is a mode of thought and perception that does not recognize a division of imagination and reality; it admits that our knowledge of nature is interconnected with the devices of fancy. It acknowledges that reality is an imaginative construct and that phenomenology requires the work of fantasy.

To study the devil is to study beliefs about nature and the nature of belief. I would like to suggest that Ovidian physics does not simply describe the local dynamics of *Doctor Faustus,* or the wider complexities of religious belief in late sixteenth- and early seventeenth-century England. Rather, Ovidian physics models the very concept of belief itself. Much recent scholarship has been invested in parsing the distinctions of Catholic and Protestant, medieval and modern. While these studies provide an important corrective to earlier work that might have overlooked the significance of such differences, we should remember that the history of belief is not a sedimentary formation, a calcified accretion of historical layers that provides a clear record of progressive change. Rather, it is, to borrow another geological metaphor, metamorphic: these layers are subject to cultural pressures that render them molten, mobile, and interpenetrating. In this sense, the world of *Faustus,* with its shifting shapes and labile coexistence of skepticism and the diabolical, offers a better model for belief than the developmental progression mapped by Rogers. Ovidian physics offers an alternative to teleology and provides an analytical mode that is not driven by etiology or genealogy.[69] It is the study of flux, not stasis, transformations rather than formations.

Notes

This essay has undergone many transformations, and its current shape has been influenced by the comments and suggestions of many people. I am grateful for feedback from audiences at Pennsylvania State University, the University of Delaware Medieval and Renaissance Workshop, the Penn Humanities Forum, the Professing Early Modernisms conference at Harvard University, and the Shakespeare Association of America conference. I benefited from the insightful readings of Jonathan Grossman, Heather Hirschfeld, Susan Zimmerman, and especially Martin Brückner. Most important, I'd like to thank the members of my writing group, in particular Scott Black, Edmund Campos, Jane Hedley, Nora Johnson, Steve Newman, Katherine Rowe, Lauren Shohet, and Julian Yates.

1. I am, perhaps, presumptuous in my assumption of disbelief. I may well have readers that do believe in the devil. Statistically, the odds are high, at least in the United States. Most Americans (64%) believe in hell; in 1997, nearly half of the people who said they believe in hell agreed with the statement, "Hell is a real place where people suffer eternal fiery torments" (and is thus, I presume, a place that requires the devil and his minions); see Jeffery L. Sheler, "Hell Hath No Fury," *U.S. News and World Report,* January 31, 2000, 45, 47. But since I do not anticipate that all Americans will be reading this essay, and since I assume that within the rarified readership of academia the percentage of people who believe in the devil is much lower than the national average, I will work with the premise that most of my readers don't believe in the devil, at least not in the same way as, say, Cotton Mather would have.

Throughout this essay, I refer to "the devil" in the singular, although I recognize that the devil has a long history of being both/either singular and/or plural. On the myriad names for the devil, see Jeffrey Burton Russell, *Lucifer: The Devil in the Middle Ages* (Ithaca, N.Y.:

Cornell University Press, 1984), 248–50. As Russell discusses, the many names and identities of the devil constantly shifted and could be used to designate one entity or many. The devil's ontological status as both one and many continued into the seventeenth century; see Keith Thomas, *Religion and the Decline of Magic* (New York: Charles Scribner's Sons, 1971), 470.

2. Edward Rogers, *Some Account of the Life and Opinions of a Fifth Monarchy Man* (London: Longmans, Green, Reader and Dyer, 1867), 13.

3. Thomas, 471.

4. Ibid., 470.

5. Jacob Burckhardt, *The Civilization of the Renaissance in Italy,* 2 vols, trans. Benjamin Nelson (New York: Harper Colophon Books, 1958), 1:143. The emphasis is originally Burckhardt's; see *Die Cultur der Renaissance in Italien* (Leipzig: E. U. Seemann, 1869), 104.

6. "A Seventeenth-Century Demonological Neurosis," *The Standard Edition of the Complete Psychological Works of Sigmund Freud,* ed. James Strachey (London: The Hogarth Press and Toronto: Clarke, Irwin, 1961), 19: 72.

7. Thomas's work is punctuated by references to Africa or "primitive" beliefs, such as his comment early in the book, "The line between magic and religion is one which it is impossible to draw in many primitive societies; it is equally difficult to recognise in medieval England" (50). The analogy between primitive societies and medieval England legitimates his turn toward anthropology; in the opening paragraph of the book, he writes, "[i]n this task [that is, 'to make sense of some of the systems of belief which were current in sixteenth- and seventeenth-century England'] I have been much helped by the studies made by modern social anthropologists of similar beliefs held in Africa and elsewhere" (ix).

8. For a discussion of the developmental teleology in Elias's *The Civilizing Process,* Weber's *The Protestant Ethic and the Spirit of Capitalism,* and Taylor's *Sources of the Self,* see Lyndal Roper, *Oedipus and the Devil: Witchcraft, Sexuality and Religion in Early Modern Europe* (London: Routledge, 1994), 4–7. As much as Roper moves away from the traditional Burckhardt-Weber-Elias model of human development, her own psychoanalytical approach and the title's emphasis on the Oedipal continues to locate the supernatural within a discourse of childhood development.

9. For a discussion of the politics of the term, see Margreta de Grazia, "World Pictures, Modern Periods, and the Early Stage," *A New History of Early English Drama,* ed. John D. Cox and David Scott Kastan (New York: Columbia University Press, 1997), esp. 9–13. Of course, one must inevitably use labels to talk about the time period, even as one is aware of the different ideological implications of the various modes of segmenting time; in this essay I move between "Renaissance," "early modern," and labeling by century.

10. "Sorcery and Subjectivity in Early Modern Discourses of Witchcraft," *Historicism, Psychoanalysis, and Early Modern Culture,* ed. Carla Mazzio and Douglas Trevor (New York: Routledge, 2000), 326. The comment appears in a discussion about how scholars have underestimated significant points of contention within early modern debates about witchcraft.

11. Clark writes that "in witchcraft matters belief and doubt were never simple alternatives, or fixed and separate compartments of thought. They varied according to specific issues and were spread out along a continuous spectrum of reactions to witchcraft phenomena. What is especially striking is how few authors can be placed confidently at the two extremes";

Thinking with Demons: The Idea of Witchcraft in Early Modern Europe (Oxford, U.K.: Clarendon Press, 1997), 182.

12. T. McAlindon, *Doctor Faustus: Divine in Show* (New York: Twayne Publishers, 1994), 33.

13. *The Devil and the Sacred in English Drama, 1350-1642* (Cambridge: Cambridge University Press, 2000), 1. As Albert H. Tricomi has discussed, a similar teleological narrative is found in the work of New Critics and cultural materialists; see "Historicizing the Imagery of the Demonic in *The Duchess of Malfi*," *Journal of Medieval and Early Modern Studies* 34.2 (2004): 347-48. Tricomi argues that *The Duchess of Malfi* "exhibits . . . the consequences of living in a world where the possibilities of spiritual intervention and demonic possession are continually in play. *The Duchess* also affords the best opportunity . . . to reengage the early modern past by apprehending ways of feeling and believing (or almost not believing) that are largely foreign to our own manner of perceiving. In treating this particular tragedy, I propose to demonstrate that the old New Criticism and to a lesser degree the cultural materialist criticism of our own day have in their discrete ways distorted or foreclosed a historicized engagement with early modern affectivity, a feature of the drama that is . . . crucial to our historical understanding" (346).

14. Cox, 2.

15. See John Parker's review in *Christianity and Literature* 52.2 (Winter 2003): 262-65.

16. E. K. Chambers, *The Elizabethan Stage*, 4 vols. (Oxford, U.K.: Clarendon Press, 1923), 3:423.

17. Chambers cites three historical documents of this event; Cox notes that there was an additional document and cites an article by Eric Rasmussen, but Rasmussen actually argues that the reference to onstage devils in *The Black Book* was most likely *not* to a production of *Faustus;* see Rasmussen, "*The Black Book* and the Date of *Doctor Faustus*," *Notes and Queries* 235 (n.s. 37): 170.

18. Ibid., 3:424.

19. (f. 556) in Ibid., 3:423-24.

20. See John Russell Brown, who uses such "stories" as Prynne's to draw parallels between Marlowe's actors and Aeschylus's Eumenides in "Marlowe and the Actors," *Tulane Drama Review* 8.4 (1964): 157; also Michael Goldman, who suggests that "the contemporary legend of the extra devil . . . was an index of how far Marlowe's original audience felt they had gone in their abandon," in "Marlowe and the Histrionics of Ravishment," *Two Renaissance Mythmakers: Christopher Marlowe and Ben Jonson. Selected Papers from the English Institute, 1975-76* (Baltimore: The Johns Hopkins University Press, 1977), 40.

21. The body of work on European and American witchcraft is extensive, and I will just cite some representative titles here. See, for example, Paul Boyer and Stephen Nissenbaum, *Salem Possessed: The Social Origins of Witchcraft* (Cambridge: Harvard University Press, 1974); John Putnam Demos, *Entertaining Satan: Witchcraft and the Culture of Early New England* (Oxford: Oxford University Press, 1982); Alan Macfarlane, *Witchcraft in Tudor and Stuart England* (New York: Harper and Row, 1970); H. R. Trevor-Roper, *The European Witch-Craze of the Sixteenth and Seventeenth Centuries and Other Essays* (New York: Harper and Row, 1969); Richard Weisman, *Witchcraft, Magic, and Religion in 17th-Century Massachusetts* (Amherst: University of Massachusetts Press, 1984).

22. Again, I offer a sampling of representative titles: Anne Llewellyn Barstow, *Witchcraze: A New History of the European Witch Hunts* (San Francisco: HarperCollins, 1994); Carol F. Karlsen, *The Devil in the Shape of a Woman: Witchcraft in Colonial New England* (New York: Vintage Books, 1989); Elizabeth Reis, *Damned Women: Sinners and Witches in Puritan New England* (Ithaca, N.Y.: Cornell University Press, 1997); Roper, *Oedipus and the Devil,* cited above.

23. See, for example, Luke Wilson, *Theaters of Intention: Drama and the Law in Early Modern England* (Stanford: Stanford University Press, 2000), chapter 5.

24. Freud, 72.

25. Freud thanks Dr. Payer-Thurn of the Fideikommissbibliothek for his help in studying the manuscript and points out that Payer-Thurn was drawn to the document for its parallels with the story of Faust (73).

26. Freud, 77.

27. Freud repeatedly emphasizes the legitimacy of the document with statements such as, "We have occasion yet again to acknowledge that in spite of the obvious purpose of his efforts, the compiler has not been tempted into departing from the veracity required of a case history" (78); "On this point, too, the [document] provides us with reliable information," and "We can see that what we are dealing with really is a case history" (80).

28. Freud, 98.

29. Ibid.

30. Ibid.

31. *A Godless Jew: Freud, Atheism, and the Making of Psychoanalysis* (New Haven and London: Yale University Press, 1987), 11–12.

32. "Premodern Sexualities," *PMLA* 115.3 (2000): 325–26.

33. All citations from *Doctor Faustus* are taken from the Oxford Drama Library edition, ed. David Bevington and Eric Rasmussen (Oxford, U.K.: Clarendon Press, 1995). I will be using the B-text, although virtually all of the passages cited are identical in A and B.

34. The B-text in the Bevington and Rasmussen edition has "old wives' tables," although the A-text has "tales." Since other editions are consistent in "tales," and since Bevington and Ramussen do not gloss "tables," I am assuming that "tables" is a typographic error.

35. The historian's tendency to present demonic evidence in terms of fiction or narrative is illustrated in a quick study of Roper's and Thomas's texts. Roper doesn't take any of the witches' testimonies as evidence of a "real" encounter with the devil. "[I]t is hard to know how to interpret documents which we do not believe to be factual. But witchcraft confessions and accusations are not products of realism, and they cannot be analysed with the methods of historical realism" (202). Instead, her entire approach assumes these particular historical documents to be a form of narrative. She writes that we must "attend to [their] imaginative themes" and "investigate two sides of the story" (202). Throughout, Roper speaks of the women's accounts as "fantasy" (227) and invokes similes such as "[l]ike the fairies of fairytale who are not invited to the baptism . . ." (209) and draws analogies with "the tendency in folktale to populate a story with evil stepmothers" (217). She invokes the theatrical as well, referring to "a certain kind of psychic dramatic script" (215), arguing that "[i]nterrogation for witchcraft . . . offered the accused a theatrical opportunity to recount and restage . . . conflicts" and asking, "But what are the themes of these dramas?" (232). Roper periodically

stops to ponder the reality factor, commenting that "[t]here is no mileage . . . in the usual historical strategy of teasing out the 'real' from the fantastic elements in this account. We cannot isolate the point at which events which we know to be 'real' . . . end, and where the fantastic begins" (233). This difficulty arises from "another salient feature of difference in seventeenth-century witch narratives: the role of the Devil. To us, the fantasies which surround him seem clearly part of the realm of the imaginary, more definitively unreal than the material I have been describing. But to them he was part of the real world" (233). This admission of reality, however, is almost immediately undermined by the subsequent claim that "[b]ecoming a witch meant engaging in an intimate relationship, usually sexual, with the Devil *as a character,* and consequently, its discovery entailed the analysis of the well-springs of the witch's own personality, motives, and emotions" (234, my emphasis). The witch's testimony is thus quickly converted back into fictional, narrative terms, offering up a text rich with psychoanalytic potential.

Although Roper and Thomas present wildly disparate modes of historiography, they share this propensity to fictionalize historical documents pertaining to the demonic. In his discussion of the devil, Thomas is clear, even emphatic, about the narrative qualities of these sources: "Medieval preachers enlivened their sermons with terrifying *stories* of the Devil's repeated appearances" (470); "Influential preachers [of the Reformation] filled the ears of their hearers with *tales* of diabolic intervention in daily life" (471); "*Stories* of Satan's personal appearance" was cited by many (472); "Most of these *anecdotes*" pertained to those who invoked the Devil in conversation (472); "Such Faustian *legends* were in common circulation. . . . They made excellent cautionary *tales*" (473); the diarist Oliver Heywood "recorded the *story* of the boy who, having read the *story* of Faustus, decided to invoke the devil" (473); "The *stories* told about his intervention in daily affairs showed him punishing perjurers" (476; all emphases mine). The devil thus moves freely through a variety of narrative genres: legend, drama, morality tales, gossip. How do we reconcile this fictional, even literary quality of the devil's appearance with what Thomas discerns as a literal early modern truth? "For most men the literal reality of demons seemed a fundamental article of faith" (475). Literary scholars might gripe that their historian counterparts often fail to see the fiction in the archives (to borrow the title from Natalie Zemon Davis's influential book), that they fail to attend to the vicissitudes of representation in their textual harvesting of facts. In Thomas (as in Roper), we find the opposite proclivity, as he positions texts originally perceived as fact—"the literal reality"—in terms of fiction.

36. Stephen Greenblatt, *Hamlet in Purgatory* (Princeton: Princeton University Press, 2001), 35.

37. Ibid., 47.

38. Bruce Smith, "Introduction," *Shakespeare Studies* 2001 (vol. 29): 22. Smith is developing the idea from Michael Schoenfeldt, *Bodies and Selves in Early Modern England* (Cambridge: Cambridge University Press, 1999), 8. Gail Kern Paster also argues that language which is "bodily or emotional figuration for us . . . was the literal stuff of physiological theory for early modern scriptors of the body"; "Nervous Tension," in *The Body in Parts: Fantasies of Corporeality in Early Modern Europe,* ed. David Hillman and Carla Mazzio (London: Routledge, 1997), 111. It should be pointed out that this distinction of metaphor and the materially "real" was being discussed within the early modern period as well. In *A Discourse*

of the Subtill Practises of Deuilles by Vvitches and Sorcerers (1587), George Gifford answers objections "that the Deuill is called a Serpent by an Allegorie, and therefore what necessity to take it there of a beast?" with the response, "I answere that the Deuil indeed is by a metaphor called a serpent in many places of holy scripture. But doth it therefore follow that in this place [for example, the Garden of Eden] was noe but he?" (sig. F3r).

39. Bate, *Shakespeare and Ovid* (Oxford: Oxford University Press, 1993), 28; Enterline, *The Rhetoric of the Body from Ovid to Shakespeare* (Cambridge: Cambridge University Press, 2000), 23.

40. The reference is to a song *Carmen de Pulice,* "popularly attributed to Ovid, although it is probably medieval in origin"; Roma Gill, ed., *The Complete Works of Christopher Marlowe,* 5 vols. (Oxford, U.K.: Clarendon Press, 1990), 2:76.

41. See *Ovid's Metamorphoses,* trans. Arthur Golding and ed. John Frederick Nims (Philadelphia: Paul Dry Books, 2000), VIII.264 passim, V.605 passim.

42. See Reginald Scot, *The Discoverie of Witchcraft* (New York: Dover Publications, Inc., 1972), 6; Johann Weyer, *Witches, Devils, and Doctors in the Renaissance (De praestigiis daemonum,* 1583), ed. George Mora, et al. (Binghampton, N.Y.: Medieval and Renaissance Texts and Studies, 1991), 165.

43. *A Preface to Marlowe* (Harlow, England: Longman, 2000), 99.

44. Clark, 168.

45. Ibid., 156.

46. See *Thinking with Demons,* Part Two.

47. Clark, 191; Charles Webster, *From Paracelsus to Newton: Magic and the Making of Modern Science* (Cambridge: Cambridge University Press, 1982), 82.

48. Clark, 191-92.

49. Facsimile reprint (Amsterdam: Theatrvm Orbis Terrarvm Ltd., 1968).

50. Cotta, 27.

51. Ibid., 28-29.

52. Ibid., 29-30. Ovid, naturally, falls well within the purview of this category of "any ancient classical Author"; it is interesting to consider what happens to *The Metamorphoses* when read through Cotta's lens of demonic metamorphosis.

53. Cotta, 31.

54. Ibid., 33-34.

55. Clark, 192. The preceding explanations of metamorphosis are also found on this page and attributed to their various sources.

56. Ibid., 167.

57. Maus, 330.

58. Wayne Shumaker, *The Occult Sciences in the Renaissance: A Study in Intellectual Patterns* (Berkeley: University of California Press, 1972), 93.

59. Such accounts are not only found in fiction; in *De praestigiis daemonum* (1583), Weyer, a skeptic voice within the period, relates matter-of-factly an instance of a monk's ill-considered contract being retrieved from hell (505).

60. Brian Easlea, *Witch-hunting, Magic and the New Philosophy: An Introduction to the Debates of the Scientific Revolution 1450-1750* (Brighton: The Harvester Press, 1980), 111.

61. Marshall, *The Shattering of the Self: Violence, Subjectivity, and Early Modern Texts*

(Baltimore: The Johns Hopkins University Press, 2002), 2; Sawday, *The Body Emblazoned: Dissection and the Human Body in Renaissance Culture* (London: Routledge, 1995), ix.

62. "Premodern Sexualities," 326.

63. The fullest exploration of the reciprocity of environment and humoralism is Mary Floyd-Wilson's *English Ethnicity and Race in Early Modern Drama* (Cambridge: Cambridge University Press, 2003). In the sixteenth and seventeenth centuries, the English climate and environment was credited with making the English people especially "pliant" (54).

64. "Melancholy Cats, Lugged Bears, and Early Modern Cosmology: Reading Shakespeare's Psychological Materialism Across the Species Barrier," in *Reading the Early Modern Passions: Essays in the Cultural History of Emotion,* ed. Gail Kern Paster, Katherine Rowe, and Mary Floyd-Wilson (Philadelphia: University of Pennsylvania Press, 2004), 116.

65. Rogers, 14.

66. "Marvelous Facts and Miraculous Evidence in Early Modern Europe," in *Questions of Evidence: Proof, Practice, and Persuasion Across the Disciplines,* ed. James Chandler, Arnold I. Davidson, and Harry Harootunian (Chicago: University of Chicago Press, 1994), 272.

67. Sprat, *History of the Royal Society,* ed. Jackson I. Cope and Harold Whitmore Jones (Saint Louis: Washington University Studies, 1958), 61–62.

68. Sprat, 340.

69. The metamorphic model allows us to better account for the lively presence of seemingly contradictory intellectual dynamics within the period; as such, it avoids the sense of paradox that has informed studies in the history of science. To us, for instance, it is an historical paradox that the height of the early modern European witch hunts corresponded with the beginnings of what we now recognize as modern science—indeed, as Easlea maintains, the scientific revolution was enabled, and even initiated, by the defeat of those who argued against witchcraft and the corresponding victory of those who believed witchcraft to be a real phenomenon (see chapter 1). Within the seventeenth century, seeming intellectual paradoxes continue to abound. There is, for example, the witchcraft debate between Joseph Glanvill and John Webster—the former the empirically driven member of the Royal Society who argued for the existence of witchcraft, the latter a believer in mysticism and the occult who argued against it; see Thomas Harmon Jobe, "The Devil in Restoration Science: The Glanvill-Webster Witchcraft Debate," *Isis* 72.3 (1981): 342–56. Most famously, there is the case of Isaac Newton, founding father of modern physics, avid alchemist. These seeming paradoxes are our own constructions, the outcome of linear, developmental models which do not easily allow for epistemological plurality and simultaneity.

Notes on Contributors

Guest Editors

MARY FLOYD-WILSON is an associate professor of English at the University of North Carolina at Chapel Hill. She is the author of *English Ethnicity and Race in Early Modern Drama* and coeditor, with Gail Kern Paster and Katherine Rowe, of *Reading the Early Modern Passions: Essays in the Cultural History of Emotion.* She and Garrett A. Sullivan Jr. are coediting a collection of essays on environment and identity in early modern literature.

GARRETT A. SULLIVAN JR. is an associate professor of English at Pennsylvania State University. He is the author of *The Drama of Landscape: Land, Property, and Social Relations on the Early Modern Stage* and *Memory and Forgetting in English Renaissance Drama: Shakespeare, Marlowe, Webster.* He is also coeditor, with Patrick Cheney and Andrew Hadfield, of *Early Modern English Drama: A Critical Companion.*

Contributors

JEAN FEERICK is an assistant professor of English at Brown University and William S. Vaughn Visiting Fellow at the Robert Penn Warren Center for the Humanities at Vanderbilt University. She is completing a book about Renaissance literature, race, and the fear of degeneration.

JONATHAN GIL HARRIS is a professor of English at George Washington University. He is the author of *Foreign Bodies and the Body Politic: Discourses of Social Pathology in Early Modern England* and *Sick Economies:*

221

Drama, Mercantilism, and Disease in Shakespeare's England and coeditor of *Staged Properties in Early Modern English Drama.* He is working
on a book project entitled *Untimely Matter: Reworking Material Culture
in the Time of Shakespeare.*

PAUL MENZER is an assistant professor of English at the University of
North Texas, where he works on text and performance. He is editor of the
collection, *Inside Shakespeare: Essays on the Blackfriars Stage,* and has
published in *Shakespeare Quarterly* and *Shakespeare Bulletin.* He is on
the board of directors of the American Shakespeare Center's Blackfriars
Playhouse.

DARYL W. PALMER is an associate professor of English at Regis University.
He is the author of *Hospitable Performances: Dramatic Genre and Cultural Practices in Early Modern England* and *Writing Russia in the Age
of Shakespeare.*

KRISTEN POOLE is an associate professor in the English department at the
University of Delaware. She is the author of *Radical Religion from Shakespeare to Milton: Figures of Nonconformity in Early Modern England,* as
well as numerous articles. Her current book project is on the intersection
of early modern eschatology and physics.

CAROLYN SALE is an assistant professor at the University of Alberta in
Canada. Other recent work includes her essay "Slanderous Aesthetics and
the Woman Writer: The Case of *Hole v. White,*" in *From Script to Stage
in Early Modern England.* Current projects include a book, *Common
Properties: The Early Modern Writer and the Law, 1546–1628,* and
investigations into early modern conceptions and representations of the
obscene.

ALAN STEWART is a professor of English and comparative literature at
Columbia University. His publications include *Close Readers: Humanism
and Sodomy in Early Modern England* and biographical studies of Francis
Bacon (with Lisa Jardine), Philip Sidney, and James VI and I. He is working
on a monograph entitled *Shakespeare's Letters* and editing the first two
volumes of the *Oxford Francis Bacon.*

WILLIAM N. WEST is an associate professor of English at Northwestern
University and taught previously at the University of Colorado at Boulder;
the University of Nevada, Reno; and the University of California at Berkeley.
He has published *Theatres and Encyclopedias in Early Modern Europe*
and is at work on a book to be called *Understanding and Confusion on
the Elizabethan Stages.*